Anti-Poverty Measures in America: Scientism and Other Obstacles

Westphalia Press
An imprint of Policy Studies Organization
1527 New Hampshire Ave., NW
Washington, D.C. 20036
info@ipsonet.org

ISBN-13: 978-1-63391-487-2

Cover design by Jeffrey Barnes:
jbarnesbook.design

Daniel Gutierrez-Sandoval, Executive Director
PSO and Westphalia Press

Updated material and comments on this edition
can be found at the Westphalia Press website:
www.westphaliapress.org

Anti-Poverty Measures in America: Scientism and Other Obstacles

Max J. Skidmore & Biko Koenig, Editors

WESTPHALIA PRESS

An imprint of Policy Studies Organization

To Those Most Devoted to Students
Around the World

Table of Contents

Introduction

The Caucus on Poverty, Inequality, and Public Policy of the American Political Science Association for some years has regularly sponsored a panel at the APSA's annual meeting. The last such panels took place at the San Francisco meeting in 2017, at the Boston meeting in 2018, and at the Washington meeting in 2019. Max J. Skidmore convened, and chaired both panels. Each was extraordinary. In view of this, the companion journal to the Caucus, Poverty and Public Policy, in 2018, published a special section for the 2017 and 2018 panels: volume 10, issue 3 for the panel from 2017; volume 10, issue 4 for those from the 2018 panel, with the special theme of scientism, defined as accepting scientific methods to the exclusion of all others, and as applying science to subjects for which it is inappropriate, such as values, aesthetics, and the like.

The 2017 panel dealt with rigid emphases on methodology, and considered whether political science remains relevant. Papers came from Anthony DiMaggio of Lehigh University; David Kingsley, retired from the University of Kansas School of Medicine where he taught research methodology; Lawrence Mead of New York University; and Max J. Skidmore of the University of Missouri-Kansas City. The papers fit together admirably, and considered the effects of scientism in the social sciences in general, and in political science in particular.

The 2018 panel adopted a related, but different, theme and examined the circumstances that create obstacles to the adoption of social legislation in the United States. For this panel papers came from Silvia Borzutzky of Carnegie-Mellon University; David Kingsley once again; Biko Koenig of Franklin and Marshall College; and, again, Max J. Skidmore.

Although the authors of all of these papers worked independently and with no coordination among them—absolutely no colluson!—the papers fit together to an astonishing extent. That made the panels extraordinarily stimulating, made the special sections in the journal especially appropriate, and led to an offer from Westphalia Press (the publishing arm of the Policy Studies Organization) to publish the papers from the two panels in this special volume. Max J. Skidmore and Biko Koenig accepted the task as co-editors.

Thus, we participants present Anti-Poverty Measures in America: Scientism and Other Obstacles.

Max J. Skidmore
Biko Koenig

Anti-Poverty & the Quantification of Political Science

Biko Koenig
Government & Public Policy, Franklin & Marshall College, Lancaster, PA

Perhaps surprisingly, my introductory course on Public Policy is, at its core, a course on values and the conflicts that arise when communities disagree over those values.

I typically begin with Stone's classic example of equity: if we bring a delicious chocolate cake to class, how ought we divide the cake among everyone present (2012:39-42)? Should every student get the same size slice? Perhaps student grades or class year should determine slice sizes. Are equal slices for all present a fair outcome for those students who had to miss class that day, or who couldn't enroll in the course? What about students who come from disadvantaged backgrounds, or who have chocolate allergies? Perhaps a fair option might be that all the students should start with the same sized fork and competition will sort out who gets what. Or, we might consider holding elections or lotteries to determine the distribution.

Stone uses this example to make two important arguments about the nature of public policy and politics. First, to achieve some greater notion of equity or fairness, we might end up with unequal distributions of some resource: equity via inequality. The second, and more important notion for this discussion, is about the root of political conflicts. On the surface we tend to see arguments about distributions: about who gets how much cake. But the distributional argument can obscure the deeper point that almost everyone strives for equity or fairness in the system. The disagreements come from the values that support different ideas of equity or fairness. We all want a fair system, but we don't often agree about what it means to be fair.

Consider the intense disagreement around immigration, especially concerning the southern U.S. border. On one level, the conflict may seem to be about the number and characteristics of those immigrants, or perhaps their perceived impact on political and economic communities. For those on the Left, the anti-immigrant positions of the Right can appear to be challenges to democracy and basic human values. Yet, many on the Right who take positions critical of immigration do so with clear referents to fairness, be it in terms of economic competition or political process. Indeed, my own research with Republicans in Northeastern Pennsylvania includes a strong narrative about the value of "legal immigrants" from Mexico and Central America based on their work ethic, family values, and religious commitments. Citizens grounded these critiques of immigration in the perceived criminality of "not following the right procedure" when others had. As Pennsylvania Republican Senate candidate Lou Barletta, the former Mayor of Hazleton, PA, put it in 2018, "we know who illegal immigration hurts most of all: legal immigrants who make our communities stronger" (Author fieldnotes 9/15/18).

This is a richer, more complicated political argument than one that simply sees all immigrants as bad people. I make this example to underline that, on some level, the political conflict over immigration is also one grounded in disagreements over what fairness and equity mean in practice, political values that can be tricky to measure with poll data and other approaches that are distant from the complexity, ambiguity, and dissonance present in how most people interact with the social world. Indeed, we can (and do) measure plenty of things about immigration, from empirical data about the immigrants themselves to opinion surveys that take the temperature of citizens regarding topics around the issue. This data is important but can obscure the deeper processes and mechanisms that influence these outcomes. Researchers can more easily access this sort of data when compared to approaches that have the intent of explaining those processes and mechanisms: explaining why certain variables correlate (or not) is a tricky proposition. Thus, like the old joke of the drunk at the lamppost, while our keys might be somewhere else, this is where the light happens to be. Our data on important issues tends to come through procedures we are comfortable with, in forms that we have worked with before, and perhaps most important, that fit into the institutional structure of our own lives.

In many respects, public policy analysis is intended to be value neutral. As Behn implies in his classic essay, the analyst takes their values from the client (1985). We don't get to decide the most equitable way to divide a cake.[1] Rather, given a particular definition of fairness, the analyst works to gather and interpret data in order to make recommendations about the impact of this or that immigration policy option. It is the process that makes policy analysis appear to be value-free, as they keep those values "outside" of the "actual" analysis. But even the most quantitative cost-benefit analysis of policy scenarios contains embedded values about what counts as fair (or democratic, or efficient, etc.). The challenge for scholars of these issues is to bring those values to the surface of the debate to have a more empirically accurate account of political conflict. I bring this up because while political science has its own debates about the role of values (and more on that later), we are well equipped to explore conflicts over political values. Indeed, discussions of both power and the outcomes of political conflicts are key topics in our discipline.

---

1   Of course there is some selection bias at play, as it is unlikely that a conservative analyst would work for the Economic Policy Institute or a left-radical at the Brookings Institute.

In this introductory essay I will offer some comments on approaches to the study of politics and how these approaches are bound up in the difficulty of changing public policy. The chapters in this volume, divided into two sections, take up both topics in turn. Here I hope to offer some synergistic commentary, primarily on how a focus on political values and conflict within the discipline offers a potentially valuable path forward for more tangible impacts on policy outcomes (and, perhaps, a more public facing political science).

The Public Face of Disciplinary Power

The challenge that researchers face who wish to make a more public or policy oriented impression is not entirely one of intent. The opportunity structures of most academic positions involves a mix of intellectual and pragmatic issues—such as getting published, making

their findings generalizable, and offering relevant theoretical insights—that usually exist apart from the everyday lives of those under study. As a result, providing socially useful information to communities is not part of the professional incentive structure of most political science researchers. Timothy Pachirat aptly frames this concern (2009, 159):

> But worst of all is the possibility that my ethnographic voice will change nothing there at all, that it will remain a form of scholasticism (Bourdieu 2000) with currency only in the particular academic field in which it was produced. This, to me, would be a realization of Burawoy's (1998, 25) concept of normalization in the most awful possible way: the normalization of an academic political science that operates in a parallel world to, and yet has little or no effect on, the relationships of power, domination, and resistance it studies (2009, 159).

Put simply, researchers face an incentive structure that does little to combat problems of scholasticism, normalization, or extraction, and these incentives create a double bind for political science writing.

A large body of political science research is, arguably, not designed to produce information that is useful to the communities we are studying, and so our findings are typically not written for, nor read by, non-academic audiences. While some research designs involve a degree of community follow-up, in the form of presentations or the circulation of written material, this is a thin version of community re-engagement if it only happens at the end of the data collection or analysis. While sharing findings may be an important step for a given project, it precludes the possibility of building iterative moments of communication into the heart of the project itself. This preclusion can reinforce the distance between researcher and community, while also making issues of extraction harder to mitigate.

Recent public discussions have criticized how academic writing on politics is often not read, circulated, or utilized beyond those in the discipline. While some locate this problem with the academics themselves (Kristof 2014), most point towards the structural issues of research, writing, quick publication times, and narrow audiences that academics face (Copeland 2014, Rothland 2014, Voteen 2015). In fact, these structures are geared to prevent non-specialist conversations or access, such as the recent failed attempt by the International Studies Association to ban its editors from blogging (Straumsheim 2015). While there has been a rise in the use of social media by academics, the same disincentives hold for more traditional forms of non-academic media, including newspapers, magazines, and trade presses.

Often the discussion of critiques of the university focuses on the cloistered, insular discussions of the social world. If we ask "who is this scholarship for?" concrete responses include the tenure committee, the funding committee, the peer reviewers. While one might toy with the idea of public intellectualism, the power dynamics of professorship come bound up in expectations of production that lead to real rewards and penalties. Layered into this basic institutional structure are those more abstract institutions of norms and practices: as many in this volume note, in Political Science this includes somewhat hegemonic practices of acceptable methods, research questions, approaches, and outlets. In such a system our work tends to look inwards, judged by internal standards of research excellent and engagement with those disciplinary topics deemed to be important. In many respects, this is not a problem, and the tremendous amount of scholarly work on display at any academic conference shows the vast extent of research and publications that push the discipline forward. The standards we keep and the research agendas we develop are key parts of honing our insights and separating our conclusions from mere speculation.

At the same time, this status quo produces some tensions in how practitioners use our research within the actual field of politics. One outcome is a gulf between disciplinary concerns and those of political practitioners, be they policy actors or citizens. Policy recommendations, where they exist, are confined to footnotes and open ended conclusions. Without a peer reviewed outlet, serious considerations of political practice are rare and have the tendency to be categorized as unimportant for tenure at best and unscientific at worst. Thus, there are clear links between the gatekeeping aspects of disciplinary hegemony and the lack of public interest in our work.

When we consider the problems involved in dealing with anti-poverty policies, we must consider the inability of our discipline to routinely interact with policy actors as part of that challenge. Indeed, given the incentive structure that scholars face, our criticisms of policy landscapes are likely to ignore the concerns and experiences of real policy actors in favor of the other academics who read and judge our work. So, many prefer a slick use of survey data or a theoretical telling point more than actionable insights for practitioners. For some, we might prefer it to be different but have tenure, promotion, and other professional concerns to consider. For others, there may be no concern about such a system. To be clear, this is not entirely a bad set of circumstances, and academics regularly offer new data and unique insights into the social world. But we are well placed to offer more to practitioners, to be more closely aligned with the empirical reality of policy production, and in some circumstances to be more targeted in how we deploy our standards for academics working in the professional world.

So What?

The discussions that have reverberated out of the Post-Perestroika movement in the discipline indicate a question bound up with some deep "So What?" tensions. As Rogers Smith puts it, the discipline is "shaped by a desire to be as rigorous a science as possible, on the one hand, and to serve American democracy, on the other" (2015). In reference to how Perestroika created new spaces for pluralist methods and publicly relevant work, Smith was not convinced the discussion was over:

> Yet despite Robert Putnam's hope for an upsurge in publicly-relevant research, and despite general disillusionment with the most sweeping ambitions of rational choice theorists, the different camps are still by no means equal in size or status. Political science has continued to trend toward the predominance of research that is most focused on achieving rigorously specified and tested findings, with only secondary concern for how far those findings are relevant to major aspects of contemporary public issues (Smith, 2015).

As the articles in this volume, as well as the experiences of the authors and some of our readers can attest to, these twin goals still live in the discipline, as does the tension between the two.

At the same time, the tension has generated a good deal of debate for those interested in the future of the discipline, either from a methodological perspective or in terms of its application.

In response to King, Kohane, and Verba's classic Designing Social Inquiry (1994), the response edited by Brady and Collier makes its point in the subtitle – Diverse Tools, Shared Standards (2010). Further, editors Yanow & Schwartz-Shea develop an approach to the interpretive turn in Interpretation and Method (2006), bringing important methodological arguments that question the suppositions of neo-positivism. And across the board, much work has been done to push the "quants vs. quals" binary into more generative debates about ontology, epistemology, rigor, and the practice of strong methods within a given methodological framework. The rise of Perspectives on Politics as a flagship journal of the American Political Science Association provides a publishing space for scholars outside of the traditional approaches to the discipline.

Adjacent to, and intersecting with, the discussion of methods and methodology is one about the applicability of social science research to the world of politics. A good example of this debate can be read in David Laitin's 2003 critique of Making Social Science Matter, and Bent Flyvjberg's response (2004). Laitin's call for a science-first approach to generating causal analysis is rejected by Flyvjberg assertion that social science must "be [a] reflexive analysis and discussion of values and interests aimed at praxis, which is the prerequisite for an enlightened political, economic, and cultural development in any society" (2004:398). Even with these tensions, the debate has provided space for scholars who think and work differently. On the methods side, action research methods and ethnographic approaches are finding more room in the discipline. Networks like research4action and the Scholars Strategy Network are explicit attempts to connect social scientists with political practitioners and policy makers.

Yet, the space that exists for scholars working outside of neo-positivist and/or statistical methods remains tenuous at best. Isaac's 2015 editorial, "For a More Public Political Science" is required reading on this point:

What do I mean in speaking of a resurgent neo-positivism? I mean, very simply, a reenergized and dynamic commitment to the idea that the most important challenge of a "progressive" political science is to promote methodological hyper-sensitivity, "scientific rigor," and expert authority (2015:274).

As the texts in this volume illustrate, the hegemonic power of disciplinary standards of neo-positivist and quantitative norms continues to dominate the discussion. Indeed, the recent debate on DA-RT ("Data Access and Research Transparency") among qualitative scholars has illustrated how some of these issues remain at the fore of deep disagreements.[2]

The Challenges of Anti-Poverty Policy

As any policy scholar will tell you, legislating is hard work. This is especially true for large programs, which as both U.S. political parties understand from recent health care debates, are as challenging to pass as they are to repeal. The reasons are legion but can be summed up in a maximalist definition of institutions, one that incorporates the formal rules of organizations like Congress as well as the norms and assumptions of our wider culture (Hall & Taylor, 1996). As Skidmore notes in this volume, the political structure of the United States was designed for slow processes and to stymie radical change. As such, policy changes to major programs often happen on the margins of enforcement, rule-making, adjustments, competing programs, or simply letting the context of society change in ways that impacts the efficacy of a given program (Hacker, 2004). The failure of Republicans to repeal the Affordable Care Act during President Trump's first term, and the moves by the administration to nonetheless weaken the Act with whatever tools they have, are a testament to this.

---

2   See the Qualitative & Multi-Method Research Spring 2015 symposium on DA-RT for an excellent discussion of its potential impacts on qualitative research.

With the right data, traditional political science can offer valuable insights into the policy making process, including the efficacy or efficiency of programs, the pathways that policies take as they undergo development, and their impacts on society. Quantitative data, in particular, can offer measurable insights into policy outcomes.

This approach is limited, however, insofar that it struggles to explain how political conflict can shape the policy making process. If we are interested in telling rich causal stories about outcomes, complicated and context-dependent discussions of politics are needed in as much as measurable quantitative data. For example, comparing the different Medicaid Expansion strategies across various states can offer important insights into how distinctive policy models can lead to better and worse outcomes (Sommers, et al. 2016). At the same time, the partisan politics around Medicaid expansion are likely a crucial variable in explaining outcomes, and one that is challenging to quantify because it rests on political values and conflict rather than clear cut inputs and outputs. Of course, political science and policy analysis has a rich history of this sort of examination, from Kingdon's classic work on policy process theory (1984) to Jacob and Skocpol's case study of the Affordable Care Act (2012). And it is in this attention to process, values, and content that we might leverage a more accessible and public political science that is geared towards service to American Democracy.

Let us turn to the content of the chapters to illustrate an example. Amidst the various challenges to passing new and stronger anti-poverty policy is the cultural institution of deservedness, a concept that appears throughout the chapters in this volume. What kinds of people deserve benefits from society, and how to political actors—citizens, politicians, and practitioners alike— make sense of deservedness and deploy it in certain contexts? What may appear to be an abstract question has real impacts on outcomes, and the examples of how deservedness lurk in the foundation of policy outcomes are legion. Military spending is typically easy to increase, while services for veterans can flounder.

When states manage welfare payment levels, those with whiter populations offer more robust benefits than those with a higher percentage of black residents. The social safety net in the United States is built on tiers of service that reward high-income work and penalized those who cannot or do not work (Campbell 2014).

These outcomes cannot be fully explained through discussions of relative efficiency or a focus on quantifiable effects. Indeed, the evidence suggests that using deservedness as a standard to provide exceedingly low benefits to the poor does not help them move out of poverty, instead functioning more like a punishment than a hand-up. Thus, if we want to understand policy outcomes, attention to the values and worldviews of political actors are crucial in explaining the whole picture. Exceedingly low TANF benefits, for example, make more sense within a logic that frames beneficiaries as fully responsible for their own straights, where they have in fact chosen to be poor. Luckily, political science has the tools to analyze these sorts of factors, be it path dependency of policy outcomes, the construction of categories, or political conflict over meaning and value.

I would posit that when we look to public debates about policy, there is very little attention paid to cost-benefit analysis or comparisons of program options. Instead, the conflict is over values. Is Medicaid For All about human rights and dignity, or is it a creeping socialism that is the antithesis of American democracy? Many actors on both sides of the debate put more stock into arguments over value than the nuances of policy work. This is not to say that we should turn away from our data-driven research, but rather that public debate is happening in a different register than scholarly debate. If we are interested in public interventions on policy, attention to the tenor of these disagreements is likely necessary. And if we are interested in more normative discussions of policy, then attention to how power shapes values and discourse is certainly necessary (Smucker 2017). Again, political science has a rich history of analyzing power relationships, the outcomes of discourse, and the process of political conflict and ideology. The challenge as researchers is that this work does not always fit into methods that solely rely on statistical analysis.

One concern is that a focus on political values and conflict can lead to work that abandons scientific and disciplinary principles of objectivity. There are many ways to approach this. At its core, this tension mirrors that which Smith discussed above—one cannot be politically neutral while also attempting to advance American democracy, regardless of the definition. Given recent concerns about President Trump's approach to political institutions and norms, this tension may need to be set aside for scholars who feel that American democracy itself is under attack (Levitsky & Ziblatt, 2018). For those new to these approaches, one might look to the interpretivist scholars cited earlier, who emphasize transparency and reflexivity as crucial ways to engage in research that requires the subjectivity of the scholar while avoiding bias.[3] But identifying the processes and mechanisms that go into policy processes are valuable and necessary components to policy research, especially if we are concerned about stagnancy or change.

Refining the Discipline

One additional line of argument is required in this discussion, namely that scholars already are engaged in work that speaks to a broader audience and seeks to make an impact in policy. Attending to

this history offers further evidence about the importance of values as well as the danger in circumscribing academic engagement with the public.

In the first instance we can look to examples of public disagreements over policy research. As Skidmore describes in this volume, Card & Krueger's 1994 study on the impact of minimum wages on employment argued in favor of minimum wage increases, and later research in different contexts have provided additional evidence to the point (Cengiz, et al. 2019). Of course, there has been

---

3 Interpretive methodologists argue that objectivity and value-neutral research is, in fact, impossible. Through the selection of the research question, methods, theory, the operationalization of variables, etc., the researcher constantly makes value judgements about what is or is not important.

disagreement and revision on the mechanisms of change and the scope of the findings, as we would suspect. However, conservative scholars and commentators reject these findings across the board. While this rejection engages some data, the clear sorting of pro-minimum wage and anti-minimum wage studies into ideological camps suggests that disagreements over values are at least partially, and probably mostly, to blame for disagreements over policy. The data itself does not exist free of values and interpretation.

As also noted by Skidmore, the story of Reinhart & Rogoff's 2010 paper on debt reinforces the need to consider values in the analysis of public policy. While their research was used to advance austerity policies across the global, later research by Herdon et al (2013) convincingly argued that the original analysis was flawed in numerous respects. This is a typical story of academic research that tests data, theories, and conclusions over time. The political world, however, reacted much differently, with conservatives rejecting the new study because it did not fit their values. The takeaway here is that for political science to engage with public debates, research needs to be sensitive to the conflicts over political values that undergird disagreements about the policies themselves. And, in fact, doing so could elevate both the relevance and usefulness of our work to the public.

A final point on public engagement is worth noting. Readers will note that throughout the chapters of this volume academics loom large in policy discussions. As noted above, Reinhart & Rogoff have had an immense impact on austerity policies. In her chapter on social security, Borzutzky notes the damaging impact of the "institutional and power and neoliberal ideas of the 'Chicago Boys,'" economic advisors trained at the University of Chicago. In his critique of mathematical models of reality, Kingsley illustrates in his chapter on long term care how the work of James Q. Wilson was not only problematic in terms of its research design but had sweeping impacts on the racist discourse of criminal justice. In his chapter that considers the status of foreign policy and neoliberalism, Skidmore discusses the rise of the Straussians, and their dominance in both penetrating government halls of power and shaping a neoconservative policy for decades.

These are noteworthy examples of scholars having dramatic impacts on policy that, for progressives and leftists as well as those committed to exemplary research, are emblematic of how policy analysis can go wrong. At the same time, recognition of these impacts could be a call to action for those who have ideological and philosophical disagreements with those conclusions. In the absence of public facing academics speaking truth to these claims, we should only expect for powerful actors to leverage our institutions to protect and cultivate that power.

In conclusion, there is work to be done. Thankfully, political scientists and policy scholars have the tools to both produce strong findings and cultivate American democracy (in whatever form that may take). In the Trump Era, this may mean unpacking decades or even centuries-old assumptions about the status quo of our political, economic, and social institutions. If things like corruption and freedom of the press are now up for grabs, then they likely have renewed usefulness as research agendas, especially if the polity is itself unsure of the value or content of these institutions.

Further, modern polarization in the U.S. is as much about values and truth claims as it is about disagreements over policy per se. From climate change to health care, from policing to tax policy, many conflicts stem from competing notions of what is right or wrong rather than which alternative has the most efficient throughput in a given scenario. Again, in our discipline we are well placed to tap into how these conflicts work, how actors make sense of them, and the kinds of decisions that are made within meaning- and institution-rich contexts. The following chapters present a compelling narrative about how the structures of the political world intersect with our own disciplinary structures. Hopefully, this discussion is one that opens space for further discussion about how our research can, and should, contribute to our political system in generative ways.

Works Cited

Behn, R. D. (1985). Policy Analysts, Clients, and Social Scientists. Journal of Policy Analysis and Management,, 4(3), 428.

Bourdieu, P. (2000). Pascalian Meditations. Cambridge: Polity.

Brady, H. E., & Collier, D. (Eds.). (2010). Rethinking Social Inquiry. Plymouth, UK: Rowman & Littlefield.

Burawoy, M. (1998). Extended Case Study Method. Sociological Theory, 16, 4-33.

Campbell, A. (2014). Trapped in America's Safety Net. Chicago: University of Chicago.

Cengiz, D., Dube, A., Lindner, A., & Zipperer, B. (2019). The Effect of Minimum Wages on Low-Wage Jobs: Evidence from the United States Using a Bunching Estimator. Cambridge: The National Bureau of Economic Research.

Copeland, R. A. (2014, February 18). Why Nicholas Kristof's Latest Column Stings So Much And Why He's Right. Retrieved June 2019, from The Huffington Post: http://www.huffingtonpost.com/rev-adam-j-copeland/nicholas-kristofs-latest-column-stings_b_4800560.html

Flyvbjerg, B. (2001). Making Social Science Matter: Why Social Inquiry Fails and How It Can Succeed Again. Cambridge: Cambridge University Press.

Flyvbjerg, B. (2004). A Perestroikan Straw Man Answers Back: David Laitin and Phronetic Political Science. Politics & Society, 32(1), 389-416.

Hacker, J. S. (2004). Privatizing Risk without Privatizing the Welfare State: The Hidden Politics of Social Policy Retrenchment in the United States. The American Political Science Review, 98(2), 243-260.

Hall, P. A., & Taylor, R. C. (1996). Political Science and the Three New Institutionalisms. Political Studies, XLIV, 936-957.

Isaac, J. C. (2015). For a More Public Political Science. Perspectives on Politics, 13(2), 269-283.

Jacobs, L. R., & Skocpol, T. (2012). Health Care Reform and American Politics: What Everyone Needs to Know. Exford: Oxfoed University Press.

King, G., Keohane, R., & Verba, S. (2012). Designing Social Inquiry: scientific inference in qualitative research. Princeton, NJ: Princeton University Press.

Kingdon, J. (2011). Agendas, Alternatives and Public Policy, Second Edition. Boston: Pearson.

Kristof, N. (2014, February 15). Professors, We Need You! Retrieved from The New York Times: http://www.nytimes.com/2014/02/16/opinion/sunday/kristof-professors-we-need-you.html

Laitin, D. D. (2003). The Perestroikan Challenge to Social Science. Politics & Society, 31(1), 163-184.

Levitsky, S., & Ziblatt, D. (2018). How Democracies Die. New York: Penguin.

Pachirat, T. (2009). The Political in Political Ethnography: Dispatches from the Kill Floor. In E. Schatz (Ed.), Political Ethnography: What Immersion Contributes to the Study of Power (pp. 143-161). Chicago, IL: University of Chicago.

Rothman, J. (2014, February). Why is Academic Writing so Acadmeic? Retrieved June 2019, from The New Yorker: http://www.newyorker.com/books/page-turner/why-is-academic-writing-so-academic

Smith, R. (2015). Political Science and the Public Sphere Today. Perspectives on Politics, 13(2), 366-376.

Sommers, B. D., Blendon, R. J., Orav, E. J., & Epstein, A. M. (2016). hanges in Utilization and Health Among Low-Income Adults After Medicaid Expansion or Expanded Private Insurance. JAMA Internal Medicine, 176(10), 1501-1509.

Stone, D. (2012). Policy Paradox: the Art of Political Decision Making. New York, NY: W.W. Norton & Co.

Straumsheim, C. (2015, March 11). After Rejecting Blogging Ban,

International Studies Association Embraces Online Media. Retrieved June 2019, from Inside Higher Ed: https://www.insidehighered.com/news/2015/03/11/ after-rejecting-blogging-ban-international-studies-association-embraces-online-media.

Symposium: Transparency in Qualitative and Multi-Method Research . (2015, Spring). Qualitative & Multi-Method Research .

Voeten, E. (2015, November 10). Dear Nicholas Kristof: We Are Right Here! Retrieved June 2019, from The Washington Post: https://www.washingtonpost.com/news/monkey-cage/wp/2014/02/15/dear-nicholas-kristof-we-are-right-here/

Yanow, D., & Schwartz-Shea, P. (Eds.). (2006). Interpretation and Method. Armonk, NY: M.E. Sharpe.

Section One
Scientism:
Speaking Truth to Power

Is Political Science Relevant? The Decline of Critical Scholarly Engagement in the Neoliberal Era

Anthony DiMaggio

Department of Political Science, Lehigh University, Bethlehem, PA

This essay relies on a participant-observation method, among other approaches, to analyze structural and professional changes in Political Science over the last few decades. I document the rise of neoliberalism in Political Science via 6 major changes to the discipline, including: the rise of scholarly "objectivity" as a means of deterring critical analysis, the decline of public intellectualism and publicly accessible studies, the marginalization of practically relevant research, the decline of methodological pluralism and the rise of methodological fetishism, the aversion to political philosophy and political theory, and the devaluation of teaching in favor of research. Proposals are provided for potential reforms to the discipline, for those interested in revitalizing the field and making it more practically relevant to politics and to the general public.

政治学具有相关性吗？新自由主义时代中批判性学术参与的下降

本文使用包括参与观察法在内的不同方法，分析了过去几十年里政治学的架构变化和专业变化。作者以该学科经历的6次重大变革，记录了新自由主义在政治学中的兴起，这6次重大变革包括：一、学术"客观性"（objectivity）为遏制批判性分析而兴起；二、公共理性主义（public intellectualism）和可公开访问研究的衰落；三、实际相关研究的边缘化；四、方法论多元主义的衰落和方法论拜物教的兴起；五、对政治哲学和政治理论的厌恶；六、对注重研究的教学进行贬低。对于公众和那些有意重振该学科领域，并使该学科更切合政治实际情况的人而言，本文就该学科的潜在改革可能提了一些建议。

¿Es relevante la ciencia política? La decadencia de la participación de académicos críticos durante la era neoliberal

Este ensayo se apoya en el método de participación-observación, entre otras aproximaciones, para analizar los cambios estructurales y profesionales en las ciencias políticas en las últimas décadas. Yo documento el alza del neoliberalismo en las ciencias políticas a través de 6 cambios importantes a la disciplina, incluyendo: el incremento de la "objetividad" académica como una forma para repeler el análisis crítico, la reducción del intelectualismo público y los estudios públicamente accesibles, la marginalización de la investigación prácticamente relevante, la reducción del pluralismo metodológico, la aversión a la filosofía política y a la teoría política y la devaluación de la enseñanza a favor de la investigación. Se proporcionan propuestas de reformas potenciales para la disciplina,

Introduction

There is no denying it: we live in the neoliberal era. And the rise of neoliberalism has meant a transformation in how higher education is structured. Critical theorists and public intellectuals have warned about the dangers of neoliberalism in higher education, as related to the decline of tenure, state taxpayer funding cuts, skyrocketing tuition, student loan debt, and the rise of the notion that students are "customers" rather than learners. Officials in both parties were responsible for this market shift, despite mounting concerns about the decline of education as a public good.

Henry Giroux, a public intellectual and scholar who has long lamented neoliberalism, believes that higher learning should serve a purpose beyond servicing corporate profits. In his essay "Thinking Dangerously," Giroux stresses the need for professors to challenge neoliberal norms. He writes: "at the core of thinking dangerously is the recognition that education is central to politics and that a democracy cannot survive without informed citizens. Critical and danger-ous thinking is the precondition for nurturing the ethical imagination that enables engaged citizens to learn how to govern rather than to be governed."[1]

Giroux calls for redefining higher learning away from the rise of anti-intellectualism. Attacks on intellectualism long predate the presidency of Donald Trump, as conservative media pundits and officials have historically maintained an antagonistic relationship with academia, attacking professors as liberally biased and for perverting the minds of the young with anti-Americanism and subversive ideas. This suspicion of higher education has grown significantly. As the Pew Research Center reported in 2017, 58 percent of Republicans and Republican-leaning independents agreed "colleges and universities have a negative effect on the country." But as recently as 2010, 58 percent of Republicans and Republican-leaning independents held a positive view of higher education. That number fell to 36 percent by 2017.[2] It does not take much imagination to conclude that the recent and rising conservative disdain for higher education is tied to the growing popularity of a reactionary, anti-intellectual culture revolving around Donald Trump.

Rather than demonstrating a far-left bias in academia, Trump's rise suggests a failure of educators and the mass media to socialize citizens to embrace critical thinking, the scientific method, and evidence-based reasoning. Trump has been attacked for his campaign and administration's routine distortions of social, economic, and political issues. His victory in the 2016 presidential election, coupled with the troubling findings from Pew's recent survey on perceptions of higher education, suggest that scholars can no longer afford to ignore the growth of anti-intellectualism and the threat it represents to higher learning. But this essay is not concerned primarily with Trump. Rather, the main issue is encouraging a discussion of the problems facing political science, and what can be done to address them.

The "professionalization" of political science, evident in the growing emphasis on research and publications, has benefited scholars and students by broadening our knowledge of political institutions and behavior, while providing instructors better-quality information in the classroom. And improvements in research methods allow for higher-quality technical research and more confidence in conclusions concerning the analysis of evidence and empirical data. However, in the push for professionalization, certain priorities have been neglected, leading to an increasingly homogenized discipline. The discipline suffers from a lack of relevance at a time when evidence-based learning and scientific knowledge are sorely needed.

In this essay, I argue that mainstream political science suffers from a variety of ills. Most of them are externally imposed, although scholars contribute to these ills by embracing, or at least tolerating, the rise of a neoliberal philosophy that is the driving force behind higher education. While I discuss six major problems that define modern political science, many of these issues also apply to other disciplines in the natural sciences, the social sciences, and the humanities. These include (i) the myth of the neutral, "objective" researcher, who sets aside his or her personal biases to discover "the truth"; (ii) the dearth of public outreach work among scholars, which has ensured that the discipline is mostly irrelevant to national, state, and local political discussions; (iii) the lack of accessibility of political science, due to the persistence of arcane language and the lack of interest in practically useful research; (iv) the decline of methodological pluralism and the rise of methodological fetishism, which have contributed to the depoliticization of the discipline; (v) the marginalization of political philosophy and political theory, leading to the dominance of technocratic research divorced from larger meaning; and (vi) the devaluation of teaching in pursuit of institutional prestige, via a growing fixation on research publications at the expense of classroom learning.

These problems are symptoms of a larger development in higher education— the ascendance of "professionalization," as defined by the market-based norms of neoliberalism. I devote this essay to exploring these problems in greater detail, while relating them back to the broader phenomenon of neoliberal change in American society.

What Is Neoliberalism? And Why It Matters

It is necessary to provide a working definition of "neoliberalism" and its relationship to academia. Generally speaking, neoliberalism refers to a market-based shift in society, in which the interests and agendas of the wealthy and corporations dominate public policymaking. It is strongly related to the concept of plutocracy, or rule by the wealthy, in that neoliberalism is criticized for enhancing the power of the affluent, at the expense of the many. Neoliberalism includes specific policy reforms, for example, tax cuts for the wealthy, government deregulation of corporations, budgets cuts for welfare programs and other social spending, support for "free trade," assaults on workers via limitations on unionization and collective bargaining, and privatization of public resources in favor of enhancing corporate profits. In the context of higher education, schools exist to train students to be the corporate workers of the future and to embrace consumerism as the dominant goal in life. Students are expected to front the costs for this opportunity to join the corporate work force, as funding for higher educational institutions shifts away from taxpayer revenues and toward a tuition-centered model, resulting in tens of thousands of dollars in debt for the average student.

Under neoliberalism, higher education is decoupled from notions that students should learn how to become better informed and knowledgeable citizens, how to think critically, and how to actively participate in a democracy. Rather, the new motto is that "learning means earning," with education devolving into credentialing in pursuit of vocational goals. Within this context, Giroux warns, higher education has "disinvested in critical education," which has led to a system of "learning" that is increasingly defined by "cultural illiteracy." In *Neoliberalism's War on Higher Education*, Giroux expands on this line of reasoning:

> Critical thought, knowledge, dialogue, and dissent are increasingly perceived with suspicion by the new corporate university that now defines faculty as entrepreneurs, students as customers, and education as a mode of training. ... [S]chools have been transformed into a private right rather than a public good. Students are being educated to be consumers rather than thoughtful, critical citizens.[3]

Many scholars—including in political science—appear not to recognize these developments, or if they do, they do not care enough to protest them.

Giroux connects the rise of neoliberalism to broader dangers. He writes:

> Across the globe, the forces of free-market fundamentalism are using the educational system to reproduce a culture of privatization, deregulation and commercialization while waging an assault on the historically guaranteed social provisions and civil rights provided by the welfare state, higher education, unions, reproductive rights and civil liberties. All the while, these forces are undercutting public faith in the defining institutions of democracy.[4]

Considering the assault on the public sphere and the very notion of the public good, educators could be playing a vital role in reminding citizens of the value of, and need for, public goods such as education. As Giroux argues: "In the present moment, it becomes particularly important for educators and concerned citizens all over the world to protect and enlarge the critical formative educational cultures and public spheres that make democracy possible."[5] However, Giroux also concedes that academics are in an increasingly precarious position to challenge the neoliberal privatization of society, considering the tendency in higher education toward "insular discourses that accompany [increasingly] specialized scholarship."[6]

By stressing the rise of neoliberalism, I do not mean to claim there is an absence of individuals in higher education who are sincerely committed to helping students learn, and to higher education as a public good. The field of political science has numerous academic journals devoted to furthering the discipline concerning not only research, but pedagogy, and to addressing "big-picture" issues in the discipline. The *Journal of Political Science Education* assists professors in developing their teaching skills, while pioneering innovations in teaching methods. *Perspectives on Politics* runs numerous articles that demonstrate a critical self-consciousness, as seen in its efforts to engage in a broader discussion of the academic discipline and the conflicting ideologies and perspectives that drive it.[7] Similarly, *PS: Political Science and Politics* addresses key issues that define the discipline, research-wise and pedagogically. In recent years, *PS* addressed many timely issues, including acknowledgment of gender bias in academia and the need for greater diversity; efforts to examine how a social science education relates to broader concepts such as citizenship; concern with the dramatic rise in student loan debt; and discussion of the vocational turn in higher education in the neoliberal era and how to promote a productive dialogue regarding efforts to improve instruction in the classroom. The journal even has numerous subsections devoted to broader questions within the discipline and to providing teaching resources for professors.[8]

But I am more concerned with dominant trends in the discipline, rather than with the efforts of specific individuals or journals, which, despite their best efforts, have been unable to reverse the harmful developments I discuss in this essay. Many of the criticisms in this essay echo those offered in the "Perestroika" movement of the early 2000s, which occurred prior to my entrance as a scholar into political science, and which related to the discipline's problems with methodological narrowness, lack of critical analysis, and disengagement from practical politics. But despite the "Perestroika" movement, which sought to confront some of the worst excesses of political science, the need for transforma-tional change in the discipline remains.[9] "Perestroika" was composed of many diverse individuals who held competing ideas about what political science should be. I go beyond the relatively narrow claims about needing more "pluralism" in the discipline, arguing that the neoliberal shift in society is responsible for the downfall of academia, with the decline of political science just one of many casualties. The neoliberal turn in higher education is about far more than any individual, department, field, or even the social sciences. It is about ideological and material trends occurring in the United States and throughout the world, in which education is increasingly valued only insofar as it can serve the interests of private corporations, private power, and private profits.

Research Design: Measuring the Neoliberal Turn

In this essay, I measure the rise of neoliberal "professionalization" of political science via one primary research method: my own experiences as an observer of, and participant in, the discipline over the last two decades. These experiences include more than five years as an undergraduate taking political science courses (1998–2003); a two-year term completing a terminal master's degree (2004–2005); another six-year term completing a PhD (2006–2012); and 13 years in the classroom as an instructor in political science and sociology (2005 to present) at two major state universities (2005–2009), a small liberal arts college (2008–2009), a community college (2011–2016), and a liberal arts university (2016 to present).

During that time, I gained extensive experience, not only in the classroom as a student and professor, but also with research obligations, serving as a peer reviewer and publishing in the field. By 2017, I had either published, or committed to publish via contract, eight scholarly books with five different publishers, and nearly a dozen book chapters and journal article; presented nearly two dozen professional conference papers; served as a peer reviewer for four different academic journals and four academic book publishers; and participated in a dozen interviews for tenure-track faculty positions. I held two permanent positions, one tenured and the other tenure-track, during this time. In total, these experiences allow me to draw on learning, teaching, research, and interview-related experiences across 12 different colleges and universities. My experiences at academic conferences, in interviews, and with mentors and other instructors meant I developed a peer network of scholars with experiences that extend to dozens of institutions of higher learning, allowing for more confidence that my conclusions are not simply anecdotal. In short, my experiences are extensive enough to allow me to generalize about how the discipline functions. I also supplement my personal experience with other information drawn from widely available national data sources, as related to hiring practices, publishing trends, and teaching priorities in the discipline. While I encountered considerable diversity in the discipline during that time regarding teaching and research styles, and philosophical outlooks, I observed numerous developments suggesting a neoliberal turn in higher education.

The Myth of Objectivity

One of the defining characteristics of neoliberalism in higher education is the demobilization of the professoriate. "Professionalization" has meant the rise of the notion that scholars can be "objective" in their analyses—by being "unbiased" or "neutral." Such claims are unsustainable on the face of it. The scientific method requires that scholars stake out claims via development of a hypothesis, which must be vigorously defended through a well-developed research design and empirical testing. Political scientists are expected to make an argument about how the world works, and that cannot be done by being "unbiased." And yet, as I can attest to in many conversations and evaluations, scholars and students regularly perpetuate the myth that social science can be pursued free from values or biases.

The "objectivity" myth is particularly effective in the graduate student training process and throughout the publication process. I was regularly subjected to lectures from mentors and other professors about the need to avoid normative engagement, and the virtues of remaining "unbiased," since the job of the social scientist is to explain how the political process works, free from personal values. On the peer review and job interview fronts, I often encountered scholars who were visibly uncomfortable with my attempts at fusing scholarship and normative engagement, to the point where it meant the rejection of publications that were under review by a publisher. Additionally, my commitment to normative engagement meant many individuals were openly hostile to my being hired by their department, as was made clear during interviews. These attacks were seldom linked to any specific or tangible methodological challenge to my work, but were driven by a more general disdain for my philosophical approach to the discipline. In the publication peer review process, I have been told that my work is too "polemical," independent of any specific substantive critique, and that normatively or critically engaged scholarship is something scholars simply do not do. However, I also attended a more unconventional graduate program for my terminal master's degree that encouraged scholars to be public intellectuals and make practical contributions to the national discourse over how to improve American society. Having this experience before entering a more conventional PhD program that stressed "objectivity" provided me with perspective on what political science could be, rather than simply accepting the status quo of "objective" scholarship.

Most all social scientists would agree that objectivity is a laudable, noble goal, if one defines it as seeking to provide the best possible explanation for how the world works with the data that are available. But to claim that this can be done by divorcing researchers from their own personal experiences, beliefs, and values, which inevitably color how they see the world and how they seek to measure it, is naive. If we are not talking about objectivity as neutrality, what is the actual role of this myth of objectivity under neoliberalism? The simplest answer is that objectivity serves as a subtle mechanism for deterring critical thinking and any possibility that scholars will challenge the central characteristics of the neoliberal system, or encourage students to develop the critical thinking and analytical skills necessary to challenge that system. Political centrism masquerades as neutrality— that is to say, individuals without strong political values or convictions one way or another mistake not having anything provocative to say with being unbiased. And this process transcends departmental political pressures. Political leaders and college administrators are well aware they are intimidating those working within public education in order to deter critical dissent against the political and economic status quo.[10]

Objectivity now serves as a filtering mechanism by those who kowtow to political power to root out unconventional views. It is a useful tool of social control for deterring criticisms of the established order. This filtering operates at various levels simultaneously, at the undergraduate, graduate, faculty hiring, and junior/senior professorial levels. It is achieved by professors' setting grading standards for undergraduate students, by establishing expectations for what scholarship is supposed to look like for graduate students, by blacklisting critically engaged scholars from being seriously considered for job interviews, by setting tenure expectations aimed at discouraging critical analysis and public engagement, and by reinforcing those standards for scholars seeking promotions following tenure.

The notion that objectivity functions as a subtle form of thought control is reinforced in political science via textbooks. These books, despite their high costs, perform poorly in encouraging critical thought. Rarely do they contain information that would lead a reader to question official or media-driven misinformation. This omission of critical analysis is intentional, since less controversial content means less potential for complaint, and better sales prospects. But omission of critical thinking and analysis is perhaps the most insidious form of bias. It establishes parameters for what students and scholars can think, and actively deters critical thinking. It displays contempt for the ability of students to decide for themselves whether they want to embrace "mainstream" values, or consider more unconventional views.

I draw on two personal experiences in documenting my claim that social scientists reinforce their own biases via omission of inconvenient perspectives. One experience relates to the study of morality and war, the other to research on political and media propaganda. My research on morality and war showcases how the "social construction" of knowledge operates in the discipline.[11] Sociologists have long written about the power of scholars to actively create and shape how knowledge is developed, by focusing on certain aspects of reality, and by marginalizing or ignoring others. In the case of war, mainstream scholarship for years focused on rising public opposition to war as a function of partisanship, ideology, casualties, or perceived prospects for victory.[12] What was systematically omitted from these studies was the possibility that citizens might be driven primarily by the perceived immorality of wars, due to the tremendous death and destruction they produce. It was not until very recently that the concept of perceived immorality gained attention in empirical public opinion studies— specifically in my work on the subject. Previous works merely focused on public assessments of war based on mainstream and pragmatic considerations about war's progress, not on the radical notion that the public may fundamentally reject war itself. This is a compelling example of how subtle biases in favor of the political status quo operate to censor critical views from scholarly discourse. Bias occurs via omission, and most students were none the wiser to this phenomenon so long as immorality was removed from discussions of public opinion and war.

Sometimes the subtle biases driving academics come back to haunt scholars, and the deficiencies in critical thought are exposed for all to see. A case in point is scholarly contempt for Chomsky and Herman's "Propaganda Model," which depicted American journalists as uncritically disseminating official rhetoric and messages, at the expense of greater diversity of views in political and media discourse.[13] Despite the popularity of their book with the public, *Manufacturing Consent* was largely ignored by major political-communication scholars, and there has been little effort to take seriously the study of media propaganda. As Robinson and Herring recount of the scholarly community's reaction to the work: "most commonly, Chomsky is not denounced, misinterpreted, or engaged with. He is simply ignored." This blacklisting meant "the marginalization of a legitimate research agenda that deserves scholarly attention and debate."[14] Prominent scholars explained the dismissal of the Propaganda Model in political terms, with Chomsky and Herman being seen as too far outside the political mainstream for academics to engage in their ideas.[15]

The study of political and media propaganda has received short shrift in numerous disciplines, including political science, communication studies, and sociology, where scholars have sought to avoid the negative consequences associated with adopting a radical research agenda that is likely to be attacked and dismissed outright. History scholars have suffered no similar pressures, since there is much more tolerance in academia and in society for looking back at wars long ended, such as World War I, the Korean War, or the Vietnam War, and understanding how propaganda was used to try and manipulate public minds. Because of these reduced pressures, historians have benefited from a proliferation of high-quality historical studies of war propaganda.[16] In contrast, there are only a small handful of recent empirical studies that document how political propaganda is used in modern times, and the number of scholars across the country working on such studies can be counted on one hand.[17]

The refusal of the social sciences to address the propaganda research paradigm means that higher education was poorly prepared to analyze the rise of Donald Trump. Trump's routine distortions and fabrications, coupled with his ironic and cynical attacks on news media for producing "fake news," suggest that the subject of political and media propaganda is more timely now than ever before. And yet, the social sciences suffer from a dearth of quality scholarship in this field, to the detriment of public knowledge and our understanding of political communication in American politics. Social sciences continue to dismiss the Propaganda Model out-of-hand, failing to learn from past mistakes. At a time when the presidency is defined by shameless lying and blatant attempts at deception, citizens would benefit from a nuanced, thoughtful, and intellectual discussion of propaganda and how to identify it. This discourse has not materialized, at least not in any way in which social science scholars have played a leading role.

British-Israeli historian Ilan Pappe does not take issue with objectivity as a concept, but with the notion that objectivity translates into being unbiased or value free. In his dispute with fellow historian Benny Morris, Pappe explains: "The debate between us is on one level between historians who believe they are purely objective reconstructers of the past, like Morris, and those who claim that they are subjective human beings striving to tell their own version of the past, like myself. When we write histories, we built arches over a long period of time and we construct out of the material in front of us a narrative. We believe and hope that this narrative is a loyal reconstruction of what happened although ... we can not ride a train back in time to check it."[18] Sociologists refer to this approach to studying the world as "positionality."[19] Scholars are open about their backgrounds and how they relate to their research, so that there is no question about underlying biases that drive one's analysis.

Political scientists would benefit from taking Pappe's words to heart. The most anyone can expect from scholars is to be honest about their own personal biases, and to present the fairest, most accurate picture of reality that they can. The hope is that, through many different scholars' attacking issues from a variety of perspectives, experiences, and research approaches, we can eventually construct an accurate enough picture of the world that it is possible to speak of "knowledge" or "truth."

Knowledge in a Vacuum: The Decline of Public Outreach

Knowledge is of no value if it is produced for its own sake, without a connection to a plan for making the world a better place. And yet this mentality—producing knowledge for the sake of knowledge—dominates political science. Scholars view it merely as their responsibility to conduct research, not to get that research into policy-relevant discussions and debates. And if much of our discipline is reluctant to even promote our work in policy circles, it goes without saying that the vast majority of political scientists do not prioritize direct political action, organizing, or protest.

Advocacy work and efforts at disseminating one's scholarship in public circles—known as public intellectualism—are not traits that are generally valued very much in graduate school, in faculty hiring, or in the tenure and promotion process. This trend is not unique to political science. Sociologists, for example, refer to the commitment to producing knowledge for its own sake as "basic sociology," as in this is the bare minimum expectation of a scholar. But then again, sociology is a more forward-thinking discipline than political science. At least there is a discussion within the field about whether the goal of scholars is to simply produce knowledge ("basic sociology"), to push political officials to pay attention to one's research and factor it into policymaking ("public sociology"), or to actively attempt to improve the world ("applied sociology").[20] This discourse is part of a basic introduction to the discipline in sociology textbooks, although one will not see anything similar in American Government introductory texts.

In the neoliberal era of higher education, citizens are viewed as atomized consumers who have no need to get involved in politics, and merely need to satisfy created wants via advertising in order to live "the good life." Under neoliberalism, political officials regularly engage in anti-government rhetoric meant to socialize citizens to be suspicious of the political system. Little wonder, then, that nearly half of the adult-age public does not pay attention to politics and the news, or vote. Political science bears unique responsibility for the rise of depoliticization and political apathy. We have not done enough to foster a passion for learning about politics, or a yearning to become engaged in the political process. This failure is likely directly linked to the myth of "objectivity." By failing to instill passion in students about the need to be informed, active citizens, scholars contribute to the problem of political disengagement.

The timidity of the professoriate regarding political or normative engagement is not surprising. It is to a large extent the product of a neoliberal effort on the part of political officials (particularly at the state level) to intimidate professors into silence. Wisconsin is only the most recent example of a state seeking to pacify professors and critical thinking through large budget cuts to higher education, with the elimination of tenure, and via state legislative efforts to dictate curriculum to suppress critical and allegedly anti-American views. Under this system, professors increasingly fear being singled out for punishment. It is no wonder, then, that most academics seek to avoid public attention and public intellectualism. In the neoliberal era, Giroux stresses, public intellectuals have not entirely disappeared. Those intellectuals who serve conservative, neoliberal, and business interests are still celebrated by right-wing political leaders and pundits. Rather, it is those who dissent against the status quo who are increasingly under attack.[21]

University and college administration have also contributed to the stifling of public intellectualism. Publicly aimed op-eds and other commentary, in addition to other forms of outreach to the mass media, while not technically discouraged, count for very little when it comes to tenure evaluation. It is not uncommon to see universities and colleges weight tenure review as follows: 40 percent research; 40 percent teaching; 20 percent service, with public intellectualism being a small component of service. At best, being active within one's community via protest, holding teach-ins, engaging in interviews with the media, publishing popular writings, or maintaining a public presence in other ways will count for little in one's tenure evaluation. At worst, these activities will actively hurt one's chances of getting hired or earning tenure. In numerous recent cases—including Native American scholars Steven Salaita and Ward Churchill, political scientist Larycia Hawkins, political theorist George Ciccariello-Maher, and sociologist Johnny Eric Williams—professors were harassed by college administration due to their visible and controversial public presence on social media and in other forms of public outreach.[22] Aside from violating basic principles of academic freedom, this singling out of professors for "bad behavior" creates a chilling effect on college campuses, as scholars rightly fear they will be next if they put forward controversial ideas. These administrators, often acting on behalf of right-wing activists, media pundits, and government officials, fostered a culture of subservience, and passivity among faculty.

In a neoliberal educational environment in which public outreach is often discouraged, esoteric research agendas divorced from the public are encouraged. In this context, we begin to see the rise of careerism divorced from social obligations. Professors become more interested in the next publication and promotion, or how to leverage an external offer into higher pay at one's home institution, or how to "publish my way into another job" that pays better and allows more time for research. There is nothing surprising about these developments, considering the values and incentive structures at work in higher education. In this process, careerism supplants the common good as the ultimate goal of faculty, not just in political science, but across academic disciplines.

I draw on two personal experiences here, in addition to broader data in the field of political science publishing, to flesh out my theme about the declining practical relevance of the discipline. It is clear via the publication peer review process that political science scholars display an obliviousness to the importance of public outreach. For example, in my most recently published book on economic policy, media bias, and public opinion, I was pressured by a reviewer to remove "the public" entirely from my book, in addition to removing any references to conservatives' claims about an alleged "liberal bias" in the news. The justification given for removing this discussion about bias was that such claims emanated mostly from individuals outside the academic community, including citizens, media pundits, and political leaders. These actors were simply not relevant to this academic work, and apparently threatened the important goal of insulating my writing from any contemporary significance.

The peer reviewer also expressed displeasure that my work analyzed the effects of media content on public opinion. It was enough, supposedly, merely to focus on academic discussions of media bias, rather than taking a more holistic approach to analyzing the effect of this coverage on public beliefs. Of course, this would have defeated the entire point of the book, which was at its core focused on media effects on public opinion, but the change was deemed necessary by the reviewer for the purposes of brevity and simplicity. A book, apparently, can only focus on one thing or another—media or public opinion—not both. This sort of needless segmentation threatens to make social science research even more irrelevant, especially when the topic analyzed is how the broader public fits into questions of media bias.

In a second example of scholars' discomfort with the public, I was pressured to remove any references in a book project to my participant observation of social movements in the post-2008 era ... in a book about social movements in the post-2008 era. The reviewer expressed discomfort with the notion that there might be first-person accounts in the book of my experiences with and knowledge of these movements, since first-person accounts are not "typical" in mainstream political science research. The completely self-defeating nature of removing primary data on social movements in a book providing a political history of modern social movements was lost on the reviewer. Nonetheless, such sentiment symbolizes just how antagonistic political science has grown toward public outreach.

Whether it is the case that much of what political scientists produce has little practical policy value, or that we professors fail to effectively "sell" our writing to a broader audience, there is little indication of any significant impact of the discipline on politics. Most scholars make little effort to promote their research findings or see that they make their way into larger policy debates. And the evidence even within the discipline is thin in terms of whether much of the research published has a significant impact. I remember a faculty mentor when I was in my PhD program speaking about various political scientists who were published in top-tier journals as "famous." I found that characterization amusing, considering how insulated the profession is, and how little tangible evidence there is that research projects are making a significant impact. I would consider my own academic career to be a success up to this point, in that I performed well academically in undergraduate and graduate school, published books and other works, and secured tenure-track or tenured positions over the years. But even my most "successful" works are not cited by more than five dozen scholars. This low level of mass appeal can be demoralizing when considering the countless hours devoted to each project.

The findings are not much different when looking at scholars who are viewed as among the most successful in the discipline. I examined citation counts via Google Scholar for three academic journals—*American Political Science Review* (*APSR*), *International Security* (*IS*), and *Public Opinion Quarterly* (*POQ*), all listed in a survey of political scientists as "top 10" journals in terms of their perceived prestige and quality.[23] These cases represent the *greatest successes* in the discipline, compared to other middle- and lower-ranked journals. In mid-2017, I looked at all the articles published by each journal for the year 2010. This allowed for nearly seven years of citations to accrue for each publication. If these "top-tier" works did not receive significant citation counts after seven years, it is doubtful they ever will.

My findings are instructive in spotlighting the limited *demonstrable* impact of academic publications. On average, each *APSR* article received 157 citations, despite the journal's being the flagship publishing outfit for American political scientists. At the lower end, it was common to see many articles receive a half-dozen citations to a few dozen, and on the higher end to receive three or four hundred citations. Results were less impressive for the other two journals. *IS* articles, on average, received 79 citations each, in comparison to *POQ* articles, which received just 56 citations each. These findings are likely much more impressive than for many middle- and lower-tier journals.

It is counterproductive to make apples-to-oranges comparisons between popular publications and scholarly ones. On the one hand, I have published in popular venues such as *Salon* and *Counterpunch*, which respectively benefit from approximately 300,000 readers and 30,000 readers per day.[24] On the other hand, my individual scholarly works have each been cited in dozens of other scholarly works. As I already discussed, this is typical for other successful scholars. But it is difficult to effectively gauge how "effective" a scholar is in making a difference in furthering the development of knowledge when assessing two different types of publishing that are wildly different in nature. Still, some general conclusions could be drawn from the above data.

First, the impact of academic publications is not very impressive, if one defines impressive to include a demonstrated broad reach and impact of one's work on contributing to national discussions of political issues. Some might claim that, while only dozens cite a typical social science piece in many highly ranked journals, hundreds, or even thousands more may read them. It is difficult to take this claim seriously without tangible evidence. It is not clear how many people who subscribe to journals even read the individual articles that are published in them. They may simply read the abstracts, or briefly skim articles of interest. They may not read or skim the articles at all. Furthermore, there is no way to know whether those who cite a piece even read it, or if they simply skimmed the piece or read the abstract. In an era in which massive numbers of publications are produced every year within individual disciplines, and professors are under more pressure than ever to "publish or perish," it is difficult to speak with any specificity about the impact of this scholarship.

The above points are not meant to denigrate research that only reaches a small number of people. As scholars, we may decide that despite small readerships, the impact of an article read by dozens or hundreds is high considering contribution to knowledge and expertise these publications have on the scholarly community. I have no interest in protesting this position. But considering the uncertain impacts of this scholarship within the academy, and the almost complete certainty that this scholarship is having little to no impact outside the halls of academia, it seems questionable to discount the value of public intellectual writings. I can say from personal experience that I have interacted with hundreds of academics over the last decade and a half via my public intellectual writings, and through these conversations I have been told many times of the value readers found in my works. This is not even considering the general or "lay" readers who also learn about politics from this writing.

The simple fact is that popular writings will teach a far larger number of Americans about politics than most academic writings. While most academic books tend to sell in the hundreds, and on occasion in the thousands, a well-placed popular article (near the top of a webpage) published in *Counterpunch* or *Salon* may be seen by tens of thousands, even hundreds of thousands of people. Dismissing these publications as insignificant is unwarranted considering their potential mass impact. Unfortunately, there was little interest in such writings among most faculty hiring committee members in the job interviews I participated in over the last half decade. Such contributions at best were seen as an afterthought regarding what scholars are "supposed" to be doing, and at times as a harmful distraction from the more "important" work of journal and book publishing.

Access Denied: Intentionally Restricting Access to Political Science

The neoliberal era is defined by the relegation of professors to a subordinate role as student trainers and certifiers, rather than as intellectuals providing citizens the tools needed to become active, informed citizens. And the decision to restrict public accessibility to our research directly contributes to the pacification of the professoriate. Most political scientists may resent this assertion, but the discipline has little practical significance to the broader public or to actual politics. This is by design, as seen in intentional efforts to divorce the public from scholarship, and in scholars' reliance on arcane, inaccessible language in their publications and talks. Academic conferences—one of the primary locations where social science knowledge is disseminated—are largely off limits to the public. Since these conferences require individuals to pay a registration fee, access is limited. And the inaccessible format of many empirical and quantitively oriented political science presentations ensures that most members of the public will not gain much from presentations even if they do attend.

Recent practices ensure that public access is even more difficult when conference and hotel representatives seek to identify individuals who have not paid to attend the conference, blocking their access to panel presentations. This behavior sends the message that making money is a more important goal in academia than disseminating knowledge to the public. This prioritization of revenues is not surprising considering that neoliberalism places profits above notions of the public good. The gatekeeping at major professional conferences is harmful to the discipline in that it ensures that scholars' findings will remain restricted to the privileged, intellectual few.

Similar problems emerge regarding public access to academic publications. Academic books are often sold only in hardcover format, seeking to capture a slice of the library book market. This means that books are often picked up by only a few hundred libraries, with members of the public unable to afford the hefty $100 to $150 price per book. Similarly, access to journals is truncated, since individuals cannot access these articles without paying an individual subscription, or without students' educational institution subscribing to these journals. The pay-based access to journals also makes it more difficult for scholars to access journals to which their employing institutions do not subscribe.

Even if academic books and journals were made accessible to the public at a low cost or for free, there is no reason to expect that these publications as written would have much of an impact. Reading has long been on the decline in the United States, and most political science research is not accessible due to esoteric language and research designs with little practical value. On the issue of arcane language, scholars are notorious for writing in a way so as to exclude the mass public, and in order to appeal to a select, initiated, intellectual few. The aura of prestige surrounding this practice allows for many academics to feel as if they are part of an exclusive club that transcends the mass public, but this practice is also harmful because it cements in the public mind that academia produces no work of value.

In his much-read book *The Structure of Scientific Revolutions*, Thomas Kuhn wrote of "normal science," or the practice of engaging in research that slowly contributes to the confirmation of an already established theory.[25] Such work fails to question the fundamental assumptions of the paradigm within which it operates. There is nothing inherently "wrong" with "normal science." To the contrary, it is incredibly important and central to the scientific method, in that broader theories and models regarding how the world works cannot be authoritatively confirmed via one or a small number of studies. Rather, it is the accumulation of knowledge, via many studies over time, that contributes to the development of knowledge. But "normal science" can also be viewed in a pejorative sense, in that much of political and social science research does not concern itself with pushing boundaries, challenging established "truths," or developing a meaningful foundation for paradigm shifts.

In political science, the problem of overspecialization has become quite pronounced, and it is tied to the kind of language used in publications. Scholars become less interested in pushing limits, taking risks, and developing new ideas and theories, and more focused on a "normal science" approach to research where they carve out a small niche within a larger body of research. Oftentimes that means increasingly smaller audiences for this work, which explains in part why most political science articles (even in top-tier journals) are cited so infrequently. The overspecialization of the discipline is an open secret among political scientists, as even a cursory review of research presentations at academic conferences demonstrates. To provide more context on the narrowness of modern research, here is a small sample of these studies, drawn from a major political science conference I attended in the early 2010s:

- "The Power of Participation: Explaining the Issuance of Building Permits in Post-Katrina New Orleans."
- "The Role of Nominal Level Legislative Careers in Explaining Constituency Service in Parliament Under Mixed-Member Electoral Rules: The Hungarian Case."
- "Self-Control and Receptiveness to Affective Framing: A Critical Test of Cognitive Load and Ego Depletion."
- "Are the Kids All Right? Evidence of the Heterogeneous Effects of Empathy-Inducing Media from Survey and Field Experiments."
- "Workload, Delegation, and the Electoral Connection: Evidence from the Interstate Commerce Act of 1887."
- "Examining the Fate of Interparty Judicial Appointments Under New York's Bipartisan System for Nominating Federal District Judges, 1877–1998."

This is, again, only a small sample, but it does speak to the larger issues of over-specialization and inaccessible language. By emphasizing topics in which the public is unlikely to share interest, and by discussing them in ways that are hard to understand for the "typical" American, political scientists actively contribute to their own marginalization.

The problem of inaccessibility has become endemic across numerous sub-fields, including political philosophy/political theory, formal modeling/game theory, and methodology. The esoteric language within political philosophy has long been known among academics across the social sciences and humanities; it is nothing new, and some strains of political theory/philosophy are almost entirely impenetrable for the layperson, including, for example, postmodern/post-structural theory. Prominent political philosophical works of thinkers such as Jacques Derrida, Judith Butler, Hans Georg Gadamer, Jurgen Habermas, and Richard Rorty, only to name a few, may be well understood by philosophers, who share an understanding of the specialized language of the field, but such works are inaccessible to most undergraduate students, as well as to the public.

But the obscure nature of the discipline does not end with political philosophy. With the rise of formal theory/formal modeling, political scientists now communicate their assumptions about how political institutions and actors function via complex game theory–based equations and symbols that are entirely unreadable to a general audience, and probably to most social scientists as well. The assumptions behind this modeling could be much more simply explained without the equations, but this would defeat the point of isolating political science in an air of exclusivity and "superiority." This critique of esoteric science is not new; it has been offered by political scientists in the past as an example of the intentional neutering of the discipline from the realm of practical relevance.[26] With the rise of the "methodology" subfield, political science's lack of public relevance has intensified. Take, for example, this set of papers, pulled at random from the "methodology" section of a major political science conference from a few years ago. They demonstrate how inaccessible much of the empirical work in the field has become:

- "Adjusting for Confounding Bias with Multi-Valued Treatments: The Covariate Balancing Propensity Score for Categorical Treatment Regimes" (2014).
- "Best of All Plausible Worlds? Checking Robustness in Time-Series Cross-Sectional Models with Fictitious Plausible Alternate Treatments" (2014).
- "Evaluating the Robustness of Item Count Technique Estimators Under Random and Non-Random Measurement Error" (2014).
- "Testing for Spatial-Autoregressive Lag Versus Unobserved Spatially Correlated Error-Components" (2014).
- "Causal Interaction in Factorial Experiments: Application to Conjoint Analysis" (2017).
- "A G-to-S Approach to Unobserved Heterogeneity in 'Short' Dynamic Panel Models" (2017).
- "Estimating Dynamic Probit Models Via the Bayesian Adaptive Lasso" (2017).
- "Copula Based Latent Variable Methods: An Application to the U.S. Senate" (2017).
- "Trajectory Balancing: A Kernel Method for Causal Inference with TSCS Data" (2017).

These titles are not only impenetrable to the "average" American; they would likely confuse many, if not most, senior scholars within political science itself, who were trained during a time when methodological fetishism was nowhere near as rampant as it is today.

One might respond to my above criticism of political methodologists by arguing that formal theory and methodology research is not *meant* to be absorbed by the general public. But this argument misses the reality that these pieces are not well received even within the political science community. Few scholars cite such works in their own research, meaning it is unlikely most methodologically centered studies are having a significant impact. For example, articles in the *Journal of Policy Modeling* (devoted specifically to political methodology research) that were published in 2010 typically received only a few dozen citations each, or fewer. This is not encouraging, considering the journal describes itself as "policy" oriented, suggesting it would retain some level of practical relevance. But ultimately, the sparse references to these pieces appears to be beside the point. In a field where methodological complexity and lack of readership are deemed a sign of sophistication, complexity, and rigor, small readership or citation counts are taken as a sign of quality and prestige.

Methodological Uniformity, Fetishism, and Depoliticization

Although there is considerable diversity in political science, the discipline has for decades seen a decline in methodological pluralism. And the obsession with methodological debates, to the exclusion of broader discussions of the significance of one's research, contributes to the depoliticization of the discipline. Increasingly, many political scientists accept the notion that to be "scientific" is to be quantitative in orientation, and that increasingly complex statistical techniques and modeling produce better outcomes. My aim here is not to rail against quantitative research—which I rely on and employ regularly, and see as potentially very valuable. I have no interest in rehashing the tired "quant-qual" debate regarding which approach to social science inquiry is "better." These methods are precisely that—methods—to be exploited to the extent that they are useful in illuminating how the political world works. But under neoliberalism, higher educational debates about research devolve into petty feuding about "whose research method or design is better," while neglecting a discourse focused on the broader significance of research findings to the world of politics. If scholars spend most of their time arguing about methods, there will be little danger of them working to spotlight bigger problems, such as the rise of American inequality, the growing authoritarianism in, and militarization of American politics, the mounting environmental crisis, and the general decline in intellectualism and critical, evidence-based reasoning.

In my experience, rarely do I hear quantitatively oriented political scientists express open disdain for qualitative research or mixed-method approaches to inquiry. Rather, it is largely taken for a given that quantitative analysis should dominate the major journals and subfields of the discipline. The fixation with emphasizing quantitative research at the expense of other methods of inquiry appears to be driven by an attempt to be "more like the hard sciences" and "more like economics," which has long prided itself as the most quantitative and "rigorous" of the social sciences, and with other disciplines such as sociology and anthropology portrayed as "softer" fields or as quasi-scientific.

Much is lost by dismissing or marginalizing qualitative analysis and mixed-methods research. As a student of social movements and the mass media, my job would be unimaginable without both qualitative and quantitative approaches to inquiry. Larger patterns in media coverage are hard to uncover without systematic content analysis of a political issue (quantitative analysis), although these findings do not provide us with many details about the nature of media discourse without a closer interpretative examination of those findings (qualitative analysis). And statistical analysis of national public opinion polls is vital to understanding whether certain demographic factors or attitudes are significant predictors of support for social movements. National polling organizations like the Pew Research Center provide vital data to scholars by surveying the public about their media consumption habits and attitudes about social movements, thereby providing the means to analyze the potential impact of media coverage on public opinion of various movements. But any understanding of social movements would be severely inhibited without scholars committing to actual participant observation of these social movements. The central point here is to say that mixed-methods research allows scholars to "hit" an issue from multiple perspectives and approaches, thereby increasing confidence in one's findings. The marginalization of such research, in favor of a singular focus on statistics, is detrimental to scholarly inquiry.

And yet, there has been little effort to promote methodological diversity in the major academic journals of the discipline. In my field, American Politics, the top-ranked journals, including *American Political Science Review*, *American Journal of Political Science*, *Journal of Politics*, *Political Communication*, and *Public Opinion Quarterly*, are almost entirely dominated by quantitative research. Second-tier journals such as *Political Research Quarterly* and *American Politics Research*, among others, display a similar bias. What is often missing from these venues is a recognition of the value that accompanies multimethod research. Political scientists are primarily interested in causality, and understanding how certain variables impact other variables within the broader context of politics. But numerous tools are marginalized or outright ignored in this effort to identify cause-and-effect relationships. These tools include a political-historical approach to understanding how political processes develop over time; interview-based analysis aimed at explaining why political changes occur and what motivates citizens to act in certain ways or believe what they do; and participant observation, which may be useful as a means of confirming larger patterns identified in quantitative research.

With the rise of methodological fetishism via the fixation on quantitative analysis, the debate in political science has shifted from the significance of one's findings on broader questions about society, governance, and democracy, to myopic and obtuse discussions that elevate debates over research designs to the primary goal of the discipline. This is not to say that research designs are unimportant—they are of huge significance. The difference between legitimate and questionable findings lies in the quality of one's research design. But ultimately, these designs are simply a means to an end, a tool used to get to broader questions about politics and society. Clearly, this point has been lost on many people in the discipline.

My experiences as a social science researcher speak strongly to the myopic turn in the discipline regarding research methods. In my experiences via presenting academic papers at conferences and hosting panels, the most heated debates inevitably end up focused on research methods and questions about research designs, and which quantitative methods are most or least appropriate for specific research projects. The intensity of these discussions is not a bad thing in and of itself, but such behavior becomes problematic when it is not accompanied by equal or greater passion devoted to deliberating on "why all of this matters" to the discipline and to politics and society more generally. In reviewing journal manuscripts and conference papers, I am regularly forced to ask fellow scholars the "so what?" question regarding the practical relevance of their findings. This question seemingly has not received much attention in many social science graduate programs. And when the "so what?" question is addressed in academic papers, it is often only briefly discussed in a paragraph at the very end of the paper, rather than incorporated into the introduction and analysis sections.

The narrow focus on methods and the neglect of broader significance of findings contribute to the depoliticization of the discipline. As perverse as it is to say, political science is no longer primarily about the study of politics so much as it is about the study of and debate over methods. I have experienced this first-hand not only at conferences, but also in the interview process. Discussions about job candidates, and decisions about which candidates to hire, revolve largely around methods, rather than about the broader significance of individuals' findings. In observing interviews as a graduate student, and as an interviewee myself, I routinely witnessed decisions over candidates being made almost exclusively based on methods concerns. To provide just one example, I was told by a colleague who had served on the committee for a job I interviewed for that the committee enjoyed both my research presentation and that of another candidate, as the job had come down to a choice between the two of us. I later found out through my colleague that a few of the committee members liked the other candidates' research methodology more, although recognizing that they were impressed with both candidates and would be happy to have either join the department. My colleague responded by asking: "shouldn't the primary determinant of which candidate we hire be how effective his/her research was in stimulating an interesting and thoughtful discussion of the findings and how significant they are to the discipline and to politics?" This claim was dismissed, with fellow committee members preferring debates over methods as the main determinant of hiring. This anecdote retains broader significance considering the discussion of my experiences over the last decade at academic conferences. In that time, I have seldom been a part of strong or passionate debates among fellow scholars about the larger significance of research presentations findings, although there is never a shortage of squabbling regarding research methods.

If our research is no longer primarily about politics, then the discipline cannot possibly retain any relevance to broader societal discussions about government. Depoliticization is increasingly evident even in the venue of book publishing. While the book format has long been the most forgiving of all in providing space needed for extended political-historical analysis, exploration of case studies, and discussion of the "big picture" significance of research, modern political science books have increasingly devolved into a glorified compilation of journal articles. It is now common to see books that are 120 to 150 pages long, with these books typically including one or two articles previously published by an author, reworked in some way, including a brief introduction, a literature review, a research "set-up," and brief conclusion. These books are so thin because they avoid much of the detail and deeper analysis of the significance of one's findings that would come along with mixed-methods research. The thinness of these works translates into the thinning out of the discipline, since academics have little interest in extending their analysis to include a more detailed qualitative, historical, or observational analysis, or to an extended discussion of one's findings and their relevance to the study of democracy, power, and other big political questions.

The Decline of Political Thought

The deteriorating commitment to, and even active contempt for political theory and philosophy flow in large part from the growing fixation on methodological fetishism. Despite academics' priding themselves in being intellectuals, members of our discipline now struggle with basic tasks such as "big picture" thinking. The inability to think in unconventional and dissident ways is a product of the neoliberalization of higher education. Academic rewards and incentives run in the opposite direction of encouraging pontificating on broader societal and political questions. As a result, academics keep their noses to the grindstone, engaging in "normal science," while churning out works that are largely depoliticized and devoid of grand efforts to theorize about the world. Little effort historically has been devoted in recent decades toward raising basic questions about the decline of democracy due to the growing dominance of politics by the wealthy few.[27] "Elite theory" is generically referenced in American government textbooks, but not incorporated in any systematic way into those texts. Only recently—following the 2008 economic crash—have political scientists begun to regularly discuss the toxic effects of inequality on the quality of democratic representation, or on the ways in which the political system itself perpetuates and increases inequality.[28]

Theory is not idealized, or generally held in high regard in political science. Some programs are so contemptuous of theory that they have banned it entirely from the discipline, assuming philosophy departments will pick up the slack, as seen with Penn State University's and Stanford University's recent actions. Other departments have allowed retirement and attrition to winnow down their focus on theory, as new hires are not made once already-employed theory professors pass away or retire. But the turn away from theory is a new development in political science. As Dyer explains in a historical review of the discipline, "At its inception, political science in the United States was principally concerned with political thought and constitutionalism, and it was taught with the public-spirited purpose of educating for citizenship in a constitutional democracy."[29] This grand focus on training students to be citizens, rather than merely careerists, requires a commitment to exploring politics, not simply as the sum of its individual parts, but in relation to larger theoretical questions about democracy, power, and political engagement.

Theory is in a state of crisis in political science—that is, unless one is talking about mechanistic, game-theoretic formal modeling, referred to as "formal

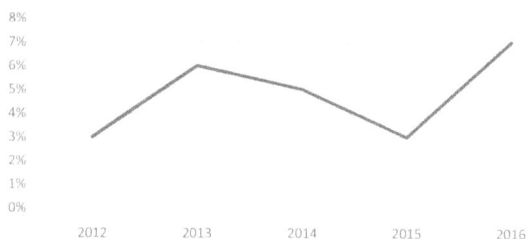

Figure 1. Devaluing Political Theory: Percent of All Political Science Job Openings in Political Theory.

theory." This form of theory, in addition to statistical modeling more broadly, have come to dominate the discipline, but neither seem to be primarily concerned with answering grand questions about who holds power in society, or about the quality of democracy and democratic discourse in the United States and elsewhere. One can see the marginalization of theory in some basic empirical indicators. In measuring how much theory is valued in an occupational sense, I examined job postings for the last half decade covering all the subfields of political science. These data are available on the "Wiki Jobs" site, which provides the public function of tracking different job postings and updating applicants on the status of those job searches. Figure 1 documents the number of all political theory and philosophy jobs as a percent of all jobs posted per year between 2012 and 2016. One can see that theory jobs make up a miniscule percent of all political science positions, ranging from three to seven percent each year. Simply stated, political theory is not valued in the job market.

But there has been pressure in recent years placed on the "flagship" journals in the discipline to become more diverse and expansive in the types of articles they publish. As a result, journal editors appear to make a significant effort to include theory pieces from time to time.

Figure 2 provides data on the percent all theory articles appearing in *APSR* each year, over the 10-year period from 2007 to 2016. An article was included in my tabulations if it referenced any classic figure in political theory or philosophy in its title, or if it made reference in the title (not the subtitle) to political theory in

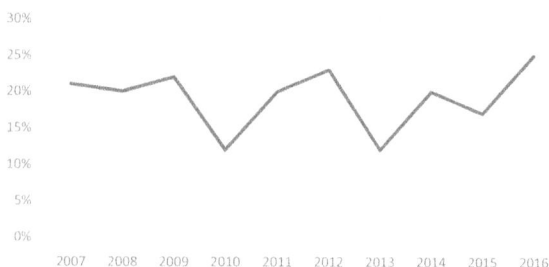

Figure 2. Theory in *American Political Science Review*: Percent of Articles Emphasizing Theory per Year.

some way, or more broadly to democracy, democratic theory, or other theoretical frameworks such as liberalism, conservatism, or authoritarianism, among others. As one can see, theory-centered pieces do appear in establishment journals like *APSR*, even if these pieces comprise a minority of all articles published. But while prominent journals have tried to diversify somewhat in terms of incorporating theory, it appears that there is little interest in this effort on the part of rank-and-file political scientists. In my review of political theory pieces appearing in *APSR*, it was typical to see perhaps a half dozen to a dozen citations for individual theory articles in Google Scholar. This suggests almost nonexistent attention to these works among scholars, considering the average citation count for an *APSR* piece in the period I analyzed was more than 150. To sum up these findings, political science departments are not interested in elevating theory to a real priority. Editors of prominent journals seek to pick up the slack by prioritizing theory to some extent. But this effort is largely in vain due to disciplinary norms that de-emphasize political theory and lead rank-and-file faculty to dismiss its value.

The banishment of political theory from political science was hardly inevitable. Other models of accepted behavior exist in other social science disciplines. For example, theory occupies a central position in sociology. Read an introductory sociology textbook, and one will see that the theoretical emphasis in the discipline is of high priority. References to the "three pillars" of the field—Max Weber, Karl Marx, and Emile Durkheim—situate sociological inquiry within broader theoretical frameworks.[30] That Marx is considered canonical to the discipline is a sign of how much more open the field is—relative to political science at least—in analyzing and considering perspectives that run contrary to neoliberal thought.

Front and center in introductory sociology texts is a discussion, woven into each chapter, of the main theories that dominate the field, including structural functionalism, symbolic interactionism, conflict theory, postmodernism/post-structuralism, rational choice, and social construction theory. In contrast, American Government textbooks briefly introduce "elite theory" and "democratic pluralism," but do not do an adequate job of consistently incorporating these frameworks into the individual chapters. To summarize, sociology has performed much more admirably than political science in terms of providing grand theoretical frameworks that aid students and scholars in making sense of the world.

The real-world implications of the failure of political scientists to teach students about theory are significant. In the neoliberal era, there is no value in teaching young Americans about political thinkers like Karl Marx, Antonio Gramsci, Eugene Debs, or other socialists, whose ideas challenge the foundations of the capitalist system. And Americans appear to be quite clueless when it comes to understanding precisely what defines socialism or Marxism. Large segments of the American public believed, erroneously, that Democratic President Barack Obama was a socialist, despite his support for the 2008 bank bailout, his call for tax cuts on businesses at various points in his presidency, his bailout of the auto industry, and his support for an expansion of market-based health insurance via the Affordable Care Act.[31] Regardless of these facts, political leaders and media pundits drummed up conspiratorial scare stories about the rise of American "socialism" under Obama, and tens of millions of Americans gullibly fell into this absurdity. This phenomenon reflects a blatant failure on the part of the education system—particularly political scientists. If those who are supposed to know about political theory do not educate the masses properly, how can one expect the public to engage in rational or coherent debates about economic issues and structures?

The Prestige Game and the Declining Value of Teaching

Most political scientists would probably deny it, but it seems clear that the discipline no longer prioritizes teaching. There are, of course, exceptions. Individually, most professors would likely say they care about teaching, even if institutions themselves increasingly devalue it. Community colleges are solely concerned with teaching, so they put little value in academic specialization and research over instruction. Furthermore, many liberal arts colleges, heavily reliant on student tuition to operate, adopt "student-centered" approaches that stress the importance of small class size and one-on-one access to professors. These practices certainly increase the quality of education.

Despite these exceptions, it has been apparent for the last few decades that teaching, generally speaking, matters less and less as a higher educational priority. Political scientist Benjamin Ginsburg documents "the fall of the faculty" in modern times, as institutions of higher education have become "professional-ized" via the rise of a small administrative class that embraces neoliberal values celebrating teaching institutions as "businesses" and students as "clients."[32] In previous decades, faculty often served in part-time administrative functions, moving back and forth between teaching and administrative responsibilities. But more recently, with the rise of the "professional" administrative class, power over university decision making shifted from faculty to administrators. These administrators, although far better compensated than faculty, often do not have teaching experience, and since they are not faculty, do not benefit from the same tenure protections as faculty. This means they are subject to various political pressures from higher-up administration, in addition to state and federal regulators in the case of public universities and colleges.

College administrators emphasize the need to "increase the prestige" of their respective institutions. The thinking here is strongly neoliberal: if schools can increase their prestige relative to other schools, that increases their ability to attract and retain students, and place those students within more prestigious or higher-paying jobs. More affluent graduates potentially means greater fundraising abilities and higher endowments, which in turn can be used to further increase the prestige of an institution. Higher rankings in the *U.S. News and World Report* allow college recruiters to more effectively hype the institution to prospective applicants in a system in which students are sought after, much the same way as businesses seek to cultivate and build their clientele. By treating colleges and universities as brand names to be built up and marketed and sold, administrators have contributed to the neoliberalization of higher education.

The obsession with chasing rankings manifests itself in various ways. First, administrators heavily emphasize the importance of the *U.S. News and World Report* rankings of schools and the need to "climb those rankings." This translates into an increasing focus on research publications, a growing emphasis on hiring PhDs from schools that are more highly ranked on the *U.S. News and World Report* rankings, and inevitably, a de-emphasis of teaching. No administrator will admit that his or her institution fails to value teaching. They—and faculty—will sound off with shopworn rhetoric celebrating the importance of "critical thinking" and "active learning" in the classroom. But by idealizing research as the primary goal of institutions, they have de-prioritized teaching.

In my last 10 years in higher education, it has become abundantly clear through my many interactions with other faculty and administrators that teaching is not valued as it once was. During my time as an adjunct at numerous universities and during my time in graduate school, faculty members routinely made comments suggesting the devaluation of education. At a major state university where I taught, a fellow professor and good friend remarked (with regard to tenure standards) that if I ever secured a tenure-track job there, I would not have to worry about being denied tenure, since "that only happens with bad teachers." This was quite a low bar to set concerning educational evaluation. Faculty could be confident that their jobs were secure, so long as they were not actively bad at their jobs. In another major university where I served as a teaching assistant, I was informed by one visibly distraught senior professor that, during his time in the institution, there was never a single professor who was denied tenure due to poor teaching. This insight was verified through my own experiences, as I saw numerous faculty, ranging between average at best to atrocious at worst in their teaching, all receive tenure due to their research and publishing accomplishments.

Nowhere was the devaluing of teaching more apparent in the discipline than in the process of interviewing for jobs. Despite having more than seven years of teaching experience across numerous institutions when I received my PhD and went on the job market, and despite regularly receiving strong evaluations in the courses I taught, I struggled to secure a tenure-track job at a four-year baccalaureate-granting institution in the first few years following graduation. This in and of itself is common today, since the number of tenure-track jobs in the field is smaller than the number of applicants for these positions. But this is only part of the story in the modern job market.

Because of my many years of teaching and strong record of student evaluations, I quickly landed a tenure-track position at a community college in Illinois where teaching was valued. But in seeking to explore my options after graduating with my PhD, I struggled to break into the four-year college "market." I had only been at my community college for a few years at that point, so I saw little reason for me to be "typecast" as "merely a community college instructor." But it became clear that for most of the jobs I applied at four-year universities, the individuals who eventually received offers had far less or no teaching experience. Typically, these candidates, while having attended more highly ranked programs, had perhaps been teaching assistants only, or at most taught one or two classes. This was an early warning sign that teaching was not being valued in the discipline.

As I secured more and more publications in the early years after my graduation, and began to secure more job interviews, it became even clearer during the interview process how little teaching was valued. When I did teaching presentations, they sparked very little discussion or excitement from faculty, who almost universally agreed that I performed admirably in these presentations, but who were mainly interested in methodological discussions about my research. Doing teaching presentations became a box to check off the interview process, not a substantive matter in and of itself. I asked one colleague and friend, who served on a committee for a tenure-track position I applied for, why my years of teaching seemed to be valued so little in the job market. He answered that, at his university, "the hiring committee assumes that candidates are already qualified to teach in the classroom when we bring you to campus, so the emphasis during the campus visit is on research and scholarship." This mind-set was confirmed in other settings as well—even in some liberal arts–oriented "teaching" schools—where committee members blatantly told me after the search had ended that the primary criteria for assessing my and other candidates' value were research, not teaching focused.

To be sure, many four-year institutions continue to value teaching, particu-larly many liberal arts colleges and universities where I interviewed. It was clear based on the structure of the interviews at these places (a teaching presentation, with no research talk required), or by the fact that faculty in those interviews prioritized discussing teaching and pedagogy, that they cared deeply about educating students. But this was not the norm. Most of the time, the focus of interviews was on research, with committee members reflexively assuming that "one applicant was as good as another" in their teaching so long as they had some experience in the classroom.

The "climb the *U.S. News and World Report* rankings" mantra that drives college administrators increasingly appears to be a losing game for most universities and colleges. The vast majority of liberal arts colleges, and even state universities and branch campuses of state public universities, will never have the resources to attract or retain (long term at least) applicants from highly ranked PhD-granting institutions. Their relatively meager endowments and other resources for scholars mean that the professors who are employed at these schools will find it far more difficult to secure the kinds of resources for data collection and research that enhance their chances of getting published in top-tier journals. Furthermore, the higher teaching loads at these schools preclude even the thought of spending most of one's time on research, short of scholars actively abandoning their teaching responsibilities. These institutions would be much better off, pedagogically speaking, by stressing the importance of quality teaching and regular student–professor engagement and collaboration, rather than playing the research–prestige game.

The devaluing of teaching in higher education is a relatively recent phenome-non. Teaching used to be much more heavily valued, and research publications less stressed, prior to the last two decades. I have had this point confirmed by many senior colleagues in the field. It used to be much more common for professors to secure tenure largely based on teaching, and with only a small number of publications, if any. To provide just one example, I was informed by two colleagues at a major state university I attended and taught at, who had come to that school during the early to mid-1980s, that professors had multiple tracks from which to choose to earn tenure. They could choose to be evaluated almost exclusively based on teaching, or via a combination of teaching and research. But "research" was defined very broadly, and this component of tenure review could be fulfilled by publishing book chapters, a book, and journal articles, or by simply presenting research at academic conferences. This system for tenure evaluation is radically different from the research-heavy expectations that currently drive tenure review at most colleges and universities.

The fixation on prestige and research at the expense of teaching is a self-defeating, harmful development. A large majority of tenure-track faculty at non-research-oriented four-year institutions will not be published in top-tier academic journals or other venues, and if they do, they are unlikely to do so regularly. Their primary impact on the field and on the dissemination of knowledge will be in the classroom, imparting their knowledge to students. If there is any chance at professors actively working toward subverting or challenging the devaluing of teaching under neoliberalism, it will need to happen in the classroom via the teaching of critical analytical and thinking skills, and through the promotion of active citizenship and engagement. But with little priority placed on developing strong teaching skills, there are few incentives for faculty to value quality instruction or the promotion of critical thinking. Individual faculty members continue to fight "against the grain" by valuing education, but that is because of their personal commitment to pedagogical integrity. The obsession with research and rankings has produced an environment in which scholarly research publications abound, but it is not clear how many of these articles are even read. Recent evidence suggests that the non-citation rate for social science articles is about a third, a severely damning statistic considering these publications are prioritized over teaching.[33]

Concluding Remarks

I am only mildly optimistic regarding the chances for the rollback of neoliberal values in higher education. Radical change and transformation within the institutions of higher learning will only occur once students and faculty become active in challenging the negative developments laid out in this essay. But there is little indication of this happening in the United States, as of this writing. Students north of the border in Canada have recently joined together to protest the rise of neoliberalism in higher education, demonstrating against proposals to radically increase tuition rates and shift from public taxpayer funding to a student-based tuition funding model. But little of this has motivated students in the United States to protest neoliberalism in higher education. Students and faculty will need to actively fight against the negative developments described here if there is any hope of seriously changing the American educational model.

Recognizing the problem of student and faculty inactivity, individual changes are certainly possible, and should be seriously discussed by those interested in an incremental shift away from the neoliberal turn in higher learning. One development that can and has helped turn the tide is the rise of idealistically minded young scholars who are willing to offer progressive research agendas that emphasize timely political issues. This has happened to an extent in the last decade. While the study of rising inequality and its negative effects on political representation and democracy received little attention in previous decades, it is now increasingly a subject of concern and analysis by various political science scholars. But more critical engagement in critical public issues of this kind will be needed moving forward.

I provide a list of individual proposals below, which could help reform political science and reverse the disciplinary turn toward irrelevance. These include:

- Restructuring tenure evaluation standards to allow faculty multiple avenues of assessment, one focusing almost exclusively on teaching (especially at liberal arts colleges and non-research institutions), and another focusing on a combination of research and teaching for those who wish to pursue research.
- The valuing of public intellectualism and outreach outside of the token contribution it currently makes to tenure and promotion review. There is a large potential value that accompanies the popularizing of social science research, even if the person doing it is not the person who originally authored the research. The valuing of public intellectualism will be vital to making political science relevant again to the world of real-world politics.
- Pushing undergraduate and graduate students to become involved in being public intellectuals and in pursuing research agendas that provide useful, practical knowledge for improving the political system and enhancing representation and the quality of democracy. This must take place early in students' intellectual development if public intellectualism is to take hold in the discipline.
- Stress a return to emphasizing theory and methodological pluralism. Academic research is not inherently better simply because it holds disdain for theory or qualitative and mixed-methods research. The diversification of the discipline means approaching questions in political science from multiple fronts, which will only improve our understanding of how the political process works.
- Renew the commitment to increasing the ranks of tenure-track lines in political science departments so that professors can feel more confident to take risks in their research and feel protected against losing their jobs due to external or internal political pressures. This advice applies outside of political science, to universities and colleges as a whole.

The neoliberal turn toward marginalizing education as a public good was hardly inevitable. But it will take a serious effort on the part of students and faculty to reverse prevailing trends that have to this point had an extraordinarily harmful impact on the quality of higher education.

Notes

1. Henry A. Giroux, "Thinking Dangerously: The Role of Higher Education in Authoritarian Times," *Truthout*, June 26, 2017, http://www.truth-out.org/opinion/item/41058-thinking-dangerously-the-role-of-higher-education-in-authoritarian-times. For an extended treatment of the need for critical thought among academics, see Henry A. Giroux, *Dangerous Thinking in the Age of New Authoritarianism* (New York: Routledge, 2015).
2. Pew Research Center, "Sharp Partisan Divisions in Views of National Institutions," July 10, 2017, http://www.people-press.org/2017/07/10/sharp-partisan-divisions-in-views-of-national-institutions/.
3. Henry A. Giroux, *Neoliberalism's War on Higher Education* (Chicago: Haymarket Books, 2014).
4. Giroux, "Thinking Dangerously," 2017.
5. Giroux, "Thinking Dangerously," 2017.
6. Giroux, *Neoliberalism's War on Higher Education*, 2014.
7. Jeffrey C. Isaac, "Political Science as a Contest of Perspectives," *Perspectives on Politics* 14, no. 4 (2016): 943–948; Jennifer L. Hochschild, "Left Pessimism and Political Science," *Perspectives on Politics* 15, no. 1 (2017): 6–19; Kennan Ferguson, "Why Does Political Science Hate American Indians?" *Perspectives on Politics* 14, no. 4 (2016): 1029–1038.
8. Emily Beaulieu et al., "Women Also Know Stuff: Meta-Level Mentoring to Battle Gender Bias in Political Science," *PS: Political Science and Politics* 50, no. 3 (2017): 779–783; Deondra Rose, "Higher Education and the Transformation of American Citizenship," *PS: Political Science and Politics* 50, no. 2 (2017): 403–407; Charlie Eaton, "Still Public: State Universities and America's New Student-Debt Coalitions," *PS: Political Science and Politics* 50, no. 2 (2017): 408–412; Ben Ansell and Jane Gingrich, "Mismatch: University Education and Labor Market Institutions," *PS: Political Science and Politics* 50, no. 2 (2017): 423–425; Bobbi Gentry, Christopher Lawrence, and Erin Richards, "The Tie That Binds: Exploring Community College Curriculum Design," *PS: Political Science and Politics* 49, no. 3 (2016): 535–540; Tania Verge, "The Virtues of Engendering Quantitative Methods Courses," *PS: Political Science and Politics* 49, no. 3 (2016): 550–553; Rebecca Susan Evans, "Men Are from Mars, Women Are from Venus, and Zombies Are from . . . Feminist Theories of International Politics and Zombies," *PS: Political Science and Politics* 49, no. 3 (2016): 554–557; Amy G. Mazur, "Mainstreaming Gender in Political Science Courses: The Case of Comparative Public Policy," *PS: Political Science and Politics* 49, no. 3 (2016): 562–565; Carol Mershon and Denise Walsh, "How Political Science Can Be More Diverse: Introduction," *PS: Political Science and Politics* 48, no. 3 (2015): 441–444.
9. Kristin Renwick Monroe, *Perestroika! The Raucous Rebellion in Political Science* (New Haven, CT: Yale University Press, 2005).
10. In talking about the conscious effort to intimidate faculty, one can look recently to the efforts of the Republican legislature in Wisconsin to dictate course and curriculum content of University of Wisconsin courses, in the name of fighting leftist bias in higher education. See Nico Savidge, "Complaining of Bias on Campus, Republicans Push for 'Intellectual Diversity' in University of Wisconsin Schools," *Wisconsin State Journal*, January 8, 2017, http://host.madison.com/wsj/news/local/education/university/complaining-of-bias-on-campus-republicans-push-for-intellectual-diversity/article_308497a3-799c-540a-a4ae-097017eb3a16.html. For examples of administrators seeking to intimidate or punish critical faculty, see Jose S. Cohen, "University of Illinois OKs $875,000 Settlement to End Steven Salaita Dispute," *Chicago Tribune*, November 12, 2015, http://www.chicagotribune.com/news/local/breaking/ct-steven-salaita-settlement-met-20151112-story.html; Colleen Flaherty, "Looking Into Tweets," *Inside Higher Ed*, April 18, 2017, https://www.insidehighered.com/news/2017/04/18/documents-show-drexel-investigating-professors-tweets-its-unclear-whether-faculty; Manya Bracbear Pashman, "Wheaton College Could Face Long-Term

Fallout Over Professor Controversy," *Chicago Tribune,* February 22, 2016, http://www.chicagotribune .com/news/ct-wheaton-college-professor-fallout-met-20160222-story.html; Colleen Flaherty, "Trinity Suspends Targeted Professor," *Inside Higher Ed,* June 27, 2017, https://www.insidehighered.com/ news/2017/06/27/trinity-college-connecticut-puts-johnny-eric-williams-leave-over-controversial.

11. Peter L. Berger and Thomas Luckmann, *The Social Construction of Reality: A Treatise in the Sociology of Knowledge* (New York: Anchor Books, 1967); John R. Searle, *The Construction of Social Reality* (New York: Free Press, 1997).

12. Christopher Gelpi, Peter D. Feaver, and Jason Reifler, *Paying the Human Costs of War: American Public Opinion and Casualties in Military Conflicts* (Princeton, NJ: Princeton University Press, 2009); John Mueller, "The Iraq Syndrome," *Foreign Affairs,* November/December 2005, https://www. foreignaffairs.com/articles/north-korea/2005-10-01/iraq-syndrome; Dominic D. P. Johnson and Dominic Tierney, *Failing to Win: Perceptions of Victory and Defeat in International Politics* (Cambridge, MA: Harvard University Press, 2006); Ole R. Holsti, *American Public Opinion on the Iraq War* (Ann Arbor: University of Michigan Press, 2011); John R. Zaller, *The Nature and Origins of Mass Opinion* (Cambridge: Cambridge University Press, 1992); Adam J. Berinsky, "In Time of War: Understanding American Public Opinion from World War II to Iraq (Chicago: University of Chicago Press, 2009); Eric V. Larson and Bogdan Savych, *Misfortunes of War: Press and Public Reactions to Civilian Deaths in Wartime* (Santa Monica, CA: Rand, 2006); Scott Althaus et al., "Uplifting Manhood to Wonderful Heights? News Coverage of the Human Costs of War from World War I to Gulf War Two," *Political Communication* 31, no. 2 (2014): 193–217.

13. Edward Herman and Noam Chomsky, *Manufacturing Consent: The Political Economy of the Mass Media* (New York: Pantheon Books, 2002).

14. Eric Herring and Piers Robinson, "Too Polemical or Too Critical? Chomsky on the Study of the News Media and U.S. Foreign Policy," *Review of International Studies,* 29, no. 4 (2003): 553–568.

15. Herring and Robinson, "Too Polemical or Too Critical?" 2003.

16. Susan Brewer, *Why America Fights: Patriotism and War Propaganda from the Philippines to Iraq* (New York: Oxford University Press, 2011); Steven Casey, *Selling the Korean War: Propaganda, Politics, and Public Opinion in the United States, 1950–1953* (New York: Oxford University Press, 2010); Toby Rider, *Cold War Games: Propaganda, the Olympics, and U.S. Foreign Policy* (Champaign: University of Illinois Press, 2016); Kenneth Osgood, *Total Cold War: Eisenhower's Secret Propaganda Battle at Home and Abroad* (Lawrence: University Press of Kansas, 2006); Nancy Bernhard, *U.S. Television News and Cold War Propaganda, 1947–1960* (Cambridge: Cambridge University Press, 2003); Laura Belmonte, *Selling the American Way: U.S. Propaganda and the Cold War* (Philadelphia: University of Pennsylvania Press, 2010); Nicholas Schlosser, *Cold War on the Airwaves: The Radio Propaganda War Against East Germany* (Champaign: University of Illinois Press, 2015); Cecilia Kingsbury, *For Home and Country: World War I Propaganda on the Home Front* (Lincoln: Univesity of Nebraska Press, 2010); Alan Axelrod, *Selling the Great War: The Making of American Propaganda* (New York: St. Martin's Press, 2009).

17. Scott Bonn, *Mass Deception: Moral Panic and the U.S. War on Iraq* (New Brunswick, NJ: Rutgers University Press, 2010); Erin Steuter and Deborah Wills, *At War with Metaphor: Media, Propaganda, and Racism in the War on Terror* (Lanham, MD: Lexington Books, 2009); Anthony DiMaggio, *Mass Media, Mass Propaganda: Examiing American News in the War on Terror* (Lanham, MD: Lexington Books, 2008); Brigitte Nacos, Yaeli Bloch-Elkon, and Robert Shapiro, *Selling Fear: Counterterrorism, the Media, and Public Opinion* (Chicago: University of Chicago Press, 2011).

18. Ilan Pappe, "Response to Benny Morris' 'Politics by Other Means' in the New Republic," *Electronic Intifada,* March 30, 2004, https://electronicintifada.net/content/response-benny-morris-politics-other-means-new-republic/5040.

19. David Takacs, "Positionality, Epistemology, and Social Justice in the Classroom," *Social Justice* 29, no. 4 (2002): 168–181; Gideon Lewis-Kraus, "The Trials of Alice Goffman," *New York Times,* January 12, 2016, https://www.nytimes.com/2016/01/17/magazine/the-trials-of-alice-goffman .html. Also see the work of philosopher Linda Alcoff: Linda Alcoff, "Cultural Feminism Versus Post-Structuralism: The Identity Crisis in Feminist Theory," *Signs* 13, no. 3 (1988): 405–436.

20. James M. Henslin, *Essentials of Sociology: A Down to Earth Approach* (New York: Pearson, 2016).

21. Henry A. Giroux, *Education and the Crisis of Public Values: Challenging the Assault on Teachers, Students, and Public Education* (New York: Peter Lang, 2015).

22. Scott Jaschik, "Final Loss for Ward Churchill," *Inside Higher Ed,* April 2, 2013, https:// www.insidehighered.com/news/2013/04/02/supreme-court-rejects-appeal-ward-churchill; Cohen, "University of Illinois OKs $875,000 Settlement to End Steven Salaita Dispute," 2015; Flaherty,

"Looking Into Tweets," 2017; Pashman, "Wheaton College Could Face Long-Term Fallout Over Professor Controversy," 2016; Flaherty, "Trinity Suspends Targeted Professor," 2017.

23. Michael W. Giles and James C. Garand, "Ranking Political Science Journals: Reputational and Citational Approaches," *PS: Political Science and Politics* 40, no. 4 (2007): 741–751.

24. These reader estimates are based on my discussions with editors at these venues.

25. Thomas Kuhn, *The Structure of Scientific Revolutions* (Chicago: University of Chicago Press, 2012).

26. Donald Green and Ian Shapiro, *Pathologies of Rational Choice Theory: A Critique of Applications in Political Science* (New Haven, CT: Yale University Press, 1996).

27. Recent publications discuss at length how American government is consistently more likely to represent the interests of the affluent over the masses: Martin Gilens, *Affluence and Influence: Economic Inequality and Political Power in America* (Princeton, NJ: Princeton University Press, 2014); Daniel M. Butler, *Representing the Advantaged: How Politicians Reinforce Inequality* (Cambridge: Cambridge University Press, 2014); Nicholas Carnes, *White Collar Government: The Hidden Role of Class in Economic Policy Making* (Chicago: University of Chicago Press, 2013); Jacob S. Hacker and Paul Pierson, *Winner-Take-All Politics: How Washington Made the Rich Richer—and Turned Its Back on the Middle Class* (New York: Simon and Schuster, 2011); Benjamin I. Page and Martin Gilens, *Democracy in America: What Has Gone Wrong and What We Can Do About It* (Chicago: University of Chicago Press, 2017); Martin Gilens and Benjamin I. Page, "Testing Theories of American Politics: Elites, Interest Groups, and Average Citizens," *Perspectives on Politics* 12, no. 3 (2014): 564–581.

28. Gilens, *Affluence and Influence*, 2014; Butler, *Representing the Advantaged*, 2014; Carnes, *White Collar Government*, 2013; Hacker and Pierson, *Winner-Take-All Politics*, 2011; Page and Gilens, *Democracy in America*, 2017; Gilens and Page, "Testing Theories of American Politics," 2014; *PS* 2017.

29. Justin Buckley Dyer, "Political Science and American Political Thought," *PS: Political Science and Politics* 50, no. 3 (2017): 784–788.

30. Henslin, *Essentials of Sociology*, 2016.

31. Derek Thompson, "Poll: 55% of Likely Voters Think Obama Is a Socialist," *The Atlantic*, July 9, 2010, https://www.theatlantic.com/business/archive/2010/07/poll-55-of-likely-voters-think-obama-is-a-socialist/59463/.

32. Benjamin Ginsburg, *The Fall of the Faculty: The Rise of the All-Administrative University and Why It Matters* (Oxford: Oxford University Press, 2013).

33. Dahlia Remler, "Are 90% of Academic Papers Really Never Cited? Reviewing the Literature on Academic Citations," London School of Economics and Political Science, April 23, 2014, http://blogs.lse.ac.uk/impactofsocialsciences/2014/04/23/academic-papers-citation-rates-remler/.

Quantification and Scientism in Political Science: Domination of Discourse by Experts Presenting Mathematical Models of Reality

David Kingsley

Department of Health Policy and Management, Kansas University Medical Center, Kansas City, KS

Mathematization has become increasingly dominant in the social sciences. Political science research reflects this trend. Unfortunately, complex mathematical models do not reflect reality and have little relevance to public political discourse. Indeed, much of the quantification in political science research is fraught with fallacies, not the least of which are reification and scientism. Even simple statistical models such as crosstabs and simple tests such as Pearson's-chi square are fallacious but not well understood by the less mathematically oriented social scientist. In addition to discussing the main problems of quantification, the author illustrates an egregious misuse of statistics by prominent social scientists relying on quantitative studies pertaining to criminal behavior.

KEY WORDS: quantification, political polling, public discourse

政治学中的定量化研究与科学主义：专家通过展示现实数学模型掌握话语主导权

社会科学的数学化趋势日益增加，政治学研究如今也呈现这一趋势。遗憾的是，复杂数学模型并不能反映现实，也与公共政治话语几乎没有关系。事实上，政治学研究中的量化过程大都充满谬误，根本算不上具体化和科学化。即使是简单的统计模型，如交叉表，或是简单的检验，如卡方检验，都是存在谬误的，但不以数学为导向的社会科学家们对此也并不太了解。　除了讨论与量化有关的主要问题之外，作者还阐述了杰出社会科学家依靠有关犯罪行为的定量研究而严重滥用统计学的现象。

La cuantificación y el ciencialismo en las ciencias políticas: la dominación del discurso por expertos que presentan modelos matemáticos de realidad

La matematización se ha vuelto más y más dominante en las ciencias sociales. La investigación en ciencias políticas refleja esta tendencia. Desafortunadamente, los modelos complejos matemáticos no afectan la realidad y tienen poca relevancia para el discurso político público. De hecho, mucha de la cuantificación en la investigación de ciencias políticas está llena de falacias, incluyendo la reificación y el ciencialismo. Hasta los modelos estadísticos simples como los crosstabs y pruebas simples como el Pearson chisquare, tienen falacias, pero no son bien comprendidos por los científicos sociales menos orientados hacia las matemáticas. Además de discutir los problemas principales de la cuantificación, el autor ilustra un uso inadecuado de la estadística por parte de científicos sociales importantes que se apoyan en estudios cuantitativos que tienen que ver con el comportamiento criminal.

Introduction

The political science profession has less visibility and influence in public policy processes than one would think a science of politics deserves. But public policy development is inextricably intertwined with public discourse. Discourse for policy discussions—especially scientific discourse—requires attention to expositions of some length and complexity; it requires critique of scholarship by peers; and, it requires openness to opposing points of view. Today, however, what passes as public discourse in the noisy, fragmented discussion of politics is misguided and often harmful.

As Neil Postman has told us, public discourse in the age of show business has become dangerous nonsense.[1] The overwhelming bulk of political debate and discussion has become a cacophony of entertainment, propaganda, shrillness, and spin on behalf of a party or politician. This mostly irrational and shallow exchange takes place on television, talk radio, and social media.

Because these media are not welcoming to lengthy, serious discussions by scholars engaged in objective examination of issues, failure of political scientists to capture much of the public's attention is not entirely the fault of the profession. However, the popularity of mathematization among political scientists has further alienated potential audiences from the science of politics. Certainly, discussion and explanation of multivariate regression models are not appropriate topics for most types of electronic media.

Although political polls—as one category of quantification—have been commoditized and become product for the entertainment industry, one does not need to be a political scientist to engage in the simple math underlying polling results. Journalists and their news organizations, private consultants, and most anyone with the drive to engage in the polling business can hang out a shingle. Although technical aspects of the validity and reliability of mental measurements are beyond the grasp of lay public without training in research methods and statistics, robust common sense should be sufficient for most individuals to see the flaws in political polls if that were part of the conversation, but it is not.

It may very well be that speaking out against the dangerous nonsense that polls and irrelevant mathematical models represent is one means for political scientists to become relevant (rather than engaging in polling themselves). However, that critically needed pushback is not happening. Mathematization, no matter how absurd and destructive it often is, goes unchecked in far too many instances. If math has become emperor of the social sciences, economics has become queen. I believe that the emperor has no clothes. The queen is naked also, but exposing the lack of validity in econometrics is beyond the scope of this article.

Mathematical models in political science literature are understood by only a few people who produce and publish them. The public will not look to the various forms of regression modeling reported in political science journals for information and ideas. Even if the public were interested in advanced mathematics in political science journals, they do not have access to them. Only academics and individuals able and willing to pay for a subscription can read them. Furthermore, the language and mathematics of articles reporting results of increasingly complex and abstruse models are incomprehensible to most everyone but a small number of cognoscenti.

Complex multivariable regression models and public opinion polls are not the only forms of mathematization causing the irrelevance of political science. Even simple models based on statistics taught in lower-level stats courses have been misused and abused, with tragic consequences. An example of how statistical malpractice through the utilization of a rather simple, stats-101, technique has resulted in tragic consequences will be discussed in this article regarding the work of the late James Q. Wilson. The relevance of this tragedy to the irrelevance of political science is that the profession had nothing to say about it—quite the opposite, they endorsed it.

While political science, other social sciences, and the humanities have been consistently reduced in importance in policy formation—as well as in higher education—economics, the most modeling-prone social science, has, as has been stated above, grown into the queen of the social sciences, and economists are the go-to professionals in policy discussions impacting fiscal and monetary policy. Because economists are enamored with quantification along with complex econometric models, mathematics and algorithms have displaced a focus on the humanistic, democratic values essential for social justice and fairness. Indeed, the process of marginalization of the humanities and social sciences—erroneously believed to have no relevance to economics and the economy—has been underway for a half century.

Political polls can be conducted, analyzed, and reported without a background in high-level math. However, critical evaluation of the validity and reliability of responses to single items is beyond the capability of the journalists who depend on them for hooking in viewers and readers. Can the political science profession generate an influential force dedicated to questioning the polling scourge? Can they climb down from their ivory castles and engage the blatherers, talking heads, entertainers, and other actors who dominate and coarsen our political discourse? I will discuss these questions in the context of common fallacies in the social sciences such as the naturalistic fallacy and scientism.

Furthermore, democracy is not well served when policy is cloaked in highly technical jargon understood by only a small number of experts. It is likely that statistical analyses will be misused and abused in attempts to foist a policy on the public. Indeed, that has happened. One example of how it has happened will be discussed in this article. It will continue to happen. Instead of deferring to the math emperor, political scientists could become the opposition and place a check on the power of the algorithm.

In this article, I will discuss quantification in political science from the perspective of a lifelong quant in the private sector, in government, and in academia (in the final stage as a professor of graduate statistics in a medical school). I believe that utilizing advanced mathematics in modeling human-group behavior is not very helpful or valid in addressing the critical problems threatening democracy and humankind at this stage of human history. Indeed, this activity does not promote a meaningful dialogue in the public sphere, which I will discuss in the last section of this article.

Scientism and the Naturalistic Fallacy

Political science is a science of grouped human behavior. Mathematization of political behavior entails a misguided view that complex social systems can be objectively analyzed and controlled through value-free research. But objective, value-free social science is a chimera.

Claims of objectivity and detachment from personal philosophies, emotions, and general psychological makeup of researchers in the social sciences are not science. Rather, it is scientism—an assumption that social science is indistinguishable from natural science.[2] This fallacy has come to be known as the "naturalistic fallacy" in the philosophy of science. And, as will be demonstrated in this article, it is a dangerous idea leading to the masking of injustice by cloaking pseudoscience in a patina of science.

No researcher of social behavior can approach a research problem without preconceived notions of what is important; without notions of what is causal; and, consequently, without notions of the overall foci of research. Specification error is indeed the most serious and intractable problem with regression models —the overwhelming technique of choice for social scientists.[3] Hence, in modeling, failing to specify relevant variables or, conversely, specifying irrelevant variables, are common problems.

In model fitting, social scientists unwittingly define reality and search for variables of interest to them. They build a model and fit data to it. Does the model reflect reality (which we call verisimilitude in the philosophy of science)? We can never know for certain if a model comports with reality. The only measure is R-squared. But that is merely the product of an algorithm.

Major shifts in human systems, whether advantageous or catastrophic, are often unpredictable and random. Furthermore, the human mind is too limited to grasp and specify the infinite number of factors that could impact an outcome. The interaction of subsystems, of subsystems and the larger system, of the environment and the overall system, and of the environment and major subsystems is beyond the capability of human research.[4] Not even IBM's Watson will ever be programmed with the ability to specify all variables that could predict future events.

Physicists and other researchers in the natural sciences are involved with deterministic models. They explain and predict processes that can be observed through tightly controlled experimental designs. Social scientists are ethically constrained to explaining behavior of human groups with stochastic models that are not amenable to a true experimental design.[5]

This constraint does not prevent some social scientists from striving for the capability of fitting deterministic models for accurately predicting the outcome of grouped human behavior. Much like economists mimic natural scientists through what they erroneously believe to be value-free research, political scientists have been beset with a natural science mentality. However, without addressing humanistic and democratic values in keeping with the U.S. constitutional framework and tradition, political science is devoid of meaning and purpose.

Because the mathematics movement has been part of a broader movement to adapt natural science techniques to social science, supposedly experimental and quasi-experimental designs have reduced the importance of philosophical and historical study of public policy from the perspective of democratic values. The most alarming consequence of societal deference to math and natural science is the influence and power of the algorithm over critical decisions in the lives of humans. Dependence on the "black box" is not only dehumanizing; it has had and will continue to have tragic consequences.

Teachers can be fired based on a proprietary, hence secret, algorithm. Groups of 30 students can randomly vary from year to year and make it appear as if a teacher has done a worse or better job. A person's chance of obtaining credit to buy a home or automobile is dependent upon a "one size fits all" algorithm. A victim of a false credit rating or random event at some point in their life over which they have no control has no means of appeal or verification of the validity of the algorithm causing denial of credit. Statistical modeling supporting the algorithm cannot account for the conscientious employee who after 20 years of impeccable attendance was unemployed because a company went out of business or a grant was terminated. An effective treatment program or some other type of program benefiting people may be ended because of poor statistical analysis or methodological procedures in general (see the discussion of James Q. Wilson below).

Reductionism and dehumanization of value-free, mathematical descriptions and prediction foreclose public discussion of issues. As explained above, this type of information cannot be communicated outside of small circles of professionals. Only the most simplistic and misguided form of modeling, that is, public polling, enters mainstream communication through television and newspapers. Indeed, political polls have become the scourge of U.S. democracy.

Mathematization in a Math-Phobic Society

It is convenient to blame the ignorance of the American public for lack of efficacy of and interest in journal articles and other sources that report the results of complex regression models. It is, however, misguided to rationalize the impractical nature of advanced mathematics in political processes this way. Most every American who completes the eighth grade is competent in basic math such as addition, subtraction, and multiplication. Those fundamentals tend to serve them well as they complete their education and training and enter a profession or become responsible employees in most jobs.

For several decades, I have spoken to lay audiences and have designed and taught master's and PhD statistics courses for students in policy and allied health professions disciplines. It has been my experience that audiences and students erroneously think they are incapable of grasping presentations of data and analysis at a level useful for political decision making. It is amazing how many bright, capable students enter a graduate-level statistics class terrified and lacking confidence.

Most of these same students do quite well at the master's degree level. They are adept at mastering the fundamentals of the mean and variance. By the end of a semester, graduate students are generally able to calculate one-way and perhaps two-way ANOVAs, and simple regression (calculation of multiple regression requires matrix algebra, which is way beyond the capability of all but a handful of graduate students).

More important than mindless calculations in master's-level stats are the logical and philosophical concepts that connect statistics to the scientific method. Indeed, I always tell statistics students that they are in a science class with mathematics as one component. Statistics courses usually devote little time to discussion of the scientific and philosophical logic of falsificationism and hypothesis testing.

Statisticians, researchers, and educators have become increasingly aware of the absurdity of p values and why they should not be reified into some material aspect of reality.[6] Nevertheless, there is still far too much mindless calculation of p values and decisions based on a misguided belief that the difference or the lack of a difference between groups has been proven because of a .05 p value. Even more worrisome is the false belief in correlations/relationships that may or may not exist. Sample size, alpha level, and effect size, as characteristics of an analysis —and hence power—are rarely explained clearly and adequately.[7] As will be discussed below, major damage and injustice can and have often happened as the result of Type I or Type II error.

In the discussion of the public sphere later in this article, suggestions for using data and numbers in informing public opinion will be provided. Numeric information and descriptive statistics are not only useful in public discourse but they are necessary. However, numeric information and simple statistics must be accompanied by caveats and clear explanations.

No doubt, society has a need for professionals with competence in advanced math. In the natural sciences, engineering, and most technological fields, algebra and calculus are required skills. Nevertheless, computer programmers need to think logically but not necessarily mathematically.

The public has a right to discuss, debate, and make input into scientific decisions affecting the overall culture and the future of the U.S. polity, as well as the need to be included in discussions about the moral and ethical implications of recommendations based on scientific expertise and mathematics.

Despite the ability of most people to be productive and contribute fully to the political, social, and economic systems of the United States, a narrative presenting the American masses as innumerate, and therefore inadequate, has become embedded in our culture. The roots of this narrative can be found in the 1950s hysteria over Sputnik. With the collapse of the Soviet Union, the U.S. math-ignorance narrative did not collapse with it. Instead, it was folded seamlessly into the global, free market competitiveness movement.

It is widely believed that making all Americans numerate in algebra, calculus, and mathematics in general will provide not only the ticket to U.S. global economic dominance but also the success of all math-competent individuals in becoming fully employed. This is an article of faith unsupported by empirical evidence. Nevertheless, teachers and students are subjected to standardized tests that will accomplish little but memorization and lack of understanding.

In a society dominated by a mythical mathematical route to a brighter future, it is not surprising that political scientists and social scientists in general came to believe that mathematical models could contribute to the understanding, predictability, and, hence, control of complex social systems—they came to believe that political scientists came to believe that math will provide the solutions that human interaction through debate and the give and take of the political process could not.

Along with a misguided faith in mathematics, higher education has become increasingly orientated toward a Weltanschauung of instrumental rationality and technocracy designed to serve extreme free market economics, which had become de rigueur by the 1980s. In the academy, humanities and critical rationality have become marginalized. In the 1980s, the summum bonum became healthy GDP growth and controlled inflation that could best be brought about through unfettered capitalism—all else took a secondary role to an unrestrained free market. Contributing to the capitalistic system became a noble act. Students became increasingly steered into business and marketing courses while history, philosophy, literature, and other disciplines came to be seen as offering little to increasing the employability of students outside of the academic setting.

With the wave of free market advocates in the form of libertarianism and other conservative and political ideologies, universities were pushed increasingly toward preparation of students for a neoliberal, unfettered, global economic system. The idea of public institutions with the mission of educating students as part of their intellectual development needed for maintaining a constitutional democracy rapidly receded with the frenzied activities supporting an instrumental, functional, rational, economic mindset.

Statistical analyses comport well with instrumental approaches to reasoning. It should not be, but it is difficult for professors to combine critical rationality and ethical issues with the results of statistical output.

A few years ago, while teaching a statistical class for graduate students in health policy and management, I lectured on conditional probability and Bayesian analysis. Through the analysis of real data, students were shown how the probability of breast cancer screening resulting in false positives was extremely high for women under age 40 (90 percent of positives are false positives). A positive result was far more likely to be in error than it was likely to be correct for fairly young women.

False positive breast cancer screens are quite problematic for the women who are subjected to them. In a high proportion of cases, biopsies are undertaken but the mental stress leading up to the result of further testing is horrific for the patient. The question posed to the class was this: Do the professionals and businesses providing screening services have an obligation to inform women about the probability of false positives, prior to or immediately following screening?

This would help alleviate the fear—perhaps panic—among those for whom the results are positive. Counseling in this regard would add a comforting, humanizing dimension to what is otherwise a technical, impersonal process.

The bigger issue for ethicists is the doubt about the wisdom of screening healthy people for a disease for which they have no obvious symptoms. These individuals will suffer for the sake of insuring that they do not have a disease for which they had no visible signs.

Although most of the students were women, the first student to respond was a young male. He said that he did not think it would be a good idea because he would be running a clinic. He opined that he would be in the business of providing screening and would need to be concerned about return on investment. If he warned women about the probability of false positives, he might scare them away and lose their business.

This student's rather dehumanizing, amoral (or immoral—depending upon how one thinks about morality), and insensitive attitude was not challenged by even one other student. The only other comment offered was that by a woman in her 30s, who said, "I want the test." Students in a class of mostly young women (and a few women in their 50s) were unwilling to engage in a discussion about statistics that could dramatically affect their lives and the lives of countless other women.

These students viewed a statistics class technocratically and instrumentally— not humanistically. They were there to learn algorithms and technology and were not concerned about the broader questions concerning the impact of statistical results on culture, the quality of life, and politics.

In the social sciences, economists through their econometric models impressed policymakers and corporations as highly useful contributors to the economic system as it evolved by the 1980s. Also by the 1980s, Wall Street workers skilled in advanced mathematics, physics, and other "hard" sciences were integrated into the financial services industry. "Quants" were seen as wizards who could devise magic models for trading financial instruments. Indeed, the Black-Scholes black box (set of algorithms) was considered the work of geniuses (although it failed spectacularly in the case of long-term capital management).[8]

Throughout the past few decades, social scientists have become enamored by a rapid advance in statistical software and, for the most part, statistics derived from regression analyses such as structural equation, hierarchical linear, Cox regression (time-to-event), and other such correlational modeling—becoming increasingly exotic by the day. Political theory, normative-ethical philosophical issues, history, social psychological, and cultural issues are being shunted aside as irrelevant, and the deference to and popularity of natural science methodology propelled the "scientific method" into dominance.

When one examines the psychology of mathematics, one finds that advanced mathematics can be a power trip. I call this phenomenon "mathematical machismo." It is generally not possible for the non-mathematician/statistician to challenge the technical and logical facets of even simple mathematical models. It is also a route to domination and control through special knowledge that few other people possess.

I remember being told in a faculty meeting that our university's PhD students in sociology were of the belief that *SPSS* (a common statistical package) was inadequate for social science research. Rather, they believed that they could not establish their statistics' street cred without *R*—a free downloadable software, which is not for the mathematically faint of heart. I teach with *SPSS*, which is plenty advanced and capable of practically all regression models but much more user friendly than *R*. I am satisfied if students become minimally proficient in it.

The reality is that most students enter PhD programs in the social sciences without an adequate background in math and the scientific method. Many of them need to know enough to satisfy their major advisor's interest or, stated differently, the particular statistical technique of interest to his or her major advisor.

Proofiness and Political Polling

Political polling is a form of low-level scientism. Major news organizations claim that their methodologies meet scientific standards. They base their claims mostly on mindless error-rate calculations and attempts at selecting random samples. Unfortunately, polls drive political decision making because politicians believe that these supposedly scientific nose counts are their guide to reelection. They vote based on what the polls say—not based on what is "right," or what is in keeping with the best interests of our constitutional democracy.

The public has plenty of reasons to be cynical and skeptical about results of polls incessantly reported on cable channels and in newspapers. Nevertheless, TV talking heads obsess on them and reify them into real characteristics of the U.S. public. Despite the poor track record of the polling enterprise, a substantial portion of the public obviously feel a need to know what they reflect. Humans have a propensity to fall into the "proofiness trap."[9]

Proofiness is the tendency of consumers of mass media to believe that numbers proffered by experts and presumed experts reflect reality. When something is presented as a measure, a poll, an average, or a percentage in the newspaper, on television, or any other form of widely viewed form of communication, it carries weight and influences the thinking of large numbers of people.

Journalists incessantly talk about President Trump's "37%" these days. Apparently, polling results suggest that his approval rating is somewhere between 35 and 40 percent (based on the work of a variety of polling firms). The questionable validity of such polling aside, journalists have reified these point estimates into "Trump's base"—some imagined entity comprised of homogenized individuals who blindly follow this particular politician, no matter what he says or does.

As a strand of the mathematization of the social sciences, polling is a scourge on democracy. Indeed, political scientists could become relevant by debunking claims by businesses and institutions such as the *New York Times*, the *Washington Post*, NBC, *the Wall Street Journal*, and a variety of universities and consultants. Until a strong movement against polling develops within the political science profession, journalists will remain the dominant source for analysis of elections and political events and issues.

The profession at this time is on the sidelines and appears incapable of countering misinterpreted polls while at the same time journalists dominate public discourse through sound bites, propaganda, fragmented information and discussion, and show business techniques.

In a math-phobic society, data analysis can be misused and abused. It is easy to foist falsehoods and erroneous "proofs" and a wide array of findings based on some sort of numeracy. Unfortunately, political scientists—having seen academic jobs disappear—have turned to work in political polling.

There is no better example of statistical malpractice. Because the public and mass media are willing to mindlessly accept polling results as meaningful, political scientists have been willing to mindlessly produce them. As this is being written, polling data, purportedly measuring public support for the Republican bill to repeal and replace Obamacare (Better Care Reconciliation Act of 2017) were displayed on a popular morning "talk program" (*Morning Joe*, MSNBC, 6/29/2017). Several polls variously indicated support for the BCRA, ranging from 12 percent (Quinnipiac) to 27 percent (FOX News). Someone badly missed the mark. The difference between 12 and 27 percent is huge.

This is not an uncommon situation among polling enterprises. The averaging of variance from polling company to polling company is one technique often employed for overcoming these differences. The concept of a "poll of polls" is an absurdity but is a common practice in the polling industry (which includes universities and political science departments).

The absurdity of this practice is glaringly obvious—it is like mixing apples, oranges, blueberries, mangoes, strawberries, and about any other type of fruit.

This is to say that polling samples always, of necessity, vary from sample to sample. They vary in terms of intensity of endorsement and the mix of gender, ethnic, and other subgroupings. They vary in terms of variance. They all could have differently worded items (questions). How can one say that the results of a poll by one company with a sloppily collected sample of 200 is validly combined with a more carefully selected sample of 1,000? Even a poll-of-poll result weighted by sample size makes no sense. You still have the mixture of fruits.

It is ordinarily claimed by media outlets that their polls are "scientific." Nothing could be further from the truth. They apparently employ some sort of representative sampling process (true randomness is impossible in the search for respondents). They operate under the mistaken belief that a sample of 1,000 will precisely measure the opinions of the entire U.S. population. They erroneously base that on a mindless binomial error rate calculation.

Typically, they take what is considered the worst-case scenario: $\pm$ (sqrt [.25/N or sample size]) * 1.96, which provides an error rate at the 95 percent confidence interval. Hence, a sample of 1,000 would yield an error rate of $\pm$3 percent. These mindless calculations are the justification used by the *New York Times* and various other media outlets and polling firms to claim that their polls are "scientific." How many ways is such a claim erroneous? In many ways. I will review the most seriously flawed among them.

When calculating error, polling companies automatically (mindlessly) assume that results will be exactly 50 percent for and 50 percent against—an exact and precisely even split. This is because the greatest error for the measure of a binomial, categorical variable will be .5. But the polls mentioned above regarding the BCRA ranged from 12 to 27 percent. One poll was 17 percent in favor, which indicated that 83 percent were not in favor. The error rate for that poll is, therefore, 2.3 percent. A poll with a 12–88 percent split would have an error rate of 2.0 percent (given a sample size of 1,000)—a huge difference from the incorrectly reported error rate of 3.0 percent.

What cannot be measured and accounted for in these types of polls is the intensity of belief in either the "for" or "against" category. Does the 88 percent in the poll split 12/88 percent feel far more or less strongly than the 12 percent? How likely is it that those respondents in the 12 percent are intense endorsers?

Controlling for a host of factors such as ethnicity, social economic status, education, and occupation is absolutely essential in reducing polling or any other type of survey error. Unfortunately, it is impossible to determine how to weight each ethnic group because many people claim "other," many are multiethnic, and some will refuse to answer these types of question.

One often hears from journalists, consultants, academics, and others that poll percentages such as the percentage in favor of one candidate versus another candidate are "within the margin of error." This is reified to mean, "there is really no discernible difference and that is a scientific fact." There may be no discernible difference, but it is not scientifically determined by polling. If the 2016 presidential race taught us anything, political polls can be widely off the mark.

The poor science, and indeed misunderstanding, on the part of pollsters and those who parrot their results is reflected in the mindless way error rates are calculated. Polls are rarely if ever binomial.

Almost always, a third category such as "don't know," "haven't made up my mind," or some such response exists. Therefore, the error rate should be based on a multinomial variable, which is much more difficult to understand and calculate and will be larger than a binomial error rate. But that rather important issue seems to be ignored by pollsters and their clients.

Mathematics and science aside, polls have become a scourge on democracy. Polling is to democracy as crabgrass is to nice lawns. They have infested our political system and have placed it at serious risk. Legislators are driven to make decisions based on what the "polls show"—not on what is morally right.

Polls measuring the fickleness of the public have become a mainstream media commodity. Journalists benefit when events generate media attention, and viewers have been conditioned to wait with bated breath for the next approval rating of the president, support for the Affordable Care Act, the BCRA, percentage of Americans who believe President Obama was born in Kenya or is a Muslim, and on and on. As I was writing this article, a marketing researcher came by my house to ask me to participate in a poll about a proposed airport about which I knew nothing and, I suspect, not many other people knew anything about.

He gave me two choices: for or against. I said that I belonged in a third category: do not know. The pollster did not have a third category. This study would be insignificant if it were not for the intention of the sponsors of the poll to influence public policy.

Republicans made the mistake of assuming, based on public polling, that the Affordable Care Act was so unpopular that they could campaign on repealing it altogether. Indeed, they had, as a minority in the Senate and with a Democratic president, voted to repeal it 16 times before taking control of both houses of Congress and the presidency. Having been put in the position of repealing the act, they set about to do just that.

As the repeal of Obamacare was put in motion, public support for the program shot up rapidly and sharply. As Gallup Polling data displayed in Table 1 indicate, overall approval for the program increased from 42 percent in November 2016 to 55 percent in a matter of months. This swift shift in public opinion regarding a

TABLE 1. Approval of Affordable Care Act

	Nov. 2016 %	Mar. 2017 %	Change (pct. pts.)
U.S. adults	42	55	+13
Democrats	76	86	+10
Independents	40	57	+17
Republicans	7	17	+10
Democrats + leaners	71	87	+16
Republicans + leaners	11	19	+8
GALLUP			

Source: Gallup Polling.[10]

major program seriously affecting an industry comprising one-fifth of the U.S. economy and the health care of hundreds of millions of Americans should convince serious political scientists of the shallowness of public polling as a driver of public policy.

The goal of legislation should be rational public policy serving the best interests of citizens in a constitutional democracy. As an aggregation of individuals' responses to an item, polls do not reflect rational thought because we humans are not rational. As Kahneman and Tversky have demonstrated through research in cognitive psychology, individuals assess risk by developing heuristic models.

The intense negativity toward the Affordable Care Act was induced by a massive, well-funded drive by wealthy conservatives. The public was inundated with anti-government propaganda and scared about big government robbing their freedom. Although the act was a good thing for a large proportion of those showing up at congresspersons' town hall meetings and screaming about death panels and "getting government out of health care," they were not thinking about what government health care was doing or would be doing for them.

When, however, they realized they would lose what the act or other government-funded health care such as Medicare or Medicaid was doing or would do for them, their risk assessment changed abruptly. Given the anti-government climate generated through libertarian and other types of conservative publicity, it is not surprising that a large proportion of the public was not terribly thrilled when the government offered to give them something. As Kahneman and Tversky established through research, people are far more averse to loss than they are motivated to seek gains.

This discussion on the polling dimension of quantification of political research can be summed up this way: polls are not scientific because they do not measure an enduring mental construct. That is, they do not and cannot be shown to have construct validity. They are recordings of emotional responses, in an instant, to a single item regarding a very narrow issue at a single point in time. Polls mostly measure white noise. Political scientists should not be staking their reputations on this nonsensical form of public discourse. Rather, their relevance would be furthered by launching an all-out effort to inform the public about the damage wrought by faux science passing off as real science.

When Math Goes Badly Awry: James Q. Wilson and Criminal Justice

During the decades between 1970 and his death in 2012, James Q. Wilson was a big deal in political science as well as in Washington policy circles. It could be said that he was the single most influential theorist of our time regarding the issue of crime and punishment—one of the most vexing problems facing U.S. democracy and social justice.

Wilson was elected president of the American Political Science Association in 1992. By that time, he had produced highly recognized and controversial publications and had become an influential policy figure in the Reagan administration. He is best known for his "broken windows" theory of community policing, which has become linked to the notorious "stop and frisk" policing programs across the United States.

Wilson's elevation to president of APSA could, in the view of serious social science researchers and victims of mass incarceration, be considered scandalous. If members of the organization seriously cared about what he published and the impact it has had, their choice may have been different. His use of terribly flawed statistics and racist pseudoscience went unchallenged. The honor of serving as APSA president added to his cachet and stature in Washington but did not enhance the association's relevance in policy circles.

In addition to being a leader of the political science profession, Wilson became enmeshed with the right-wing "think tank" movement that began to flourish in the 1970s due to funding from wealthy archconservatives. He was a board member of the Manhattan Institute, a conservative propaganda organiza- tion (which passes itself off as a research organization). As an example of what the Manhattan Institute puts out, Heather McDonald, one of its current star "scholars," recently published a book entitled *War on Cops*,[11] in which she claims that a disproportionate number of African Americans are in jails and prisons because they "commit most of the crime."

That is a patently false statement, which can be easily debunked with a quick check of FBI arrest statistics. In absolute numbers, whites overwhelmingly are arrested in greater numbers than African Americans. What has not been clearly studied is why, given that so many more whites are arrested, that African Americans are imprisoned.

Wilson's career and his endorsement by APSA is a case study in deference to mathematical and methodological jargon no matter how subpar or nonsensical it may be. He represents one dimension of the multidimensional problem of reducing complex social systems to mathematical models and algorithms— referencing statistical modeling without attention to validity and quality of the studies referenced. As stated above, Wilson himself did not originate quantitative studies in which he engaged in design of statistical analyses. I know of no research originated by him based on an experimental or quasi-experimental design, data collection, statistical analysis, and interpretation. Rather, he bor- rowed from others—many of whom engaged in egregiously invalid statistical analyses and/or discredited pseudoscience.

He either did not understand the scientifically unacceptable quality of his source material or he did understand it and did not care. I would suggest that the former was the case. If it was the latter, he engaged in serious unethical conduct. Although legislatures produced the legal framework for mass incarceration, Wilson, despite the utter absurdity of most of the science on which he relied, supplied the theoretical justification for more and harsher punishment and less treatment and rehabilitation.

By borrowing the statistical analysis of others, Wilson demonstrated how mathematical models can, in the words of one mathematician, be turned into "weapons of math destruction."[12] As was his wont, he searched for studies confirming his theories and, consequently, supporting his attempts to translate his ideology into policy. The quality of the supposedly scholarly work he referenced seems to not have been of major concern.

For instance, he ignored a purportedly effective program for treating juvenile offenders until after faculty researchers in the Department of Applied Behavior Analysis at the University of Kansas published devastating statistics indicating the program was not any more effective than other similar programs. This was after nearly 20 years of glowing evaluations by the same researchers.[13] Furthermore, an extremely flawed evaluation of the program funded by the National Institute of Mental Health was published in 1992.[14]

Wilson, in his publications throughout the 1970s and 1980s, promoted the theory that criminals are not amenable to rehabilitation and that programs designed for that purpose would fail.[15] In borrowing subpar research, he used the mass media to make his case that punishment rather than rehabilitation is the most suitable public policy directed at criminal behavior.[16]

Wilson was willing to use math that suited his purposes, but he displayed considerable math ignorance. Consulting with a competent statistician at Harvard where he was a professor would have served him well. Despite p values slightly greater than .05, reported in one of the articles pertaining to the juvenile offender program mentioned above on which he relied, common sense should have led even the normal layperson to conclude that the program at issue was clearly more effective than the programs to which it had been compared.

As stated above, Wilson published his most noted work in mass media publications such as the *Atlantic Monthly*. He co-authored his 1985 magnum opus, *Crime and Human Nature*,[17] with Richard Herrnstein. This book was aimed at a lay audience. It is remarkable that discredited biological determinism and racism are proffered in *Crime and Human Nature*.

In the early 1970s, Herrnstein, borrowing from Arthur Jensen's racist IQ theories, published his own incendiary theories regarding IQ, elites, and success —a claim that racism, classism, sexism, and other isms are unrelated to achievement.[18] The 1960s revolution had not run its course by the time Herrnstein published his thoughts about "meritocracy." The view that inequality is driven by inherited biology stirred up considerable faculty and student outrage at Harvard and other universities. However, the counterrevolution had begun to spring into action at the same time that Professor Herrnstein was propounding his views regarding IQ.[19]

By the mid-1980s when *Crime and Human Nature* was published, the 1960s revolution was spent and a well-financed, right-wing juggernaut had put the Reagan Revolution into motion. As part of the reactionary forces propelling U.S. public policy to the right, eugenics and biological determinism were reappearing in a seemingly more palatable form. The new biological determinism and its association with the crude eugenics of the 1930s sterilization movement in the United States and the panoply of Nazi policies in Germany were for the most part ignored by the mass media, politicians/policymakers, and the public in general.[20] Awareness of the connection was certainly not evident in the APSA elevation of James Q. Wilson to president of the association.

In *Crime and Human Nature*, Wilson and Herrnstein repackaged some very old and discredited science aimed at proving that criminal behavior is driven by genetics. Neither of these two social science professors could claim expertise in the field of genetics. In fact, real geneticists have uniformly rejected the notion that criminal behavior could somehow be explained by a human's genes.[21] Nevertheless, the anthropometry of Lombroso, Hooten, W. H. Sheldon, and others provided the basis for Wilson's and Herrnstein's theories concerning "human nature" in crime. Indeed, chapter 3[22] is a defense of these relics of a less admirable time in the social sciences and is replete with Sheldon's pictures of nude males posed in a manner to elucidate the mesomorphic, ectomorphic, and endomorphic body types. The conclusion was that mesomorphic body type was associated with a propensity toward crime, which should not be surprising since the most likely age of criminal offending is late teen years through the 20s. Individuals are more in shape—buff, so to speak—and have not experienced the type of bodily changes that result in the more pear-shaped (soft and round) endomorphic body type. It is absurd that bodies of humans can be classified into only three types. It is just as absurd to believe that a connection can be made between anthropometry and genetic propensities to commit crime.

I first encountered the name of W. H. Sheldon in 1965 in an undergraduate anthropology class. The professor explained that he was known for his experiments involving the participation of college freshmen at various universities. Sheldon was able to convince the University of Washington and Yale and perhaps some other universities to make it a requirement that freshmen pose in the nude for him as part of a research project. Apparently, he was attempting to establish a connection between body type and success in college.

Sheldon was forced to cut his University of Washington research short when a mom and dad discovered that their daughter was required to be one of his research subjects. The university was compelled to abruptly end cooperation in Sheldon's "body-success" research. Yale University did not, however, encounter an angry parent. Sheldon was given carte blanche to photograph the incoming freshmen— some of whom would become quite famous. It was said that nude pictures of George W. Bush, Hillary Clinton, John Kerry, and perhaps others existed in Sheldon's research files, even after they were ensconced at the Smithsonian Institute. The latest word on the street is that they have been destroyed.

In 1965, my anthropology professor considered Sheldon's work to be laughable and befitting of a crackpot. Nevertheless, some 20 years later, his theories formed the basis for one of the most influential books on crime in the late twentieth and early twenty-first centuries—co-authored by one of the most influential political scientists of the past half century. Seven years after publication of *Crime and Human Nature*, Wilson was elected president of APSA.

Wilson was a neoconservative. Like neoconservatives in general, he was obsessed with African Americans as a race.[23] In their chapter on race in *Crime and Human Nature*, Wilson and Herrnstein assert, without any empirical evidence, that African Americans are genetically prone to a mesomorphic body type. They were sly about broaching the subjects of race, genetics, and criminal behavior. Readers were left to draw their own conclusions about biological determinism in crime from claims regarding mesomorphic body types, crime, and race.

Wilson implied that African Americans are genetically predisposed to criminal behavior. However, he was not subtle about the efficacy of rehabilitation. He had spent a large part of his career claiming that criminals were not amenable to rehabilitation and that punishment, incapacitation, and incarceration were the only viable approaches to criminal behavior.

Wilson was not a quantitative researcher. He designed no studies, collected no data, and conducted no statistical analyses. He looked for studies confirming his preconceived ideas and supporting his ideology. In a classic example of confirmatory bias, the statistically subpar studies mentioned above pertaining to Achievement Place were incorporated into the book as supporting evidence for the biological determinism underlying the thesis that criminals could not be rehabilitated.

Among a few other resources, Wilson and Herrnstein relied to a great degree on a couple of simple mathematical models based on 2×2 crosstabs and a chi-square statistic (produced by faculty in the Department of Applied Behavior Analysis at the University of Kansas).[24] Based on the conclusions of these faculty researchers, Wilson and Herrnstein made the claim that these simple models based on a very small sample of youthful offenders were proof that offenders could not be rehabilitated.

As it turned out, these were not just any old crosstabs from which a chi-square statistic and a couple of p values were derived. Wilson elevated them to a level of absolute proof that criminals cannot be rehabilitated.

These KU faculty had also created and operated the juvenile treatment program from which the data were collected. The program was designed to keep youth offenders in their community and attending the schools they were attending when adjudicated. The mode of treatment included placement of adjudicated youth in a residence overseen by a husband and wife trained in behavior modification techniques. Only eight boys or eight girls lived in a home. The initial home, Achievement Place in Lawrence, Kansas, was initiated in 1967. It was replicated in 200 homes throughout the United States by the 1980s. The Achievement Place model was adopted by the legendary Father Flanagan's Boys' Town in the 1970s and has remained the treatment modality there.

After nearly 20 years of publishing articles demonstrating the effectiveness of the Achievement Place program in reducing recidivism (compared to other community-based treatment programs), the faculty researchers did an about-face and published an article in which they concluded that the program was no more effective than comparison group home programs.[25]

This conclusion was based on p values greater than .05 but still rather small. Unfortunately, Wilson and Herrnstein accepted the KU findings at face value—without challenge or serious critique.

Crosstabulation of count data and the calculation of a chi-square statistic are taught in introductory stats courses. Any competent graduate student would notice the folly in accepting a *p* value slightly larger than .05 as proof that a null hypothesis should be accepted. Indeed, the power of the statistics accompanying the models was too low for justifying the authors' conclusions.

Wilson was not responsible alone for the bad math he rendered consequential in policies leading to mass incarceration—disproportionately of African Americans. University faculty producing studies and the National Institute of Mental Health were complicit in claiming this work as conclusive proof of biological determinism in crime.[26]

There is no better example of dangerous nonsense than that produced by Wilson and his co-author Richard Herrnstein. Their "incendiary" book—which is filled with "junk science"—buttressed claims that criminal behavior has an underlying genetic cause. That Wilson and Herrnstein's influential work has not been challenged and treated as the scandal that it is speaks volumes about the political science profession.

Wilson and Herrnstein received the imprimatur of APSA, and that imprimatur was placed on the resurgence of racist pseudoscience in the 1980s. APSA members may not see the situation in quite the same way. However, Herrnstein went on to write *The Bell Curve* with Charles Murray—a racist tome in which the authors claim that IQ is heritable and that African Americans have genetically determined lower IQ than whites.

Support for *The Bell Curve* was provided by the American Enterprise Institute and the extremist, right-wing Bradley Foundation. Much of the reference material cited in *The Bell Curve* had been produced by the eugenics-oriented Pioneer Fund, an organization much admired by the German, Nazi government in the 1930s.

Murray and Herrnstein claims were accompanied by logistic regression models that supposedly proved their nonsensical theories. The model results, as reported, did not support their claims to genetic-caused, racially distinct, IQ.

A year after publication of *The Bell Curve*, William Bennett, John Dilulio, and John Walters relied on Wilson's view that society was beset with a coming wave of dangerous, feral, incorrigible African American youth in their now infamous book *Body Count*,[27] which combined these fearful traits into the meme "superpredator." Even Hillary Clinton, first lady at the time, sounded alarms about these dangerous kids who needed to be "brought to heel."[28] The wave of "superpredators" did not materialize as predicted by *Body Count*, but the damage done to African American youth in the juvenile justice system continues to adversely impact and disgrace the United States to this very day.

Political Science and Math in the Public Sphere

The public sphere is that realm of our culture where political discourse occurs—even if more and more of that discourse is absurd. Saying that political science is not as relevant as it should be is, in effect, saying that the profession is not adequately engaged in the public sphere. At one time, this cultural realm was confined to the typographic media (pamphlets, news-papers, books, etc.), and public events such as Lyceums, Chautauqua's, and political oratory.

Compared to the public sphere before the age of television and Facebook, the current public sphere is entertaining, shallow, often disrespectful and vulgar, and based on bits of disconnected information requiring very little concentration. In the long history of humankind, it has been only recently that political communication occurred in short, fragmented, entertaining bits. Much of this is due to the rapidity of change in the technological sphere. Not all that long ago, in the 1850s, the public sphere was public in the sense that it demanded the presence of an individual in a public setting at which politicians and others would debate or orate for several hours. The audience attending affairs such as the Lincoln-Douglas debate would listen to the spoken word in the form of complex, sophisticated sentences.

The Lincoln-Douglas debates could last for several hours. Members of the audience would be required to remember, mentally process, and comprehend words spoken by orators who were capable of framing their statements in long, complicated sentences and paragraphs.[29] William Greider, in *Secrets of the Temple*[30] (a history of the Federal Reserve), writes about how the prairie populist farmers of the 1890s packed their families into covered wagons and met in a grove of trees or other suitable location. They camped for days and conducted lectures and discussion pertaining to monetary policy and the role of the federal government in banking regulation. Rather than passive consumers of lectures by experts, they were self-educated and knowledgeable about the finer points of monetary policy.

The oral and written traditions of the sixteenth to nineteenth centuries in the United States required a form of mental processing that is far different from the electronic media dominant in late twentieth- and early twenty-first-century America. Television does not lend itself to serious discussion in depth of a topic such as Social Security, unemployment, poverty, individual liberty, and the myriad other issues of importance today.

As we approach the third decade of the twenty-first century, political discourse is in sync with information dissemination in general. Entertainment and show business are paramount. People tend to tune out a television program that requires focus and concentration on a particular topic for more than a few seconds. Images flash across the screen and allow mere seconds for viewers to process their meaning in relation to the topic discussed (*presented* is a better word). None of this requires serious examination of what is presented for the purpose of ferreting out error, misinformation, and the inane and irrelevant content.

The public sphere in the United States is sick and suffering from many maladies caused by electronic communication. I suggest that political scientists can begin a strong movement toward a healthy public sphere. In my view, a healthy public sphere would be a constellation of fora for serious, in-depth exposition and debate. The public would have access to these fora and have an opportunity for meaningful participation in them. A forum in this constellation is not necessarily a physical space such as an auditorium or other type of room.

For several reasons, complex quantification is not a suitable form of communication in the public sphere just described. The same thing could be said about even the simplest models beyond basic math: crosstabs, comparison of averages between groups (think ANOVA and T-test). Practically everyone understands the percentages reported by pollsters; however, practically no one, except experts trained in psychometrics, understands the major validity and reliability issues.

I do believe that basic math in the form of counts, sums, averages, and medians must be an integral part of discourse in the public sphere. It is imperative, however, that numbers be presented in a forum characterized by critical thinking. Politicians and interest groups have a tendency to slant budgetary and other forms of data of critical importance for the purpose of achieving their political objectives. Dishonesty in discussion of numbers pertaining to public policy is pervasive.

For instance, it is often said by politicians, faux scholars in think tanks, and misinformed journalists that 60 percent of the federal budget is allocated to programs for the elderly, which is false. This demagoguery and/or ignorance causes the public to believe that the nearly $1 trillion of Social Security expenditures is part of the federal budget. It is not. Furthermore, one half of the Medicare budget is fully funded by beneficiary payroll taxes (it is a social insurance program) and out-of-pocket expenses. The other half is budgetary and requires a transfer from the U.S. Treasury.[31]

Practically all discussions of the budget lump total expenditures on Social Security and Medicare into one sum and claim that it accounts for the highest budgetary expenditure (approximately $1.5 trillion of the approximately $3.8 trillion budget in 2016). This false narrative has entered public discourse and has led to ageism and scapegoating of the elderly.

Political scientists can take a leadership role by pressing for public fora in which budgetary misinformation pertaining to the elderly and myriad other destructive false narratives corrupting public discourse can be debunked. Who would be better qualified than political scientists to help the public understand the truth by presenting objective information and facilitating reasoned discussion in which the public participates.

Today, the public sphere is generally a radio station, a television station, a newspaper, or some form of social media. However, at its best, the public sphere is an auditorium or other space where people can come together for mature, serious discussion and debate. Indeed, members of the public have exhibited a "hunger" for learning from interesting lectures and for participating in discussion of issues of importance to them.

It is apparent that a large proportion of the U.S. population does not want to just sit home and watch programs on CNN, MSNBC, Fox, and other cable channels or surf the internet. The Kansas City Public Library lecture series is often packed to capacity and beyond. For instance, a recent lecture by Thomas Frank, author of

Listen Liberal, was overflowing, as are all lectures by authors speaking in the library series. There is no dearth of individuals asking intelligent questions during the short question and answer sessions at the end of the lectures.

CSPAN is the best public forum for discussion of serious political issues. Although TV audiences are passive viewers and unable to participate in CSPAN events, attendees are able to make comments and ask questions. Unfortunately, most TV political fare is dominated by journalists and performers. Although some journalists have covered a particular area of government for a long time and have developed expertise in their beat, such as foreign policy, defense, health care, and so forth, it is not uncommon for reporters for leading newspapers and television networks to appear on the various talk shows and comment on almost any subject.

The hosts also hold forth on any subject likely to grab the interest of viewers. Performing is of the utmost importance. Without attracting an acceptable number of viewers each day, they will be out of a job. Therefore, they entertain by loud, provocative interchanges in which people are rudely interrupted (by the host usually). They regularly include "man bites dog" stories with no relation to any larger political context. This keeps viewers entertained.

Age and race appear to be more characteristic of those experts, journalists, and hosts receiving the most face time on the leading network political shows than educational training, expertise, and experience. The hosts and the guests booked on the shows—but particularly the hosts and regular journalists—are usually young with the "right TV appearance." They are also overwhelmingly white.

The television space also depends on political polls to keep viewers interested on an ongoing basis. Even if not much of interest or consequence is happening, a political poll on almost any ridiculous subject can be conjured up.

Today the public sphere is a cacophony of social media, television, protests, politicians' town halls, and email. Newspapers and public affairs magazines such as *Time* and *Newsweek* still exist but have eliminated text and replaced it with photographs. Indeed, photo-journalism has continuously gained a larger share of the space in both newspapers and weekly magazines.

Despite the lack of validity associated with public opinion polls (discussed above), this phony mathematized form of communication drives policy considerably more than most people realize. Pushed by journalists and highly paid political consultants, these pseudoscientific measures of public opinion actually influence opinion through their unfounded claims about what is broadly believed. Journalists who depend on "events" for maintaining viewer interest use polls to evoke fear, relief, or anticipation. Politically interested individuals wait with "bated breath" for the next set of diverse polls regarding President Trump's approval rating.

These polls, along with "man bites dog" spectacles (such as outrageous statements or behaviors on the part of politicians) are useful events for ratings—critically important in competition between networks and their cable channel ratings. With survival in office and/or winning an election as major purposes of politicians, legislators, and candidates, they are fearful of public opinion.

Political scientists can enhance their relevance and contribute to a more mature, reasonable public discourse by:

1. Leaving the ivory tower and castles in the sky. Social science academics can move beyond writing papers for other academics. Among academics producing abstruse, multivariable, quantitative models, only a tiny number of their peers understand and/or have an interest in their esoterica.
2. Proposing, organizing, and facilitating public fora (characterized by sober, serious, mature consideration of issues). Political scientists can work with local libraries and their own institutions in designing and presenting lectures and public discussions. It would be necessary to establish ground rules for behavior at these events. After decades of deterioration in public discourse, interrupting, disrespecting, and even screaming at adversaries have become standard fare on television—the current primary forum for political discussions.

A large share of the public has an interest in knowing about such matters as how the Federal Reserve works, monetary policy, and a host of legislative and policy issues. Of course, in the age of show business, presenters must have the ability to relate well to attendees.

3. Questioning elites inside and outside of the academy. A professor may be a big deal in academia and outside of the academy, but a professor at an elite institution such as Harvard, and with considerable cachet in government, should not be given a pass from peer review and critique. For example, the American public—especially the African American subpopulation—has a right to be fully informed about the racialist social science that served as the raison d'être for mass incarceration.

Certainly, these three ideas for action, if put in motion, will not thrust the political science profession to the pinnacle of attention in this age of show business. But they would be a good start in moving political science toward relevance.

Summary

Unfortunately, the political science profession has displayed a lack of leadership and deference to quants and their amoral, scientifically questionable, and often irrelevant, mathematical models. Not only has the American Political Science Association failed to confront dangerous pseudoscience, in the past they have endorsed it by making James Q. Wilson president of the association in 1992. Wilson's impact on criminal justice through statistical malpractice and the damage it has wrought were discussed in this article as a case study of the political science profession's blind eye turned toward racist, classist, and scientifically ill-informed theories foisted on the public through the mass media and a trade publication. It is an illustration of the danger of unchallenged mathematization, which is far too often the case.

To support this harsh criticism of a rather famous political scientist, an appendix is attached to this article for the purpose of demonstrating the misuse and abuse of a *p* value and statistical significance in making the case for biological determinism. Wilson did not collect the data or conduct the statistical analysis. He merely found a study that supported the reactionary social science and criminology he needed to further his ideological political agenda. The question for this article is "Where were his peers?" That is to ask why Wilson's obviously ridiculous claims have gone unchallenged.

In addition to the pseudoscience reported in scholarly journals, claims of objectivity and scientific presumptions by the polling industry have deceived journalists and the public into believing that they are an adequate measure of reality. They are not. Rather, they are junk science and should be debunked as that by political scientists.

Political scientists can become far more relevant by initiating public fora in which pseudoscience is debunked and the public has an opportunity to interact with scholars in discussions of historical, social science, and philosophical issues as they impact governance and democracy. Numbers and mathematics are pertinent to that discussion. However, the language of advanced math and statistics will prevent meaningful participation by the lay public.

Notes

1. Postman, N. (1985), *Amusing Ourselves to Death: Public Discourse in the Age of Show Business*. New York, NY: Penguin Books, pp. 23–29.
2. Cook, T., & Campbell, D. (1979), *Quasi-Experimentation: Design & Analysis Issues for Field Settings*. Boston, MA: Houghton Mifflin, pp. 91–94.
3. For a discussion of specification error, see, for example, Pedhazur, E. (1982), *Multiple Regression in Research*. Fort Worth, TX: Harcourt, Brace, Jovanovich College Publishers, pp. 35–36, 226–229.
4. Bertalanffy, L. (1968), *General System Theory*. New York, NY: George Braziller; Buckley, W. (1967), *Sociology & Modern Systems Theory*. Englewood Cliffs, NJ: Prentice-Hall.
5. Bradley, W., & Schaefer, K. (1998), *The Uses & Misuses of Data & Models: The Mathematization of the Human Sciences*. Thousand Oaks, CA: Sage, pp. 30–32.
6. See, for example, Ziliak, S., & McCloskey, D. (2011), *The Cult of Statistical Significance*. Ann Arbor, MI: The University of Michigan Press.
7. Lipsey, M. (1990), *Design Sensitivity*. Newbury Park, NJ: Sage.
8. An excellent discussion of the failure of quants and their advanced math can be found in Lowenstein, R. (2000), *When Genius Failed*. New York, NY: Random House.
9. *Proofiness*.
10. http://www.gallup.com/poll/207671/affordable-care-act-gains-majority-approval-first-time.aspx.
11. MacDonald, H. (2016), *War on Cops*. New York, NY: Encounter Books.
12. *Weapons of Math Destruction*.
13. Kingsley, D. (2006), "The Teaching-Family Model and Post-Treatment Recidivism: A Critical Review of the Conventional Wisdom." *International Journal of Behavioral Consultation & Therapy*, 2(4), 1–16.
14. Ibid.
15. See, for example, Wilson, J. (1983), *Thinking About Crime*. New York, NY: Basic Books.
16. See, for example, Wilson, J. (1983), "Raising Kids." *The Atlantic Monthly*, October 1983.
17. Wilson, J. & Herrnstein, R. (1985), *Crime and Human Nature*. New York, NY: Simon & Schuster.
18. Herrnstein, R. (1974), *IQ in the Meritocracy*. Boston, MA: Little, Brown & Company.

19. Ibid.
20. Kuhl, S. (1994), *The Nazi Connection: Eugenics, American Racism, and German National Socialism*. New York, NY: Oxford University Press. Terms such as "Nazi" and "German National Socialism" may seem hyperbolical, but the repackaging of biological determinism and white supremacy, especially by Herrnstein, was characteristic of the racialist theorizing included in a body of right-wing literature supported by think tanks such as the American Enterprise Institute and the Manhattan Institute. The Pioneer Fund, a pro-eugenics and Nazi-favored organization in the 1930s, funded much of the research referenced by Herrnstein and Murray in *The Bell Curve*. Wilson was less "out front" on white supremacy, but 12 of the 44 references in *The Bell Curve* chapter on crime were to *Crime and Human Nature*.
21. Griffiths, A., Wessler, S., Lewontin, R., & Carroll, S. (2008), *Introduction to Genetic Analysis*. New York, NY: W. H. Freeman, pp. 652–653; Lewontin, R., Rose, S., & Kamin, L. (1984), *Not in Our Genes*. New York, NY: Pantheon Books; Mukherjee, S. (2016), *The Gene: An Intimate History*. New York, NY: Scribner, pp. 300–301.
22. Wilson & Herrnstein, *Crime and Human Nature*. pp. 69–103.
23. Kingsley, D. (2016), "Neoconservatives and the Demise of a Humane Juvenile Justice Program: A Conversation About Social Science & Racism." *Poverty & Public Policy*, 8(4), 330–367.
24. Kirigin, K., Braukmann, C., Atwater, J., & Wolf, M. (1982), "An Evaluation of Teaching-Family (Achievement Place) Group Homes for Juvenile Offenders." *Journal of Applied Behavior Analysis*, 15, 1–16.
25. Kingsley, D. (2006), "The Teaching-Family Model and Post-Treatment Recidivism: A Critical Review of the Conventional Wisdom." *International Journal of Behavioral Consultation & Therapy*, 2(4), 1–16.
26. Wolf, M., Braukmann, C., & Ramp, K. (1987), "Serious Delinquent Behavior as Part of a Significantly Handicapping Condition: Cures and Supportive Environments." *Journal of Applied Behavior Analysis*, 20, 347–359.
27. Bennett, W., DiLulio, J., & Walters, J. (1996), *Body Count*. New York, NY: Simon & Schuster.
28. The first lady's statement can be viewed on YouTube at https://www.youtube.com/watch?v=j0uCrA7ePno.
29. Postman, *Amusing Ourselves to Death*, pp. 23–29.
30. Greider, W. (1987), *Secrets of the Temple*. New York, NY: Simon & Schuster, p. 244.
31. Kingsley, D. (2015), "Aging & Health Care Costs: Narrative Versus Reality." *Poverty & Public Policy*, 7(1), 3–21.

Reforming Political Science

Lawrence M. Mead

Department of Politics, New York University, New York, NY

Political science is in decline because it has become too focused on methodological precision, has lost contact with public policy, and recruits only among academics. To become more vital and relevant, it must use a wider range of methods, recover a voice on policy issues, and expect much more government experience from its recruits.

政治学改革

由于政治学太过于追求方法论的精确性，忽略了对公共政策的关注，并且只招募专业学术人员，导致它正在走向衰落。为了加强其重要性和相关性，政治学必须采用一系列更广泛的方法，重新为政策议题发声，并招募具备更多政府工作经验的人员。

Reformando las ciencias políticas

Las ciencias políticas están en decadencia porte se han enfocado demasiado en la precisión metodológica, han perdido contacto con las políticas públicas y solo recluta a académicos. Para ser más vital y relevante, la disciplina debe utilizar una gama más amplia de métodos, recuperar un a voz en los temas políticos y pedir mucha más experiencia de gobierno de sus reclutas.

Paper prepared for presentation at the conference of the American Political Science Association, San Francisco, CA, August 31, 2017.
[Shorter version published in German in *INDES: Zeitschrift für Politik und Gesellschaft*, Fall 2011].

Introduction

Academic political science[1] appears to be successful, yet it is deeply troubled. On the one hand, it is a vast enterprise. The American Political Science Association has over 15,000 members, most of whom teach or study political science in colleges and universities across the United States. But on the other hand, the discipline is deeply divided. A few years ago, a virtual civil war broke out between the political science establishment, which favors highly mathematical research, and a "pere-stroika" movement demanding a return to more diverse methods.[2]

More important, the discipline commands little attention. Few political scientists have an audience outside academe. Few indeed are known beyond their own narrow specialty. Hardly any political scientists are visible authorities on public issues in the way economists are. To many Americans, politics may be important, yet the professional study of politics is ignored. Obscurity may be one reason why morale in political science is low. One survey from the 1980s found political scientists less excited about recent developments in their subject than the followers of 31 other disciplines.[3]

I propose three explanations for this state of affairs: Political science has become scholastic, meaning overly specialized, and ingrown; it has too little to say about public policy; and the recruitment of political scientists is too narrowly academic. To recover standing and morale, political scientists must take on broader subjects, address policy issues, and gain more practical experience of government.

Scholasticism

Political science suffers from scholasticism, meaning that its research pursues refinement at the expense of substance. Like medieval philosophers who debated the details of Thomism, political scientists tend to devote excessive attention to small subjects in which few other scholars—let alone ordinary people—have an interest. Scholasticism is a general problem in academe, not only in political science. In recent articles, I described what scholasticism means and documented its growth.[4] I mean by the term four developments in research:

1. *Specialization*: Compared to several decades ago, academics today tend to work on narrower subjects and interact only with other specialists in their fields.
2. *Methodologism*: Today's researchers are far more self-conscious about the procedures of inquiry, often focusing on method to the detriment of substance.
3. *Nonempiricism*: In part due to methodologism, today's research often has little evidence behind it. Some "research" is entirely mathematical, without any substantive content at all.
4. *Literature focus*: Today's scholars typically take their questions and methods from earlier research in their specialty, rather than forming their own view of reality.

Of these trends, specialization is the most fundamental and the easiest to document. One sign of it is growth in the number of journals. In political science, there was only one journal in 1886, but there are 42 today, many of them specialized. Since 1981, the American Political Science Association (APSA) allowed "sections" for different specialties to form, and 35 of them have organized. The annual APSA conference has similarly become fragmented by specialty.

To document the trends, I coded articles in the *American Political Science Review*, the leading journal in political science, for whether they showed the four scholastic features in five separate years over 1968–2007. During that interval, there was a sharp increase in specialization and literature focus and a smaller rise in nonempiricism.[5] By 1998, 85 percent of *APSR* articles were specialized, and

60 percent had a literature focus, figures that fell to 70 and 41 percent by 2007. These were among the articles that I classified as scholastic:

1. A study of the theory of tyranny in the ancient Greek polis.
2. A rational choice analysis of how to combat terrorism with limited resources, without data.
3. A reestimation of the effect of campaign spending on Senate elections.
4. A critique of recent literature on "the state."[6]

Such articles would be likely to interest only other specialists doing closely similar work—not political scientists in general, let alone the broader public. Rising scholasticism was not confined to fields that often use quantitative methods, meaning multivariate statistics or rational choice (game theory); it advanced in all fields, even those, like political theory, where argument is qualitative.

Thus, today's political science research is increasingly aimed at minor issues within narrow specialties. I have heard and read of similar trends in other disciplines. Today's academic research serves values of *rigor* derived from the "hard" sciences—the idea that inferences must be definitely provable and replicable. But to achieve rigor, researchers subdivide inquiry into tiny subjects, leading to results that are often trivial or unrealistic. They neglect the values of *relevance*—addressing problems that the outside world perceives, not just academe, and where there is an audience beyond the researchers themselves. The pursuit of rigor has become a dead end, the chief immediate reason why today's political science lacks importance and audience.

However, scholasticism did not happen by accident.[7] Deep-seated forces in academe lie behind it. These include:

1. *The exhaustion of research*: With so many political scientists doing research, the important findings in most fields have already been made. Thus, scholars must seek out ever narrower and more obscure topics if they are to say anything original, as the usual canons of research require.
2. *Research over teaching*: American higher education has increasingly assessed faculty for research publications rather than teaching, which further raises the number of researchers and promotes obscurantism.
3. *Peer review*: Review of academic articles for journal publication is dominated by specialists, forcing authors to pursue specialization and rigor if they want to publish. Tenure reviews have also focused increasingly on journal articles in specialized fields.
4. *The vogue for mathematics*: Quantitative methods (statistics and game theory) are more prestigious than other methods in academe and have come to dominate research in all the social sciences.[8]
5. *Academic prestige*: The American university enjoys such prestige that it has escaped accountability to the wider society. This has allowed faculty to pursue arcane subjects that are of little interest to anyone but themselves.

Scholasticism has tended to drive intellectual life out of the university, toward other venues, such as non-journal publications, think tanks in Washington and elsewhere, and the blogosphere. In all these settings, political scientists can make broader arguments on important issues and seek broader audiences than they can in the journals.

The Neglect of Policy

A more long-standing problem is that political science has little to say about public policy. Unlike economists, political scientists seldom claim to know anything that would improve policy or help government function better. All they know about is politics, but most people in and around government think they already know enough about that. Economists have much more to say about policy, so they get much more attention in government and the media.

One worrisome sign of political science's irrelevance is that, since 2009, conservatives in Congress have made repeated attempts to cut NSF funding for political science, which they view as a waste. One cut in 2013 eliminated such funding except for research on national security or economic development.[9]

This is a change from the past. The ancients treated politics as the master science. To them, politics was crucial to whether society attained the good life. That was partly because politics was important in itself. As Aristotle said, "man is a political animal" who naturally seeks involvement in politics. But politics is also a means to social ends outside politics. Society cannot achieve the good life unless it is well governed.[10] Thus, the major test of politics is policy—whether it governs society so that ordinary people can live well.

A concern for policy, however, dropped out of American political science at an early point. In its first decades, in the early twentieth century, the discipline focused on understanding the formal institutions of American government. After World War II, it shifted toward analyzing the informal processes within those institutions, including public opinion, interest groups, and parties. But at no point did political scientists treat their subject as a master science—a craft that might improve governance, to the benefit of society. Recent mathematical methods such as statistics or game theory have not changed this.

Why was policy ignored? In part because American government was always too successful, at least compared to regimes in most other countries, to force a focus on policy and governance. American political scientists also feared that to take policy positions would be to second-guess the democratic political process, which they had no authority to do. Above all, they feared that involvement in policy disputes would embroil the discipline in advocacy and thus compromise its ambitions to become a true science. So today, very few political scientists are known as policy experts, and those who are have little standing in academic political science.[11]

This reticence about policy was the principal reason why, when policy analysis developed as a field after World War II, its main basis was economics rather than political science. Economists had no hesitation about advising government about policy, even though their discipline—based as it is on the marketplace—had only limited relevance to the public sector.[12] Economic models of policy are effective in areas where market behavior can be assumed, for example in business regulation, but much less so in areas like social policy where behavior is less economizing and programs must be more highly administered. Economism also counts for little in areas where strong moral beliefs may override any desire to optimize economic utility.

For a brief period in the 1950s and 1960s, Harold Lasswell developed an idea of the "policy sciences," in which political science alongside other disciplines would help society solve public problems.[13] But the idea was too vague to be broadly persuasive, and political science never developed models linking policy to outcomes in the rigorous way economists claimed to do. In today's political science, there is a subfield called "public policy," but its members largely study policymaking without making arguments about best policy. Their focus is on process, not outcomes. In this, they resemble the rest of political science. So what they write is largely ignored by both policymakers and the broader public.[14]

I do not mean that political scientists are totally passive or lacking in normative concerns. Many of them criticize American politics for failing to achieve the democratic ideals set forth in the nation's founding documents. In a common view, American politics is so dominated by economic interests and the rich that the people govern only in name.[15] Other political scientists are more sanguine, saying, not that the public interest is ignored, but that we disagree about how to achieve it.[16] But in any event, this is a dispute *about politics* and not about how to *use* politics to achieve the social good in any more practical sense. How to improve policy is the political question that average Americans care most about. By failing to address it, political scientists consign themselves to obscurity.

Ironically, the retreat from policy has occurred at the very time when the potential of political science as a policy science was never greater. In today's Washington, the major impediment to effective policymaking is not ignorance of what government should do, as economists assume. Rather, it is difficulty in motivating government to "do the right thing" for institutional reasons. One cause of paralysis is rising polarization between the political parties. Another is a breakdown in the budget process, which helps to explain the rising national deficit. And, after an era in which the major trend in economic policy was to deregulate markets, today's need is to restore enough controls to prevent another financial crisis. Donald Trump's disturbing election as president in 2016 suggested wide public disillusionment with government's performance in *policy* terms.

In anti-poverty policy, the major goals are to get poor adults to work more consistently and avoid unwed pregnancy. Economists believed that changing economic incentives could achieve this, but the effects have been negligible. Accordingly, government has taken to enforcing work and promoting marriage through political and administrative means, which have more effect.[17] Those forces were largely responsible for driving most welfare mothers off the rolls into jobs during the American welfare reform. Most experts opposed the reform, in part because they were mostly economists and sociologists who knew little about politics or bureaucracy.[18]

Government also faced chronic administrative problems. The intergovernmental grant system is tangled, and how best to implement local programs is unclear.[19] The idea of "reinventing government" has generated progress at the local level, but how to apply it to federal administration is unclear.[20] On all these fronts, institutions are critical to effective policy, and research is needed. Of all disciplines, political science has the best hope to connect reforms to improved outcomes, as the public wishes. But few political scientists even attempt to do this.

Academic Recruitment

A third, and related, reason for problems in political science is the way political scientists are formed. Their training is overwhelmingly academic. They usually proceed straight from their undergraduate studies to graduate programs where they learn research methods and specialties within political science. Few have any direct experience in government, apart, perhaps, from volunteering in political campaigns. The research they do for their dissertations will typically be highly specialized, due to the fragmentation of the discipline already mentioned. They then hope to be appointed to junior positions in political science departments, where again they will do specialized research to gain tenure. This trajectory perpetuates the political science we have—a scholastic craft, remote from actual government or policy, in which outsiders take little interest.

These tendencies are strongly enforced by the overproduction of PhDs in graduate programs. Only a small share of new political scientists can hope to get a permanent (tenure track) academic job, where they are paid to teach political science and do research. Competition for those few slots forces candidates to generate publications even before they finish their degrees. That in turn forces them to specialize much more sharply than they once did. Their research must be highly methodological, as the journals require. They cannot take the time to address broader questions or policy, let alone experience government firsthand. All this perpetuates the status quo.

One might think that the development of policy analysis as a field would have countered these trends, but it has not. Traditionally, American public administration showed the same diffidence about policy as political science, with which it was closely allied until the postwar era. Mostly, public officials have viewed themselves as expert implementers of policy, but they left the content of policy to democratic politicians. In the late 1960s and 1970s, public policy graduate schools developed that were more forthright about recommending policy—but they were dominated by economists rather than political scientists. Most of the PhDs they produce are essentially economists, skilled at data analysis, but largely out of touch with actual government operations. These schools have not yet produced a more relevant, more policy-oriented political science.

Policy scholars, also, are subject to scholastic pressures themselves. Most of them do quantitative research, based on existing databases, because then the methodology can be precise, hence more acceptable to the journals. They tend to ignore institutions because to study them requires methods such as field interviewing that are costly, time consuming, low-tech, and tougher to defend. Thus, the institutional side of public programs largely escapes serious study.[21]

Reforms

How could political science recover its heritage as the master science?

Curbing Scholasticism

The first step is to reverse the narrowly focused, strongly methodological bent of current research. To do more substantive work and to get more attention, political scientists must take on broader, more important topics. They must seek greater relevance, addressing problems that are visible outside academe and commanding a wider audience—even if it means some loss of rigor. Here, some large political questions that, to my knowledge, the discipline is effectively ignoring, often because they call for broader reasoning than scholasticism allows:

1. How to reframe normative political theory to address the real issues in the politics of rich countries. These seldom are about "justice" in John Rawls's sense, much more often about crime, welfare, education, and other issues of social order.
2. How to reconcile a Western political tradition, which originally considered only class differences within the political community, with today's politics, in which differences in race and ethnicity are much more important.
3. How to explain the increasing alienation of Western publics from voting and political involvement. Answers are elusive because there has been little unstructured research into public attitudes and motivations, only endless, empty analysis of existing survey data. Few public opinion specialists, for example, anticipated Trump's surprising election.
4. How to explain the weakness of political development outside the West? Why did reasonably honest, efficient, and democratic regimes arise essentially only in Europe and its offshoots, and in Japan. Students of development have mostly ignored important world cultural differences.[22]
5. How to grapple with the profound implications of massive Third World immigration for Western politics.

Serious research in political science should at least shed light on some question as important as these, if not the whole of it. In my experience, political scientists are widely aware of such questions and interested in them. But— shackled as they are by scholastic assumptions—very few do anything to address them.

To address such issues takes a wide-ranging argument that refers in depth to history, social science theory, and world cultural differences—exactly the dimensions that today's political science shuts out. The only political scientist of any prominence who writes at that level is Francis Fukuyama.[23] He has a vast audience both in and outside political science but is largely ignored within the discipline.

Opponents of obscurantism must make a case against it, as I have tried to do in this and other articles cited above. But change will also require outside pressure. Resistance will come most immediately from outside funders of research, as congressional efforts to cut NSF funding suggest. There will also likely be pressure from business, which opposes the neglect of teaching by faculty absorbed in narrow research, causing many university graduates to lack the skills that employers need. And if graduates cannot be hired, their parents will also demand change.[24]

Reclaiming Policy

A focus on policy tends to restrain scholasticism, because it requires addressing real-world problems visible outside the university, rather than narrow academic concerns. Thus, a second essential change is for political science to say more about public policy. Rather than just study politics and, at most, criticize it in its own terms, political scientists must connect political and administrative factors they know about with desired policy outcomes. We need a science, not just of politics, but of statecraft. Here are some of the urgent policy issues facing American government:

1. How to restore the federal budget process so the national budget deficit can be curbed.
2. How to tame exploding costs in the big health programs, Medicare and Medicaid, which are bankrupting the government.
3. How to create more directive social programs, able both to support poor adults while requiring that they work and do other things to support themselves.
4. How to rationalize the complicated system of intergovernmental grants that largely funds American domestic programs.
5. How to apply performance management techniques to the federal government.
6. How to achieve large performance improvements in big public agencies, such as the American military realized after the Vietnam War.

Right now, policymakers address these questions based on ad hoc experience, largely without the benefit of research. They are advised, at best, by economists who can recommend best policies but know little about institutions. Political scientists—if they were willing—could do much better.

To address such questions requires broadening policy analysis to include political analysis and vice versa.[25] Orthodox policy analysis—usually written by economists—tells government what to do to solve policy problems. It seldom addresses whether the recommendation could be politically accepted and implemented. Preferably, policy analysts should make the case for their recommendation on the merits as they do now—but then *go on* to discuss the political and bureaucratic constraints on realizing that policy. Perhaps changes in the policy process will be needed before government can "do the right thing." Conversely, one can argue the other way, showing how government's goals must be trimmed to fit what the institutions can deliver. Whereas orthodox policy argument largely excludes institutions, this wider conception includes them. Policy analysis becomes a form of systems analysis, where best policy is traded off against the capacities of government.[26]

Admittedly, this idea requires greater breadth than today's political scientists usually display. One must master both policy analysis and political analysis, each with its own methods and assumptions, rather than just one of them. Indeed, a hands-on grasp of actual government is so important that service in government is desirable as well. So political science as a policy science may be something that only fairly senior scholars can do. On the other hand, this is a conception open to political scientists within government as well as academe. In their daily struggles to reconcile best policy with what Congress or the bureaucracy can deliver, political scientists who work in government already practice the master science. Their work should be much more visible and honored than it is.

This conception entails, as well, a *rapprochement* between political science and public administration. In their early days, the two disciplines were closely linked, and public administration was a respected field even within academic political science. In the postwar era, academic political science broke with administration, finding it insufficiently rigorous. But given the rising complexity of American government, political science demands insights from modern public administration if it is to say anything about improving policy.[27]

Broadening Recruitment

Currently, obscurantism and neglect of policy are driven by the fact that new PhDs enter political science at a point when they are harshly specialized, due to the competition for academic jobs, and know very little about actual government. Ideally, the production of new PhDs should be reduced to the number of junior academic positions available. That would allow graduate students to study more broadly, avoid early publication, and take on broader subjects in their dissertations, without fear that they would be jobless at the end of their studies. This is unlikely since universities depend on large numbers of graduate students and postdocs to teach courses and staff research projects at low cost.[28]

A more practicable solution would be to appoint junior faculty, not straight out of graduate school, but only somewhat later. New PhDs would be expected to leave academe and work in or around government for several years so that their academic training was leavened with real-world experience. They would then compete for junior academic positions on the basis of this record plus a research agenda growing out of their experience. They would later be judged for tenure based on how successful this research turned out to be. Universities already name some senior politicians and other notables to endowed professorships when they leave government. Junior appointments should be made on the same basis, although without tenure and with lesser expectations about visibility than at the senior level.

Think tanks choose their scholars in much this way. They recruit from among experts who have already shown that they can address important issues and reach a sizable audience, going beyond other specialists. Some of these scholars come from the congressional staffs or from government agencies, others from nongovernmental organizations that follow certain issues. Academic appointments should be made by similar criteria rather than in the current narrowly scholastic way. Political science would gain vastly in substance and audience. A combination of academic training plus hands-on knowledge of government allows one to frame bigger and more important research questions than is possible solely from inside academe.[29]

Conclusion

The three problems of political science, and the solutions I propose, are all closely connected. It is partly because political science became scholastic that it never addressed public policy. A discipline preoccupied with rigor cannot encompass the complexity that mastering public problems requires. Conversely, the neglect of policy confined the discipline to the study simply of politics, without policy, thus simplifying its problems and promoting its claims to rigor. A political science confined to the academy has then been confirmed by the formation of political scientists almost entirely within that world.

Political science must trade off the values of rigor to achieve greater relevance, so that it can take on larger problems that are of interest outside academe. That would permit addressing policy questions, while the world of policy also generates pressure against scholasticism. And to play these roles, political scientists must broaden themselves. They can no longer be just academicians but must draw insight, and even employment, from government itself. The effect is to merge research with some of the problem-centered advisement seen in business scholarship.[30]

In and out of government, those who work to reconcile best policy with institutional constraints can practice the master science. They seek to understand government in order to use it to improve society. That was always what political science should have set out to do.

Notes

1. These comments are confined to American political science, which I know best, but my impressions are that political science in Europe suffers from similar problems.
2. Jonathan Cohn, "Irrational Exuberance: When Did Political Science Forget About Politics?" *The New Republic*, October 25, 1999, pp. 25–31.
3. Lee Sigelman, "The Coevolution of American Political Science and the *American Political Science Review*," *American Political Science Review* 100, no. 4 (November 2006): 474.
4. The following is based on Lawrence M. Mead, "Scholasticism in Political Science," *Perspectives on Politics* 8, no. 2 (June 2010): 453–464; and idem, "The Other Danger... Scholasticism in Academic Research," *Academic Questions* 23, no. 4 (December 2010): 404–419.
5. Methodologism fell slightly, probably because I defined it restrictively. An article was "methodological" only if it made a point of advanced methods, as against merely using such methods.

6. For details on these articles, see Mead, "Scholasticism in Political Science."
7. The following is based on Lawrence M. Mead, "Scholasticism: Causes and Cures," *Academic Questions* 24, no. 3 (Fall 2011): 300–318.
8. My coding of the *APSR* did not show these methods to be strongly associated with scholastic features at a point in time, but they probably have promoted obscurantism over time, chiefly by causing scholars to focus more on the methods of inquiry than on their question.
9. Patricia Cohen, "Field Study: Just How Relevant Is Political Science?" *New York Times*, October 20, 2009, C1, C7.
10. Aristotle, *Politics*, trans. Earnest Barker (New York: Oxford University Press, 1962), pp. 111, 119–120.
11. Besides myself, some other political scientists known for involvement in actual policy include Graham Allison, John DiIulio, Paul Light, Richard Nathan, Allen Schick, and James Q. Wilson. Except for Wilson, who has died, none of us has seen much recognition by the American Political Science Association. And the rest of us are now toward the end of our careers.
12. Richard R. Nelson, *The Moon and the Ghetto* (New York: Norton, 1977).
13. Harold D. Lasswell, "The Policy Orientation," in *The Policy Sciences*, ed. Daniel Lerner and Harold D. Lasswell (Stanford, CA: Stanford University, 1951). chap. 1; idem, "The Emerging Conception of the Policy Sciences," *Policy Sciences* 1, no. 1 (Spring 1970): 3–14.
14. Dennis J. Palumbo, "Bucking the Tide: Policy Studies in Political Science, 1978–1988," in *Policy Studies Review Annual, Volume 10: Advances in Policy Studies Since 1950*, ed. William N. Dunn and Rita Mae Kelly (New Brunswick, NJ: Transaction, 1992), chap. 2; James M. Rogers, "Social Science Disciplines and Policy Research: The Case of Political Science," *Policy Studies Review* 9, no. 1 (Autumn 1989): 13–28. Public policy is one of the "sections" of the APSA mentioned above.
15. Charles E. Lindblom, *Politics and Markets: The World's Political-Economic Systems* (New York: Basic Books, 1977); Theodore J. Lowi, *The End of Liberalism: The Second Republic of the United States*, 2nd ed. (New York: Norton, 1979); Grant McConnell, *Private Power and American Democracy* (New York: Vintage, 1970); H. Mark Roelofs, *Ideology and Myth in American Politics: A Critique of a National Political Mind* (Boston, MA: Little, Brown, 1976).
16. Steven Kelman, *Making Public Policy: A Hopeful View of American Government* (New York: Basic Books, 1987); James Q. Wilson, *Political Organizations* (Princeton, NJ: Princeton University Press, 1995).
17. Lawrence M. Mead, ed., *The New Paternalism: Supervisory Approaches to Poverty* (Washington, DC: Brookings, 1997).
18. Lawrence M. Mead, "Research and Welfare Reform," *Review of Policy Research* 22, no. 3 (May 2005): 401–421.
19. Lawrence M. Mead, "On the 'How' of Social Experiments: Using Implementation Research to Get Inside the Black Box," in *Social Experiments in Practice: The What, Why, When, Where, and How of Experimental Design & Analysis*, ed. Laura R. Peck, *New Directions for Evaluation*, no. 152 (Winter 2016), pp. 73–84.
20. David E. Osborne and Ted Gaebler, *Reinventing Government: How the Entrepreneurial Spirit Is Transforming the Public Sector* (Reading, MA: Addison-Wesley, 1992); Donald F. Kettl, "The Three Faces of Reinvention," in *Setting National Priorities: The 2000 Election and Beyond*, ed. Henry J. Aaron and Robert D. Reischauer (Washington, DC: Brookings, 1999), chap. 13.
21. Lawrence M. Mead, "Policy Research: The Field Dimension," *Policy Studies Journal* 33, no. 4 (November 2005): 535–557; idem, "Only Connect: Why Government Often Ignores Research," *Policy Sciences* 48, no. 2 (June 2015): 257–272.
22. Lawrence M. Mead, *Burdens of Freedom: Cultural Roots of American Power*, forthcoming, chaps, 1, 8.
23. Francis Fukuyama, *The End of History and the Last Man* (New York: Free Press, 1992); idem, *State-Building: Governance and World Order in the 21st Century* (Ithaca, NY: Cornell University Press, 2004); idem, *The Origins of Political Order: From Prehuman Times to the French Revolution* (New York: Farrar, Straus and Giroux, 2011); idem, *Political Order and Political Decay: From the Industrial Revolution to the Globalization of Democracy* (New York: Farrar, Straus and Giroux, 2014). I have recently addressed most of these same high-level questions in *Burdens of Freedom*, currently under review by publishers. I rely heavily on Fukuyama but depart from him in giving greater stress to world cultural differences.
24. Lawrence M. Mead, "The Universities: Avatars of Modernity," *Society* 50, no. 2 (March–April 2013): 167–175.
25. I have worked out the following conception in several articles, of which the most recent is Lawrence M. Mead, "Teaching Public Policy: Linking Policy and Politics," *Journal of Public Affairs Education* 19, no. 3 (Summer 2013): 389–403.

26. For an ambitious attempt to apply this perspective to recent federal government failures, see Paul C. Light, "Vision + Action = Faithful Execution: Why Government Daydreams and How to Stop the Cascade of Breakdowns That Now Haunts It," *PS: Political Science and Politics* 49, no. 1 (January 2016): 5–20.

27. H. George Frederickson, "The Repositioning of American Public Administration," *PS: Political Science and Politics* 32, no. 4 (December 1999): 701–711.

28. Andrew Hacker and Claudia Dreifus, *Higher Education? How Colleges Are Wasting Our Money and Failing Our Kids—And What We Can Do About It* (New York: Times Books, 2010), chap. 3.

29. My own career anticipated this pattern. After graduate school, I worked in the federal government, a think tank, and the Republican National Committee for six years before moving to NYU. There I teach public policy in a political science department but also in NYU's Wagner School, its public policy graduate program. My subsequent research chiefly addressed questions about anti-poverty policy and welfare reform that I brought with me from Washington.

30. Andrew H. Van de Ven, *Engaged Scholarship: A Guide for Organizational and Social Research* (Oxford, England: Oxford University Press, 2007).

Advancing Toward Science: Retreating From Responsibility?

Max J. Skidmore

Department of Political Science, University of Missouri-Kansas City, Kansas City, MO

Political scientists currently devote considerable effort to forecasting, but when it comes to policy, they rarely deal with content as opposed to efficacy, efficiency, or cost-effectiveness. Similarly, they hardly ever consider "speaking truth to power" to be their obligation. This article suggests that policy and ethics would benefit if political scientists, like economists, would utilize their skills to do so. Caution, though, is necessary.

KEY WORDS: truth to power, retreating from responsibility, quantification, preoccupation with methodology, intellectual rigidity

走向科学：躲避责任？

政治科学家目前将相当大的精力投入在了预测方面，但就政策而言，相对于政策功效、政策效率或政策成本效益，政策内容却是科学家所基本忽视的。相似的是，他们几乎不把 "对权力讲真话" 视为他们的义务。 本文指出，如果政治科学家能像经济学家一样利用自身技能去做事的话，那么相关政策和道德规范制度就会因此受益。当然，他们也需要慎重行事。

Avanzando hacia la ciencia: ¿retirándonos de la responsabilidad?

Los expertos en ciencias políticas ponen mucho esfuerzo en la predicción, pero cuando tiene que ver con la política, muy infrecuentemente lidian con el contenido, en vez de la eficacia o efectividad de costo. Similarmente, casi nunca consideran que "decirle la verdad al poder" sea su obligación. Este artícullo sugiere que la política y la ética podrían beneficiarse si los expertos en ciencias políticas, como los economistas, utilizaran sus habilidades para ello. La cautela, sin embargo, es necesaria.

Originally presented at American Political Science Association, Caucus on Poverty, Inequality, and Public Policy, San Francisco, September 2017.

Some years ago, it not only was possible, but would have seemed almost mandatory, to ask the following:

What Role for Political Science?[1]

The role that political science tends to play in recent times must be troubling for those of its practitioners whose interests trend toward policy. The inside-the-Beltway mentality that permeates the news media frequently stresses method and process, rather than content. To a large extent, political science reflects similar tendencies.

Consider the example of Jacob Hacker, an exception among political scientists, who has been active in health policy, including advising policymakers on health care reform. After passage of the Affordable Care Act (ACA), he wrote an excellent article discussing among other things how reform happened, why the legislation took the form it did, how the intense polarization occurred, and what obstacles the bill faced.[2] Most interesting for purposes of this article, he asked whether it all had been worth it. The toll his activities took on his private life was excessive, but, although he conceded that "the healthcare bill was incomplete and imperfect in many ways," he judged it also to have been "a vital first step" and wrote that he had no "regrets about stepping into the realm of policy advocacy."[3] As for the law's restrictions, he conceded that he believed that it might have been possible to have had a stronger ACA, but considering the circumstances, not stronger by much.

Hacker in no way complained about his own situation, nor about his own treatment. On the contrary, he praised the institutions where he was based, had nothing to criticize with regard to his personal situation, and paid tribute to the many scholars and others who supported him "tirelessly." Despite this, obvious though it surely is to others in the profession, he had to stress that, with regard to policy advocacy, "this sort of work is not highly valued within political science." The reason for this, he said, "may seem self-evident—policy recommendations seem to be a breach of objectivity and a distraction from real scholarship." Undoubtedly this is the case, but, as he points out cogently, "that does not explain why academic economists routinely engage with public issues while political scientists appear more reticent. Political scientists," he stressed, "have the potential to say at least as much as economists do about how institutions and policies are structured—and might be better structured—as economists do." Moreover, in a comment that he phrased beautifully, he reminded our historically challenged discipline that "our profession once had far less reluctance about speaking the truth that it discovered to the power that it studied."

Now, it should seem necessary to press the question much further. Why is it that even the discipline most directly related to the study of politics provided no hint that the most fundamental political institutions of the world's oldest democracy, its oldest constitutional system, were vulnerable—perhaps even to an existential level? Why were practitioners of the only discipline devoted—presumably exclusively—to politics unaware that the system's safeguards built so carefully through the centuries were so fragile as to be shaken to their foundations so suddenly?

Why could political "scientists" not have foreseen, and warned, that a new president could be selected over the opposition of clear voter preference, and then could simply ignore restrictions, and proceed to use the office openly for personal gain? How could they not know that a candidate could openly urge the participation of a foreign power in the election and still be placed into office? How could they not have been aware of the potential from the enormous warping of the electorate that simple tools of gerrymandering and voter suppression would generate? How could they not have warned that the willingness of a party to disregard all precedent and constitutional provisions could be rewarded by control of the Court? Were they so committed to their narrow view of "science" and value-free study that they were compelled to ignore what some other observers—journalists, policy analysts, novelists, playwrights, poets, and the like —might have recognized as obvious? Did their devotion to "objectivity" make it impossible for them to understand that warnings were in order? Or if they did become aware of the potential for danger, were they so repressed by fear that their objectivity might be questioned that they did not have the courage to speak out for fear that the discipline's major figures might disapprove?

Political science, one must concede, is certainly not the only discipline to go astray. Southern "Vindicators" dominated American history throughout much of the twentieth century. Seeking to clean up the South's sordid record, Confederate apologists succeeded for far too long in making obvious nonsense seem convincing to the racist and the gullible. Slavery had little or nothing to do with the Civil War, they insisted, as they glorified Robert E. Lee and vilified Ulysses S. Grant. Similarly, scientists as well as most of the social sciences should do penance for their history of condemning same-sex orientation, praising eugenics, employing lobotomies, toying with insulin shock therapies, providing treatment by radiation for acne and other nonthreatening conditions, encouraging radio-graphic studies of fetuses to provide better preparation for birth, and accepting lifetime incarceration for Hansen's disease (or leprosy, a condition that turns out not to be highly communicable, and now is easily curable).

The flaws that may have afflicted other disciplines, though, in no way excuse those of political science. As the elections of 2016 demonstrate so clearly, political science offered little or nothing of help to the public, professionals or otherwise. Not only did confusion and imprecision reign below the projected veneer of confidence, but few, if any insights, came from the work of political scientists. Their work produced virtually no warnings, when there were clear dangers that should have been readily apparent.

Andrew Gelman of Columbia University—himself a professor of both statistics and political science—wrote of lessons that political scientists should have learned from the 2016 debacle.[4] First among these was that the party no longer decides, although experience with primary victories by, say, David Duke for the Republicans in Louisiana (1991), and followers of Lyndon LaRouche for the Democrats (1986), should have demonstrated that long before 2016. This hardly requires a scientific study to verify, any more than the other astute observations on Gelman's list. These include such things as the existence of survey nonresponse, the reality of polarization, the minimal effect (so far, at least) of demographics, the lack of correlation between elite and popular opinion, the clear existence of an authoritarian dimension to American politics, the difficulty of persuading relatively apathetic citizens to cast votes, the exaggerated role played by overconfident commentators, and the like.

It does not diminish Professor Gelman's work in the least to point out that most, if not all, of these are easily ascertainable simply by acquiring general political knowledge. It is telling that he has made real contributions—contributions that did not emerge from formal scientific studies, and in fact exceeded any insights from such studies. No doubt Professor Gelman's expertise in statistics enables him to be more realistic—more perceptive—than most political scientists when considering statistical approaches. Perhaps it is not too much to suggest that the profession's excessive preoccupation with method, as opposed to content, may have obscured the obvious and prevented observation of the "big picture." One suspects that this is especially true among the less sophisticated—and hence, likely more dogmatic—of political scientists.

Much post-election commentary (including comments from many Democrats), in fact, would suggest that there had been a landslide favoring the Republicans ("Democrats ignored working-class voters," etc., even though a cursory glance at the Democratic platform and at Hillary Clinton's speeches suggests that this is untrue). Actually, however, although the Republicans certainly remained extremely strong at the important state and local levels, the Democrats took a substantial majority of the popular vote. Moreover, they succeeded in gaining seats in both the House and the Senate. If this were a landslide, it was a very odd one. Whatever national "landslide" there was seemed exclusively to be an electoral college phenomenon (and the electoral vote itself— despite Mr. Trump's perception of a crushing victory—was hardly overwhelming, exceeding only 11 others out of a total of 58). There was no national landslide among the population at large.

Immediately after the election, another political scientist, Jason Blakely of Pepperdine University, had speculated that there was a fundamental misconception at the root of modern political science.[5] Whether the study of politics is truly a science is a question, he submitted, but one that goes largely unasked. He pointed out that he was not objecting to the use of polling and such techniques. These, he said, "can be an extremely useful tool for gaining snapshots of widespread beliefs and practices within society." What he did object to was using them to forecast, which he described as "the attempt to report predictions as supposedly scientific or quasi-scientific findings akin to work that happens in the natural sciences." He, and humanists in general, argue for including the study of politics in the humanities because, they say, political knowledge is far closer to history "than to physics or biology." This is because, he says, quoting the philosopher Charles Taylor, "human beings are 'self-interpreting animals.'" Thus, as creative agents, their interpretations can always change, and do not reflect the regularity of the natural sciences. Nevertheless, regardless of what he calls its spectacular errors, "the attempt to turn the study of politics into a science continues to be one of the biggest and most well-funded intellectual projects of our time," and those "who present themselves as 'scientists' are given much larger platforms than political historians, cultural experts, or legal theorists."[6]

One of those legal theorists, Jacqueline Stevens of Northwestern University (who also is a Professor of Political Science there), in a devastating *New York Times* op-ed, had previously—more than two years before the 2016 elections—pointed out the failure through the years of political scientists as forecasters.[7] She wrote that it was an "open secret" among political scientists that her disciplinary colleagues had "failed spectacularly" at making "accurate political predictions," and that these were "the field's benchmark for what counts as science." The effect of all this, she maintained reasonably, was the waste of "colossal amounts of time and money." She pointed to political scientists' "insistence, during the cold war, that the Soviet Union would persist as a nuclear threat to the United States." The historian John Lewis Gaddis, she noted, had written that this was an issue of such huge importance that "no approach to the study of international relations claiming both foresight and competence should have failed to see it coming," yet all did so. Regarding domestic politics, she said, the record was no better. In 1992, just before the Democratic victory of Clinton's election that year, and the Republican congressional victories of 1994, Morris Fiorina had reflected the conventional wisdom of the time when he wrote that we appeared to be facing a long period of Republican presidents and Democratic congresses. She noted that a political psychologist, Philip E. Tetlock, more than a decade before had questioned in depth some 284 political scientists on basic issues. His book *Expert Political Judgment: How Good Is It? How Can We Know?* won an APSA prize (the *Robert Lane Award for 2006), but concluded that "chimps randomly throwing darts at the possible outcomes would have done almost as well as the experts," most of whom had PhDs in political science. Stevens favored studies of probability and statistical significance, and urged continuation of governmental funding, but warned against continuing to assume that they provide knowledge that can lead to accurate forecasting.[8]*

When confronting the pretensions of many American political scientists, it might be well to consider a comment from Peter Taylor-Goodby, Professor of Social Policy at the University of Kent, when addressing the Academy of Social Sciences on July 5, 2012.[9] "Social science," he said, "deals with areas where the world outside needs answers but by the nature of the case it cannot provide the sort of simple, definitive, directive answers that are wanted because the knowledge it produces isn't like that." It is time to stop pretending that it does.

In terms of practical effects, consider the elections of 2000. Political scientists had been caught unaware of the imprecision of vote counts in the United States. To add to that, their work did nothing to warn against, let alone to prevent, Republican leaders from skillfully replacing a valid concern for accurate counting with a spurious one that asserted widespread existence of the virtually nonexistent "voter fraud." In 2016, nothing came from political science that could alert the political system to the vulnerability—even the fragility—of the most basic, the most fundamental, political institutions of the United States.

Jacob Hacker engaged in policy, specifically in health reform, because "of something that students of American politics too often forget or trivialize: Policy substance matters. It matters most obviously because what government does has an enormous effect on Americans. But it also matters because of the political ramifications of this obvious but oft-neglected fact. Fights over policy are fights over who gets to exercise government authority toward what ends." When political scientists "treat policy as a black box or an ideological label," they miss the "extent to which it is policy substance itself—'who gets what, when, and how,' in Harold Lasswell's famous phrasing—that is the key concern of political contestants."[10]

Hacker conceded that political scientists should not merely leave their desks and jump into the fray (unless, he said, the "calling is so loud it cannot be ignored"), but argued that they should be more "attuned to the contours of public policy and the process by which it is made." This will make political scientists more relevant, but that is not the real reason to engage, which is to make for better political scientists. Hacker warns wisely not to expect professional rewards, but to be "guided a little more by the fascination with what government does that first sparked the profession." In this way, the profession might see a broader, if not always prettier, "picture of how and for whom our democracy works."[11]

One may note that to do this, political scientists must remember the roots of their discipline—why politics is the field of study in the first place—and retreat from the effort to convert it into something narrow, completely mathematical, and largely unconnected to human beings. The arrogance of one of the former pillars of the discipline who said, "if ya' ain't doing math, you ain't doing political science," echoes down through the decades to become admonitions from self-appointed gatekeepers of today who forbid (impotently, of course) anyone who comments on the nature of policy proposals from self-identifying as a political scientist.

From ancient times, there has been much thought devoted to justice and ethics. As far back as Aristotle, the study of politics was the "Architectonic Science," and dealt with the good life. Centuries later, it came to involve speaking truth to power. Both of these require dealing with values, and in politics this means that the substance of policy—not merely its process—is relevant.

Today, however, concerning itself primarily with procedure or forecasting, American political science rarely deals with the actual substance of policy. "Speaking truth to power" apparently (so the reasoning goes) would require sacrificing the "Most Important Criterion": scientific objectivity. Therefore, as political science strives to become more scientific, it simultaneously becomes more inclined to avoid critical analysis.

This certainly is not to oppose scientific techniques in general, or quantification in particular. Both are valuable, and often are necessary, in the study of politics. Rather, it is to call for recognition that such approaches are not the only ones with relevance or worth. To limit studies to "scientific" approaches, narrowly defined, is simultaneously to deny researchers many insights, while simultaneously reducing—or in many instances even virtually eliminating—any ability to have influence. Forbidding all approaches other than those that bear the imprimatur of the academy's current power holders is troublesome for many reasons.

Additionally, restricting approaches creates many opportunities for error when scientific techniques are used inappropriately, applied without appreciation of nuance, or concentrated upon the easily quantifiable—which is likely also to be trivial. What such an approach does achieve, however, is to relieve researchers from any obligation to move political knowledge in the direction of "the good life," and also to protect researchers from the consequences of their own findings.

In general, even in political philosophy, one now would have to search far and wide to find the concrete as opposed to the abstract. Similarly, because the phrase "ethics in politics" currently would seem almost to be an oxymoron in the real world (and almost completely lacking as a concern in the literature of political science), it would appear as though the discipline could play a key role. Nevertheless, both popular media and disciplinary journals tend to avoid comments that could subject them to criticism for indulging in value judgments—or perhaps even to fear critical analysis of any sort. This avoids the danger of being seen as partisan or, in the case of scholarly journals, being judged to be "journalistic," which academic political scientists might conclude is even worse.

That damning term, "journalistic," now seems to be an all-purpose fallback to use as the basis for rejecting conclusions without going to the trouble of considering them on their merits—or their consequences. The term often appears in reviews of any study that lacks rigorous quantitative analysis, or that involves evaluation of policy content with reference to values. Sadly, it may be applied simply when the work under scrutiny is too clearly written, too accessible, too inexcusably lacking in jargon, and too active with avoidance of the passive voice.

To perform their vital functions, both political analysis and political science must have relevance to the real world. A telling example took place in 2006 when the elections involved furious arguments over the use of embryonic stem cells in research. In Missouri, State Auditor Claire McCaskill challenged sitting Senator Jim Talent, who had taken a firm position against the use of such stem cells as "destroying human life." Former Senator John Danforth, a fellow Republican, had attempted to inject some realism into the argument when he commented that no one attempting to rescue a person from a burning building if forced to choose between saving stem cells or an actual human being would fail to choose the human being. Senator Talent responded to a reporter's question that the rescuer would have to make a value judgment to determine which to choose.

State Auditor Claire McCaskill became U. S. Senator Claire McCaskill.

Note that Senator Danforth is an Episcopal clergyman, as well as a lawyer. Note, also, that political science as a discipline had nothing to contribute to the discussion.

This is not to say that the issue was spurious, or to deny that thoughtful people may arrive at many differing opinions on the subject. The point is that the very discipline that has politics as its subject did not concern itself with the controversy that was at the heart of so much discussion. Could political science have made a contribution? If so, should it have done so? Would it have been able to distinguish between matters that are completely abstract, and those that have real-world effects? The Scholastics have been the butt of jokes because of allegedly spending much time and effort debating the number of angels that might be able to dance on the head of a pin, but does modern political discourse bear some similarities? If so, could political science help to clarify matters? Does the tendency to avoid values make political science irrelevant? It would seem that in refusing to deal with the substance of policy, political science comes close to ignoring the heart of the field of study that justifies its own existence as a discipline.

It not only is appropriate, but even vital, to ask, then, whether under such circumstances political science can have a role to play in politics beyond political behavior. Can the discipline contribute to political ethics? Can it participate in the evaluation of policy content as opposed merely to that of process? More fundamentally, can it even find ways to contribute to policy? Is it possible to engage in criticism and to produce policy advances without sacrificing scientific objectivity? Beyond that, is it not possible to be reasonably objective without being formally scientific? Can the discipline help in moving toward the good life?

The purpose of this argument is to raise questions, with the aim of generating recognition that political science should indeed engage in the substance of policy. It does not attempt to determine the form of this engagement, which of course would vary according to the specialty and preference of each investigator.

There are exceptions to the reluctance to engage in policy. We will examine two: one was an effort to affect public policy for the general welfare; that is, it sought to contribute to achievement of the good life. The other is a major exception, and it comes from political philosophy rather than from political science. However major, it is only a partial exception, in that instead of speaking truth to power, it was an overt seizure of power in a manner that suppressed any truth directed its way.

First, consider again the example of Jacob Hacker. He is an exception among political scientists: one who has not let disciplinary prejudice prevent him from being active in health policy. Not only do his studies concentrate on the issue, but also he has been a key adviser on health care reform to policymakers. He made substantial contributions to the Affordable Care Act and subsequently examined just how reform took place, how it was that the legislation emerged as it did, why there was such enormous polarization, and what were the specific obstacles that the bill faced.[12]

He dealt with the effort it took and considered whether it had been worth it. There were intense pressures on his private life, but, however much "the healthcare bill was incomplete and imperfect in many ways," he was happy that he made the decision to participate. The law that emerged was, he argued, "a vital first step." He thus had no "regrets about stepping into the realm of policy advocacy."[13]

Given America's political dynamics at the time, the Affordable Care Act probably was about all that could have been accomplished. For a full century, progressives and others had sought universal health care. The effort began when former president Theodore Roosevelt, in the unlikely venue of Osawatomie, Kansas, in 1910, gave what was arguably the most progressive speech by any president in history (or in his case, former and hopeful future president). The substance of that rousing talk became the foundation of his 1912 "Bull Moose" program. Decades passed. When, in 2010, the Affordable Care Act passed after a century of failed efforts, many impediments were to have been expected, and should surprise no one that they shaped and weakened the legislation.

It should be clear that Hacker was grateful for the way the universities where he had been based had treated him, and had nothing but praise for the support he had received. Many scholars had supported him "tirelessly," he said, and he gave them hearty tribute. His own personal situation had been all that he could have hoped. Nevertheless, he had to make it plain—as though it were not already apparent to those in the discipline—that "this sort of work is not highly valued within political science."

Certainly, he said, the reason for this "may seem self-evident—policy recommendations seem to be a breach of objectivity and a distraction from real scholarship." There is no doubt that this is true, but "that does not explain why academic economists routinely engage with public issues while political scientists appear more reticent. Political scientists," he stressed, "have the potential to say at least as much as economists do about how institutions and policies are structured—and might be better structured—as economists do." He reminded political scientists that "our profession once had far less reluctance about speaking the truth that it discovered to the power that it studied."

Hacker's example demonstrates what could be. He deserves our praise for what he has accomplished, and also for making it plain that political science has great unrealized potential. Certainly, he can serve as a model for those seeking a more engaged political science.

The second example, as indicated, comes from political philosophy. Rather than demonstrating the capacity for public good, however, it should be taken as a warning that the potential of a more engaged political science is not all on the beneficial side of the ledger; there is potential for harm as well.

Emerging from that example was one of the greatest foreign policy disasters in American history, the war in Iraq. It no doubt had become inevitable because the Republican officeholders, with assistance from many Democrats, threw caution aside and insisted on pursuing it against all evidence that should have counseled caution. Political science provided no guidance whatsoever; political philosophy (or what purported to be political philosophy) encouraged the reckless adventure. An early candidate for the party's 2016 nomination was Jeb Bush, the brother of the president, George W. Bush, who had taken the country into that war. The former president's brother had trouble answering whether he would have taken us into that war, and essentially his response was that he would have, *even if he knew then what he now knows.*

The story of the road into that war is uniquely one built upon what bears many of the marks of a cabal, one from deep within perhaps the most obscure segment of political philosophy in America. The story is not complete without examining how that group emerged from the ivory tower to capture the foreign policy of a presidential administration. The late Leo Strauss, perhaps more so even than most superb teachers, had many students, most of them admiring students. Those behind what almost could be branded a coup were more than Strauss's students, or students of his students; they were, as Anne Norton puts it, disciples.[14] We can use the name they apply to themselves, "Straussians." Norton says she is sorry for the name "Straussian" because "it implicates Strauss in views that were not always his own, but it is best to call people what they call themselves. Straussian is the name these disciples have taken. The Straussians have made a conscious and deliberate effort to shape politics and learning in the United States and abroad."[15] Their detractors argue that they bear the marks of a cult: insistence on across-the-board agreement, willingness to shun those whom they consider apostates, the practice of taking over academic departments by gaining positions of authority and then employing only other Straussians, and so forth.

Those who self identify as Straussians have formed their own society, taking over academic departments, securing key governmental positions, and going far beyond what their master taught. The teaching skill of Straussians is legendary. I can vouch for this, because during my doctoral work, I had five courses from a professor who had studied with Strauss himself at the University of Chicago. The technique that they employ is close textual analysis, concentrating upon classic writings and ignoring secondary interpretations of those writings. They read slowly and deliberately, going over their selected material line by line. Norton says that Strauss taught American students a new way to read a text that was a very old way.[16] It is "a way of reading that has fallen out of favor in the universities," but "in the *shul*, the *madrassa*, in seminaries and in Bible study groups, sacred texts are still studied in this way."[17] This can lead to fascinating teaching, and to deep insights. It also, however, denies students the insights that may come from other scholars, and risks leaving them to make the same mistakes that previous scholars have made without any correction that could be available from subsequent wealth of scholarship.

The more questionable aspects of Strauss's teaching come from his notion of hidden messages. Strauss taught that the masters of political philosophy wrote overtly for the masses, but covertly in the same texts for those capable of understanding and dealing with the disguised truths. Those truly capable readers, of course, were the Straussians. Strauss taught the search for truth, but also accepted the necessity of the "noble lie."

"Straussians" tend to have much in common besides having studied with Strauss or having studied with those who did. They reflect a preoccupation with national strength, and advocate aggressive foreign policies. They also appear to be especially concerned—here I carefully avoid the pejorative "obsessed"—with a version of masculinity that Harvey Mansfield, Jr., describes in his book of that name as "manliness."[18] This is somewhat odd, because many Straussians, while strongly urging military action on the part of others, avoid military service or anything exposing them to personal risk.

Take Mansfield, himself, for example. He is a widely respected political philosopher, but his life seems hardly to be one that would lead him to extol "manliness." To be sure, his definition, maintaining "confidence in risky situations," is a worthy quality, but is one that surely is reasonably distributed between the sexes. Mansfield has no experience in the military, and in fact has spent virtually his entire life at Harvard. Not only does he teach there, but he lived there growing up when his father before him was on the Harvard faculty. This was no doubt somewhat responsible for the tone of Walter Kirn's review of *Manliness* in the *New York Times*. Kirn seems to have difficulty deciding whether to be amused or astonished by Mansfield's "fussy" treatment of a subject that would seem not to come naturally to him.[19] Similarly, Mansfield did himself no favors with his answers to "Questions for Harvey C. Mansfield: Of Manliness and Men," by Deborah Solomon, in the *New York Times Magazine*.[20]

Presumably he was attempting to be humorous, but it isn't clear. Asked if his "left-leaning colleagues" were willing to talk with him, he said that people listened to him, but didn't pay attention. "I should punch them out, but I don't." Dick Cheney, he said, was manly because "he hunts. And he curses openly." Asked when was the last time he did something that required physical strength, he replied: "It's true that nothing in my career requires physical strength, but in my relations with women, yes."

"Such as?" Solomon asked.

"Lifting things, opening things," he said. "My wife is quite small."

There you have it. Perhaps mentioning Theodore Roosevelt here could be seen as a digression, but it is one that is directly relevant to this discussion of Straussians. TR was assistant secretary of the Navy, which put him in the number two position of what was then a cabinet department. He resigned that post in order to fight physically—to accept a combat position in the Spanish-American War, a war that he had encouraged—so that he put himself in the place of danger along with others who were there in a conflict that he had urged upon the nation. As William Harbaugh remarked, TR "had read the bulk of his own country's literature and knew personally perhaps a majority of the nation's best writers."

This not only was a "rare quality in any man of action," but was a "unique quality in a President." No one else, regardless of the pretentions of the Straussians, has practiced what Harbaugh so aptly calls "virile intellectualism."[21] That made it possible, as biographer John Milton Cooper remarked, for TR to "pursue during his presidency what historian Jacob Burkhardt had called 'the state as a work of art.'"[22] These accomplishments could have been worthy of praise from Strauss himself; certainly, though, no Straussian has duplicated or come close to them, except perhaps in their own imaginations. Paul Wolfowitz, for example, long before the Bush-Cheney administration took office, had urged that the United States attack Iraq. In the Bush-Cheney administration, as deputy secretary of defense, Wolfowitz was in a position to a large extent paralleling that which TR had held. Can any sober observer seriously believe that Wolfowitz ever for a second entertained the thought that he, personally, should be in physical danger in the war for which he had been so enthusiastic?

However snide it may sound, perhaps Norton was not exaggerating when she wrote of her experience with Straussians in graduate classes, that "tiny little men with rounded shoulders would lean back in their chairs and declare that Nature had made men superior to women. Larger, softer men, with soft white hands that never held a gun or changed a tire, delivered disquisitions on manliness. They were stronger, they were smarter, and Aristotle had said so. This may not have been entirely successful in warding off the evil eye of sexual rejection, but it seemed to furnish some consolation."[23]

Norton lists a huge number of Straussians who have held positions in think tanks, lobbying firms, and political actions as well as Republican administrations from Ford and Reagan through—especially—that of George W. Bush. "This is no scattered and disorderly influence," Norton writes. "There is [this was in 2004] a powerful and long-standing Straussian presence at several sites. The first is military. Straussians shape policy at the Department of Defense." Paul Wolfowitz was deputy secretary, and there were many others there, such as Richard Perle, who were influential, and they were heavily represented in intelligence as well. I. Lewis "Scooter" Libby, Vice President Cheney's key aide, was a Straussian. Another, William Kristol, former aide to Vice President Dan Quayle, was one of the founders of the Project for a New American Century.

In George W. Bush's first term, journalists began sounding warnings about the Straussians, the neoconservatives. Writing in the *New York Times*, James Atlas identified an American school of thought that saw the Iraq invasion as "nothing less than a defense of Western civilization—as interpreted by the late classicist and political philosopher, Leo Strauss" (Atlas spoke of the "neo-cons" as "Leo-Cons"). He noted that President Bush paid tribute at the conservative think tank the American Enterprise Institute to the "cohort of journalists, political philoso-phers, and policy wonks known—primarily to themselves—as Straussians. 'You are some of the best brains in our country,' Mr. Bush declared." Bush went on to say, "my government employs about 20 of you."

Atlas noted that many would argue that "employs" is too weak, and that Bush's foreign policy seemed to them to be "entirely a Straussian creation." He cited Wolfowitz and Bill Kristol, "founding editor of *The Weekly Standard*, a must-read in the White House." He asked how the obscure Strauss came to be the motivating fact of the neoconservatives, and said that it stemmed from the publication of Allan Bloom's *The Closing of the American Mind* in 1967. Bloom was a student of Strauss's, and although his polemic was not a call to action, it was "a celebration of the classics as a civilizing force," and the agenda "became "politicized when it was appropriated—some might say hijacked—by a cohort of ambitious men for whom the university was too confining an arena." Although Strauss might not have favored the policies of his disciples, he served as the symbol that motivated our rush to war.[24]

Almost at the same time as Atlas's article in the *New York Times* came another, this time in *The New Yorker*.[25] Seymour Hersh wrote that "they call themselves self-mockingly, the Cabal—a small cluster of policy advisers and analysts now based in the Pentagon's Office of Special Plans." Deputy Defense Secretary Paul Wolfowitz had conceived the operation that within the previous year had "brought about a crucial change of direction in the American intelligence community." Beginning their work after 9/11, they "helped shape public opinion and American policy toward Iraq," relying heavily on information from other agencies, "and also on information provided by the Iraqi National Congress, or I.N.C., the exile group headed by Ahmad Chalabi." Rapidly, the group came to rival "both the C.I.A. and the Pentagon's own Defense Intelligence Agency, the D.I.A., as President Bush's main source of intelligence regarding Iraq's possible possession of weapons of mass destruction and connection with Al Qaeda."

As of that writing, no such weapons had been found, and much of the intelligence was already in question. Now, more than a decade later, it is clear that there was nothing to be found, and that the information was more than questionable; it was totally false.

The head of the Office of Special Plans was a Straussian, Abram Shulsky, who had been a staff member on the Senate Intelligence Committee in the early 1980s, and had worked with Richard Perle when Perle was assistant secretary of defense in the Reagan administration. Pentagon sources told Hersh that Defense Secretary Donald "Rumsfeld and his colleagues believed that the C.I.A. was unable to perceive the reality of the situation in Iraq," and that Special Plans therefore was to examine CIA information and "reveal what the intelligence community can't see. Shulsky's carrying the heaviest part."

This it did, providing support for "what Wolfowitz and his boss, Defense Secretary Donald Rumsfeld believed to be true—that Saddam Hussein had close ties to Al Qaeda, and that Iraq had an enormous arsenal of chemical, biological, and possibly even nuclear weapons that threatened the region, and, potentially, the United States." Unfortunately, "there was a close personal bond, too, between Chalabi and Wolfowitz and Perle dating back many years. Their relationship deepened after the Bush administration took office, and Chalabi's ties extended to others in the administration, including Rumsfeld; Douglas Feith, the Under-Secretary of Defense for Policy; and I. Lewis Libby, Vice-President Dick Cheney's chief of staff." There were other ties, also. Chalabi and his group through the years had received millions of dollars from the CIA, but those funds halted around 1996 when the CIA came to doubt Chalabi's integrity, and those in the agency recognized that his group was a "political unit—not an intelligence agency," and manipulated information for its own purposes.

Norton writes that the "necessarily intimate links between defense and intelligence enhance the influence of the Straussians, for Straussians have a prominent place in the intelligence community." Shulsky, she says, is "the most prominent of these," but notes there are many others as well. "Gary Schmitt has occupied several positions in the intelligence community. Carnes Lord now teaches at the Naval War College. Straussians have also advised congressional committees on intelligence. Each of these sources of influence reinforces and extends the others," and, in fact, Straussians have written many of the speeches of Republican secretaries of defense, vice presidents, and even presidents.[26]

Hersh remarks that it may not be "immediately obvious" just how Strauss's views might pertain to intelligence gathering, but that "Shulsky himself explored that question in a 1999 essay, written with Gary Schmitt, entitled 'Leo Strauss and the World of Intelligence (By Which We Do Not Mean *Nous*)'—in Greek philosophy the term *nous* denotes the highest form of rationality." Shulsky and Schmitt argued that Strauss's notion of hidden meanings suggests the deception that is at the heart of political life.

Regardless of whether Strauss and his ideas may or may not be directly related to the preoccupations of the Straussians, those outside the group should be able to view them with fewer presuppositions, and thus be more objective in their conclusions. A number of former intelligence operatives, according to Hersh, "believe that Shulsky and his superiors were captives of their own convictions, and were merely deceiving themselves." They really have no friends other than those within their own group, and they constantly reinforce one another. This is certainly plausible. As Hersh notes, "this has been going on since the nineteen-eighties, but they've never been able to coalesce as they have now. September 11th gave them the opportunity, and now they're in heaven. They believe the intelligence is there. They want to believe it. It *has* to be there."

But it wasn't. Strauss would likely have known better. Norton goes to the heart of the issue. "The idealization of the state of Israel was the work of Straussians, not of Strauss. The alliance with Christian fundamentalists in a latter-day crusade against Islam was the work of Straussians, not of Strauss."[27] Before Strauss, Norton writes, the dominant account in the United States of political philosophy was that of George Sabine (although Mulford Sibley's *Political Ideas and Ideologies* is the better treatment). It was entirely European in its orientation. "In Strauss and Cropsey, things are otherwise," she says. "There are chapters on Plato, Aristotle, and Kant, and there are chapters on al Farabi and Maimonides. The chapter on Marsilius of Padua, written by Strauss himself, notes the importance of ibn Rushd to an understanding of Christian and European thought." In fact, Norton says, "Strauss revived the study of Islamic philosophy in the West."[28] Kristol and others can present "the meeting of Islam and West" as "defenders of civilization against civilization's opponents," or as George W. Bush cast it, "as a crusade. Nothing in Strauss's writing endorses a Judeo-Christian crusade against Islam. Strauss saw Jewish and Muslim philosophy as closely linked."[29]

In 2015, when Republicans vying for their party's presidential nomination of 2016 were having to deal with the incentives for going to war in Iraq, many argued, incorrectly, that everyone agreed at the time that Saddam Hussein had "weapons of mass destruction," and that he had ties to al Qaeda. The attacks on 9/11 meant that Iraq posed a massive threat to the United States, and that it was reasonable to assume that the United States had to remove Hussein from power.

Few people now remember that PNAC, the Project for a New American Century, was urging invasion of Iraq long before 9/11, and, in fact, before the administration of George W. Bush came to power, or was even elected. The PNAC was a Washington, DC, think tank that Bill Kristol and Robert Kagan formed in 1997. By all accounts, it was a neoconservative (read "Straussian") organization—which, considering who the founders were, was to have been expected. It lasted until 2006, when it was officially dissolved, soon to be superseded by a "Foreign Policy Initiative." Kristol was the chair, and the directors included Kagan and John Bolton, who was to become George W. Bush's irascible ambassador to the UN by recess appointment.

Other directors were Devon Gaffney Cross and Bruce P. Jackson, while Gary Schmitt was "executive director of the Project." In September 2000, during the last year of the Clinton administration, PNAC issued a report of some 90 pages, calling for increased military expenditures. Although it noted that the United States was the sole remaining superpower, and no longer faced a powerful antagonist, it urged expanding the military in order to maintain world domination. The tone was alarmist, and suggested that threats flourished. The core missions that it called for were to defend the homeland; "fight and decisively win multiple, simultaneous major theater wars"; perform "constabulary" duties for the world; and "transform U.S. forces to exploit the revolution in military affairs." The latter had to do with "rebuilding" forces that were "ill-prepared," adapting new equipment, and translating "U.S. military supremacy into American geopolitical preeminence." It called for increasing military budgets by more than a third.[30] The list of project participants numbered 27, including the three Kagans (Donald, the father, of Yale, and his sons Fred, of the U.S. Military Academy at West Point, and Robert, of the Carnegie Endowment for International Peace). Others included Abram Shulsky, then of the RAND Corporation, Paul Wolfowitz, then at SAIS, Johns Hopkins, and I. Lewis "Scooter" Libby, later to become Vice President Cheney's powerful chief of staff.

On January 26, 1998, the PNAC sent what can only be described as an arrogant letter to President Clinton. It charged that his administration's Iraq policy was dangerously inadequate, and called openly for war.

"The only acceptable strategy," it said, was "one that eliminates the possibility that Iraq will be able to use or threaten to use weapons of mass destruction. In the near term, this means a willingness to undertake military action as diplomacy is clearly failing. In the long term, it means removing Saddam Hussein and his regime from power. That now needs to become the aim of American foreign policy."[31]

Those who signed the letter numbered 18, most were Republicans, and all were those who had held, or were to hold, key positions in the military and intelligence establishments of Republican administrations. Straussians were prominent among them, as were those who later were to use 9/11 as an excuse for the administration of George W. Bush to invade Iraq. Francis Fukuyama, Robert Kagan, William Kristol, Richard Perle, Donald Rumsfeld, and Paul Wolfowitz were to become especially famous, or infamous.

The following month, PNAC sent yet another letter to President Clinton.[32] This one reiterated the weaknesses, as the signatories saw them, of the policies toward Iraq and repeated the demands of the first letter. It expanded those demands to say that the "vital national interests of our country require the United States," among other things, "to: Recognize a provisional government of Iraq based on the principles and leaders of the Iraqi National Congress (INC)" and followed with the laughable description of INC—Chalabi's political interest group—as "representative of all the peoples of Iraq." The letter ended with a flourish to the effect that the policies it recommended would "save ourselves and the world."

The latter missive had even more signers, 40 in all, still nearly all Republicans, and still many Straussians. They included former and future cabinet members, significant names from publishing, members of Congress, the defense establishment, and the intelligence and diplomatic communities—again, from former or future Republican administrations. Among them were Eliot Abrams, Richard V. Allen, John Bolton, Frank Carlucci, William Clark, Doug Feith, Frank Gaffney, Fred C. Ikle, Robert Kagan, William Kristol, Robert McFarlane, Donald Rumsfeld, Gary Schmitt, Caspar Weinberger, and Paul Wolfowitz. Nearly all of those who signed the first letter signed the second one also. It is ironic—considering the high opinion that Straussians tend to have with regard to their own intellects—that this letter's gushing confidence in Chalabi's INC reflects not brilliance, but naiveté.

Based upon these clear statements from the PNAC, there is no doubt that the will to invade Iraq was there long before 9/11. Years earlier, the same powerful voices that participated in the decision to invade Iraq after 9/11 were urging a different—and apparently more prudent and less ideological—administration to invade Iraq. They were urging this without the excuse of the traumatic events that took place early in the second Bush's first term.

For purposes of the argument here, it is sufficient to have examined the PNAC and its role in attempting to stimulate action against Iraq long before the administration of the second Bush. It should not be assumed, though, that this was the beginning of Straussian efforts to push the United States into a war against an Arab state that posed no threat to America. It takes little digging to trace such efforts back long before PNAC was even formed. Any thoughtful and thorough study of the first Gulf War will discern the pernicious efforts of Straussians in positions of authority. Similar analyses of the Reagan administration will reveal the influence of Straussians to shape, and add belligerence to, American foreign policy more than a quarter century before 9/11.

Virtually all authorities now recognize what should have been clear at the time, that Iraq was in no way involved in 9/11. Moreover, it seems odd for the United States of America, the most powerful nation-state in world history, to react with near hysterical fear of a small, poorly developed, country in the Middle East with very limited resources. Regardless, political scientists should have been able to supply crucial information that would have corrected the Bush administration's misstatements that were duly repeated in the *Washington Post* and the *New York Times*.

Surely, the discipline should encourage its Jacob Hackers, and begin again to contribute to sound policy formation across the board, as Hacker did in the realm of health care. What he did was to contribute ideas and sound principles—to improve policy.

The discipline also should have been in a position to counter the ideological influence of the Straussians. What they were doing was not to contribute ideas for the purpose of improving policy. The study of political philosophy had led a cultish group to inflict great damage. The Straussians were not speaking truth to power. They were demonstrating their own hunger for power. Political science did nothing to halt them, nothing to alert the public, nor anything even to alert others within the discipline.

In 2016, the dynamic was, if anything, potentially even more destructive, and political science was equally impotent. The Republican candidate came from outside; he appealed to, and represented, the worst features of American culture: xenophobia, racism, scorn for all opponents, bullying of women and the disabled, and on and on. The news media gave him constant coverage, but as an entertainer, not as a serious political figure. No warning came from the academy.

There was no attention to the effect of a quarter century of demonization of Hillary Clinton that led many voters to think a vote for Trump would be preferable because they associated *her* with scandal. There was no response from political science when the press reported that "political scientists" viewed Senator Sanders as representing views too far out of the mainstream to be acceptable. "Political scientists," though, according to some scholars who should have known better, were admonished not to respond. A response indicating that there was disagreement among political scientists would have been unacceptable; it would be "partisan," or "biased."

Those familiar with American political history should easily have recognized that Senator Sanders was more mainstream in his views than popular discussion indicated. He expressed views consistent with those of the New Deal, Fair Deal, and Great Society—his views in fact were less "radical" than those of the "Bull Moose" platform of Theodore Roosevelt in 1912 or Richard Nixon's call for a guaranteed annual income. Yet to some offended political scientists, a simple evaluation of the Sanders program was not possible; it was not "scientific."

Perhaps the most revealing response to the observation about the characteristics of the Sanders proposals was an attempt at humor. It sarcastically mentioned the "scientific breakthrough" that the observation represented, and said, "it's huge that we are finally able to classify policy proposals in a common left-right policy space all the way back to the early 20th century. How many bills have you coded from Theodore Roosevelt to the present?" it asked. "Would you share the methodology of how you figured this out? When will the data be available?"

The "methodology of how this was figured out" was simple. An intelligent reading of platforms made the conclusion obvious, although to be sure it required a familiarity with American political history as well as with the Sanders proposals. The one making the comment was too single-minded, or perhaps too simple-minded, to recognize that many things can be readily clear, that face-validity exists.

Then, because of the dynamics of American politics that political scientists overlooked, the electoral college brought us President Donald J. Trump. To borrow words from Trump himself, "who could have known?"

Notes

1. From Max J. Skidmore, "'Bi-Partisanship' as a Detriment to Anti-Poverty Efforts: Some Contrarian Comments," *Poverty and Public Policy*, 5:4 (2013), 281–291.
2. Jacob Hacker, "The Road to Somewhere: Why Health Reform Happened," *Perspectives on Politics*, 8:3 (2010), 861–876.
3. Ibid., p., 872.
4. Andrew Gelman, "19 Lessons for Political Scientists from the 2016 Election," *Slate* (December 8, 2016); http://www.slate.com/articles/news_and_politics/politics/2016/12/_19_lessons_for_political_scientists_from_the_2016_election.html
5. Jason Blakely, "Is Political Science This Year's Election Casualty?" *The Atlantic* (November 14, 2016).
6. Ibid.
7. Jacqueline Stevens, "Political Scientists Are Lousy Forecasters," *New York Times Sunday Review* (June 24, 2014), SR6.
8. Ibid.
9. Peter Taylor-Goodby, "The State of Social Science: Only Itself to Blame?" *Academy of Social Sciences* (July 11, 2012); http://www.socialsciencespace.com/2012/07/the-state-of-social-science-only-itself-to-blame/.
10. Hacker, quoted in Skidmore, "'Bi-Partisanship," p. 872.
11. Ibid.
12. Hacker, "The Road to Somewhere."
13. Ibid., p. 872.
14. Anne Norton, *Leo Strauss and the Politics of American Empire*, New Haven, CT: Yale University Press, 2004, p. 6.
15. Ibid., p. 7.
16. Ibid., p. 2.
17. Ibid., p. 6.
18. Harvey Mansfield, Jr., *Manliness*, New Haven, CT: Yale University Press, 2006.
19. Walter Kirn, "Who's the Man? Review, '*Manliness*,' by Harvey C. Mansfield, *New York Times Books* (March 19, 2006); http://www.nytimes.com/2006/03/19/books/reviews/19kirn.html.
20. "Questions for Harvey C. Mansfield: Of Manliness and Men," interview by Deborah Solomon, *New York Times Magazine* (March 12, 2006); http://www.nytimes.com/2006/03/12/magazine/312wwln_q4.html

21. William H. Harbaugh, *The Life and Times of Theodore Roosevelt*, rev. ed., New York: Oxford University Press, 1975, p. 434; quoted in Max J. Skidmore, *Presidential Performance*, Jefferson, NC: McFarland, 2004, p. 183.
22. Skidmore, ibid., pp. 9, 195; for Cooper's original comment, see John Milton Cooper, *The Warrior and the Priest*, Cambridge, MA: Belknap Press of Harvard University Press, 1983, pp. 87–88.
23. Norton, *Leo Strauss*, p. 63.
24. See James Atlas, "The Nation: Leo-Cons; A Classicists Legacy: New Empire Builders," *The New York Times*, "Week in Review" (May 4, 2003); https://www.nytimes.com/2003/05/04/weekinreview/the-nation-leo-cons-a-classicist-s-legacy-new-empire-builders.html.
25. Seymour M. Hersh, "Selective Intelligence: Donald Rumsfeld Has His Own Special Sources. Are They Reliable?" *The New Yorker*, "Annals of National Security" (May 12, 2003); https://www.newyorker.com/magazine/2003/05/12/selective-intelligence.
26. Norton, *Leo Strauss*, p. 18.
27. Ibid., p. 216.
28. Ibid., pp. 224–225.
29. Ibid., p. 226.
30. Donald Kagan and Gary Schmitt (Project Co-Chairmen); Thomas Donnelly (Principal Author), *Rebuilding America's Defenses: Strategy, Forces, and Resources for a New Century*," a report of Program for a New American Century, September 2000; see esp. pp. 26ff.
31. Available at http://www.informationclearinghouse.info/article5527.htm.
32. Available at http://www.iraqwatch.org/perspectives/rumsfeld-openletter.htm.

Section Two:
Considering the People

Privatizing or Annihilating Social Security: What the United States Can Learn From Chile's Privatization

Silvia Borzutzky

Carnegie Mellon University, Heinz College of Public Policy and Management, Pittsburgh, Pennsylvania

This article argues that based on Chile's 38-year experience with a privately administered, fully funded, defined contribution system, the adoption of this kind of approach in the United States will be very damaging. We argue that this policy will be especially harmful to low-income groups, to women, to both racial and gender minorities, and to those who have part-time employment or find themselves in and out of the labor market. Additionally, this kind of policy does not solve the financial problems of the Social Security system. In fact, transferring either the entire, or a part of the payroll tax to private accounts will add a new burden to the fiscal coffers via transition costs, as fiscal receipts will diminish and the obligation to pay pensions to old and new retirees will continue. From the standpoint of the insured and potential retiree, the cost of administering the retirement accounts will increase, but there is no certainty that the benefits will increase due to the unpredictable nature of the market and the increase in administrative costs. Most importantly, for lower-income groups, the redistributive effect that Social Security has today will be eliminated.

KEY WORDS: Social Security, pension, privatization, United States, Chile

本文提出，借鉴智利在过去38年来奉行私人管理、完全资助的养老金计划经验，美国采用这种做法将是非常有害的。笔者认为，智利的政策将特别损害低收入群体、妇女、种族和性少数群体、从事兼职的群体，以及那些不稳定就业群体的利益。此外，这种政策并没有解决社会保障制度的财政问题。实际上，将工资税的全部或部分转移到私人帐户会产生转移成本给财政库房带来新的负担，因为财政收入会逐渐削减，政府依然有义务向新老退休人员支付养老金。从投保人和潜在退休人员的角度来看，管理退休帐户的费用将增加，但由于市场的不可预测性和行政成本的增加，无法确定这些福利是否会增加。最重要的是，对于低收入群体来说，当今社会保障的再分配效应将被废除。

关键词： 退休金计划, 美国社会保障制度, 私有化, 确认债券

Este documento sostiene que, según la experiencia de 38 años de Chile con un sistema de contribución definida, totalmente financiado y administrado por el sector privado, la adopción de este tipo de enfoque en los EE. UU. será muy perjudicial. Argumentamos que su política será especialmente dañina para los grupos de bajos ingresos, para las mujeres, para las minorías raciales y de género y para aquellos que tienen empleo a tiempo parcial o se encuentran dentro y fuera del mercado laboral. Además, este tipo de política no resuelve los problemas financieros del sistema de seguridad social. De hecho, transferir la totalidad o una parte del impuesto sobre la nómina a una cuenta privada agregará una nueva carga a las arcas fiscales a través de los costos de transición, ya que los ingresos fiscales disminuirán y la obligación de pagar las pensiones a los jubilados antiguos y nuevos continuará. Desde el punto de vista del asegurado y el posible jubilado, el costo de administrar las cuentas de retiro aumentará, pero no hay certeza de que los beneficios aumentarán debido a la naturaleza impredecible del mercado y al aumento de los costos administrativos. Más importante aún, para los grupos de menores ingresos, se eliminará el efecto redistributivo que tiene hoy la seguridad social.

PALABRAS CLAVES: Chile, sistema de contribución definida, sistema de seguridad social de Estados Unidos, privatización, bonos de reconocimiento

Introduction

Since the 1990s, a group of policy experts and politicians in the Republican Party has proposed either a partial or a total privatization of Social Security. The proponents of this approach have argued that due to the changing dependency ratio, the future financial stability of Social Security is at risk and what needs to be done is to transfer either the entire payroll tax, or a part of it, to privately administered savings accounts. These proposals, which were abundant during the Bush administration, died down during the Obama years, but it is reasonable to assume that given the Trump administration's political and social environment, these proposals will reappear, especially if the Republican Party remains in control of Congress after the November 2018 election. Thus, while the Trump administration has not touched Social Security or Medicare during the first 16 months, it has not sought to find any solutions to the financial issues facing the retirement system either. Additionally, given the expected large budget deficit created by the new tax law, there is a real concern that after the November 2018 elections, there are going to be proposals geared to reduce the fiscal contribution to these programs in order to ease the deficit and the push for either total or partial privatization will re-emerge.

This article strongly argues that based on Chile's 38-year experience with a privately administered, fully funded, defined contribution system, the adoption of this kind of approach in the United States will be very damaging. We argue that this policy will be especially harmful to low-income groups, to women, to both racial and gender minorities, and to those who have part-time employment or find themselves in and out of the labor market. Additionally, this kind of policy does not solve the financial problems of the Social Security system. In fact, transferring either the entire, or a part of the payroll tax to private accounts will add a new burden to the fiscal coffers via transition costs, as fiscal receipts will diminish and the obligation to pay pensions to old and new retirees will continue. From the standpoint of the insured and potential retiree, the cost of administering the retirement accounts will certainly increase, but there is no certainty that the benefits will increase due to the unpredictable nature of the market and the increase in administrative costs. Most importantly, for lower-income groups, the redistributive effect that Social Security has today will be eliminated. Thus, the accounts' rate of return will be subject to the vagaries of the market, and the only winners will be the financial institutions involved in the administration of the private accounts.

The first section of the article reviews proposals to privatize Social Security in the United States and the promises made by their proponents; the second section provides a thorough analysis of Chile's fully funded, defined contribution system; and the last section provides an overview of the current problems of the U.S. Social Security system and proposed solutions. The article concludes by strongly opposing either a partial or a total privatization of Social Security because of their detrimental effects on those who need social security the most.

The United States: Proposals to Privatize

Early proposals to privatize Social Security were made by the CATO Institute in mid-1995, following the "success" of the Chilean model. According to CATO's plan for Social Security privatization, supported at that time by various Republican politicians, workers should be free to choose between the private option and Social Security. The framers of the plan added that for those who choose the private plan, workers and employers would each pay 5 percent of wages, instead of the current Social Security payroll tax of 6.2 percent paid by each of them. According to the plan, the monies would be deposited into private investment accounts, resulting in an eventual payroll tax cut of 20 percent. Besides supporting retirement benefits, the accounts would finance privately administered life and disability insurance, thus replacing Social Security survivors and disability benefits. "Workers who opt out of the current Social Security system would receive recognition bonds from the federal government that would pay them a proportion of future Social Security benefits equal to the proportion of lifetime taxes they had already paid" (Ferrara, 1997).

Many experts immediately objected to privatizing Social Security because of the potential cost of the transition to a privatized system. However, its proponents argued—much like in Chile in 1980—that the transition could be financed without imposing new taxes and without cutting benefits to recipients. Indeed, the CATO Institute's analysts argued that the transition deficit would be eliminated in 14 years, and that after 14 years, the reform would actually start producing a surplus for the federal government. According to Ferrara (1997),

> Apart from the tax cut, the net transition deficit would be eliminated in only 14 years. Before that point, the transition deficits can be financed in part by issuing new government bonds, or selling existing Social Security trust fund bonds, totaling no more than $500 billion (in 1996 dollars). However, privatization would produce sufficient net surpluses by the 22nd year after it begins to completely pay off and retire all the bonds previously sold to finance the transition. The remaining net transition

deficits in the early years can be offset by reductions in government spending totaling approximately $60 billion per year, or approximately 4 percent of total federal spending. Perhaps most remarkably, once the bonds issued to finance the transition are paid off, privatization would actually start producing large surpluses that would reduce the federal budget deficit. Consequently, rather than producing concern over the short-term budgetary impact of the transition, Social Security privatization should be seen as the only means of eliminating the currently projected, enormous, long-term federal deficits, and indeed ultimately producing large additional surpluses that can be used to cut taxes or to reduce the national debt.

The CATO analysis reads very much like the promises made in Chile by Minister Piñera, who is a prominent member of this organization. Thus, according to Ferrara (1997), privatization would not only secure the solvency of the system, but also contribute to reducing the fiscal deficit. Additionally, privatization would provide Americans with the freedom to choose, would benefit the poor and the young workers, and would reduce the payroll tax. Ferrara adds that privatization would bring about equity and a comfortable life to all retirees because essentially the market will make everyone rich. As noted by Ferrara (1997), the same distinguished economists who advised the Chilean government in the early 1980s supported this proposal. Among them were Harvard Professor Martin Feldstein and Nobel Prize–winning economists Gary Becker, James Buchanan, and Milton Friedman, as well as University of Chicago Distinguished Professor Arnold Harberger, who played a critical role in Chile's privatization.

In conclusion, the CATO document proposed to remove Social Security from the budget and to establish a private option that would "allow workers the freedom to choose to provide for their retirement, survivors, and disability benefits through a private investment account, like an IRA or 401(k) plan, rather than through Social Security. For those who choose this option, the worker and employer would each pay 5 percentage points of the current 6.2 percent Social Security tax on each into the private account up to the maximum taxable limit calculated, as is the case today" (Ferrara, 1997).

Concerns with the feasibility of the CATO plan prompted others to explore alternative options. For instance, the Investment Company Institute (ICI) that represents mutual funds, exchange-traded funds, closed-end funds, and unit investment trusts, as well as the Securities Industry endorsed more moderate ideas and legislation that is more moderate. For instance, the bill introduced in the Senate by Democrat Robert Kerrey of Nebraska and Republican Alan Simpson of Wyoming proposed to channel not the entire payroll tax, but only 2 percent of the tax into private investment accounts. Testifying in support of the Kerrey-Simpson plan, ICI's Matthew Fink warned that urgent action was needed to deal with a "widespread sense of 'no confidence' in the current Social Security system" (Dreyfus, 1996). According to Fink, not only would workers get a better return if their money was invested in the personal investment plans (PIPs) envisioned in the bill, but "the shifting of these funds from Treasuries into stocks, bonds and mutual funds would provide much needed capital for private industry." Departing from CATO, ICI believed that anything more than 2 percent would lead to unaffordable transition costs, draining too much money from the system and making it impossible to pay benefits to current retirees (Schieber & Shoven, 1999, p. 279). The Kerrey-Simpson bill proposed to reduce some of the cost-of-living adjustments (COLA) benefits, to increase the retirement age, and to dedicate 2 percent of the payroll tax to the establishment of PIP accounts. Barry Bosworth, on the other hand, also proposed the creation of a form of PIP structured with an additional 2 percent; in other words, the payroll tax would increase by 2 percent (Schieber & Shoven, 1999, p. 279).

President George W. Bush, after defeating John Kerry in the 2004 election, proclaimed that he was going to reform the Social Security system because it was facing bankruptcy. Thus, he advocated replacing Social Security with privately owned personal savings accounts and called for the establishment of an "ownership society" through the partial privatization of Social Security accounts. In Bush's 2004 State of the Union address, he declared, "Younger workers should have the opportunity to build a nest egg by saving part of their Social Security taxes in a personal retirement account. We should make the Social Security system a source of ownership for the American people" (Galston, 2007). Much like the CATO plan, this proposal was geared to reduce government involvement in the administration and provision of Social Security and other retirement benefits following the writing and ideas of both Milton Friedman and Frederick von Hayek. According to Friedman, Social Security had to be a privatized effort because this is a function that can be better accomplished by the private sector. Supporters of privatization had a powerful ally in the financial industry, which stood to gain a lot from the expected flow of funds.

President Bush, who had mentioned the issue repeatedly during the 2004 campaign, was then arguing that his reelection represented a mandate to move forward on what he called personal accounts. After the election, President Bush made it clear that he was totally committed to Social Security reform, and he asserted that "I earned capital in this campaign, political capital, and now I intend to spend it" (Galston, 2007). As noted by Galston, soon after the election, White House advisors Karl Rove and Ken Mehlman launched a massive initiative geared to mobilize public opinion and build public support for Social Security reform. The initiative involved a number of presidential tours. However,

> it soon became apparent that it would be a tough sell. Within weeks, observers noticed that the more the President talked about Social Security, the more support for his plan declined. According to the Gallup organization, public disapproval of President Bush's handling of Social Security rose by 16 points from 48 to 64 percent—between his State of the Union address and June. (Galston, 2007)

Lack of popular support also meant lack of congressional support, not even from many Republicans who understood the political and economic implications of these ideas, including the commitment of important voting groups to maintaining social security and the fact that these personal accounts were going to be subjected to the vagaries of the market. In fact, given the high-technology crash of 2000–2001 and the 2008 Great Recession, the privatization of retirement accounts would have been a disaster for workers and would have devastated retirees. The fact that the current Social Security system promises fixed benefits, whether the stock or bond markets rise or fall, and has paid them faithfully since its beginnings in 1935 is certainly an advantage for both current workers and retirees (Madrick, 2015). By the summer, a Republican-dominated Congress let the plan die.

The Heritage Foundation has also proposed the creation of personal retirement accounts because they are "practical and feasible. More important [according to Heritage analysts], the money in those accounts would be yours, and not subject to the whims of a politician." Among the arguments developed by the Heritage Foundation are that if you died young, it would go to your family, and that while the system will cost money to set up, it was not as much as argued by those who opposed it (Heritage Foundation, 2004). In another article, Heritage analysts not only cite the success of the Chilean case, but also argue that

> Privatization would not require any reductions in benefits for those who already are retired or nearing retirement. It would enable America's future elderly to retire with dignity, in addition to bringing enormous benefits to the economy overall. Replacing the payroll tax with a system of private savings accounts would boost the anemic level of savings in the United States. It also would boost the creation of jobs by sharply reducing the tax penalty imposed on employment. The resulting increase in economic growth would add thousands of dollars to the average family's income. (Heritage Foundation, 1997)

As the Chile experience indicates, there are many problems associated with the establishment of these accounts, including the fact that these proposals place the risks for managing investments on the workers, who have very little or no experience with the market. Moreover, privatizing Social Security would have not by itself reduced the future deficit because it does not add revenues to the system. On the contrary, as workers drop out and move their payroll taxes to private accounts, the reform creates a shortfall in financing benefits for current retirees, thus increasing the deficit.

In the wake of the 2001 market decline, CATO analysts argued again that privatizing Social Security was a good idea because they could be sure that "most workers would invest in a balanced portfolio that included both stocks and bonds. Given a portfolio of 60 percent stocks and 40 percent bonds, the stock market would practically have to be wiped out to make individual accounts a worse deal than Social Security" (Biggs & Tanner, 2001). The insistence on the part of CATO and Heritage Foundation analysts and others on the virtues of privatization continues through today, as noted in a 2018 article by three CATO analysts (Dayaratna, Greszler, & Tyrrell, 2018).

While this sector of the academic community continues to push for privatization, since the election of Mr. Trump, a potential privatization of Social Security has not been discussed by members of Congress, or prominent political figures. In fact, after calling for privatization for years, Speaker Ryan's latest version of his "Path to Prosperity" program does not include a privatization proposal. However, we foresee a renewed effort to privatize the system given the large budget deficits created by the 2017 tax law. The deficit is expected to increase to about $1 trillion because the amount of corporate taxes collected by the federal government has dropped to historically low levels (Tankersley, 2018). As noted by an analyst,

> Income-tax revenue is important to Social Security because it is free cash flow that is forecast to grow rapidly. In the latest trustees' report, the authors projected that the system would gather about $35 billion in revenue from income taxes in 2017. While this sum is currently over-shadowed by payroll tax revenue, income-tax support for Social Security is projected to grow at more than three times the rate of the economy to more than $80 billion over the coming decade. That figure approximates the payroll taxes of roughly 20 million active workers The tax cuts ignore this impact on Social Security's finances. (Smith, 2017)

The next section analyzes the impact of Chile's privately administered, fully funded (FF), defined contribution (DC) system based on its 38-year experience.

Chile

Chile's Retirement System in Historical Perspective

Chile, a country of almost 18 million people with an economically active population (EAP) of about 8.5 million, was a pioneer in pension privatization. Its 1981 reform, inspired by the ideas of the so-called "Chicago Boys," in turn, motivated the World Bank and other countries to recommend and pursue similar policies.

Between 1924 and the early 1970s, Chile's social security system was structured around a unique pay-as-you-go (PAYG) Common Fund system. By 1973, the system covered about 75 percent of the EAP through more than 600 small and 35 major funds, and through substantial legislation geared to provide special benefits to those interest groups that could exercise political and/or economic power (Borzutzky, 2002). As a result, the provision of social security became expensive for the state and the employers, it was unequal, and it was very inefficient from an administrative standpoint. In fact, the multiple funds reinforced patterns of socioeconomic inequality present in the wider Chilean society. Attempts to reform and rationalize the pension system during the Alessandri and Frei administrations (1958–1964 and 1964–1970) were frustrated by powerful interest groups and their representatives in the Chilean Congress (Borzutzky, 2002).

While it is clear that the social security system needed a major reform, it is also clear that the reform enacted by the military dictatorship of Augusto Pinochet (1973–1989) was not what the country needed. As I have argued elsewhere, the 1980 social security reform was a by-product of the institutional power and neoliberal ideas of the "Chicago Boys," General Pinochet's economic advisors. The ideology of the free market and individualism expounded by the military dictatorship's economic policymakers, supported by high levels of repression and the destruction of Chile's political institutions, produced a far-reaching transformation of the role of the state, its socioeconomic policies, and the country's economy and society (Borzutzky, 2002).

The reform was designed and implemented by Labor Minister José Piñera with the support of Professors Martin Feldstein and Arnold Harberger. Piñera is a member of the CATO Institute, and he has written extensively on the benefits of social security privatization. Piñera replaced the PAYG system with a privately administered, compulsory, FF, DC pension system. Because of its free market commitment and its aim to reduce labor costs, the reform eliminated the portion of the social security tax paid by the employer. The newly created compulsory "savings/pension" scheme was to be privately administered, but supervised by the state to protect the interests of the corporations responsible for managing workers' pensions (Borzutzky, 2002). The transference of the administration to the private sector involved the creation of a new type of for-profit enterprise: the Administradoras de Fondos de Pensiones (pension fund managing corporations), or AFPs. The AFPs' function is to administer the pension funds in return for hefty commissions.

Central to the FF, DC pension reform was the elimination of the principle of social solidarity and its replacement by the notion of individual responsibility—but in this case, it was compulsory individual responsibility because the privatized scheme was made mandatory for all workers in the private sector. It is noteworthy that while the reform took place under a military regime that had adopted a free market mantra, the military and the police retained their state-administered PAYG pensions that had existed since the 1920s.

The individual pension accounts are financed by a 10 percent wage tax paid by employees and that the employers do not contribute to the pension plan. In addition, workers are permitted to make additional voluntary contributions above the mandatory 10 percent, which are administered in separate funds established by the AFPs, with the sole purpose of managing voluntary contributions (Gobierno de Chile, Decree-Law 3500). A new bureaucracy was created to administer the Bono de Reconocimiento, or Recognition Bond, which represents the amount of money accumulated in the PAYG system. These monies are transferred to the individual account at the time of retirement.

At the time of retirement, pensions are provided directly by the AFP through programmed withdrawals, indirectly through an annuity bought from an insurance company with the funds accumulated in the account, or through a combination of the two. If the retiree exhausts his or her account assets, he or she qualifies for a state-provided minimum pension (Asociación de AFPs, 2000, pp. 1,2). In the case of disability and survivors' pensions, the benefit is paid directly by the AFP. Thus, the state acquired the obligation to provide minimum pensions to those in the private pension system who did not have enough money saved to have a pension equal to the statutory minimum. To supplement and complement the pension system, the 1981 reform established a means-tested welfare pension for those who are below the poverty level and had not contributed to the system.

The Impact of Privatizing Pensions: More Losers Than Winners

Over 35 years of data on the socioeconomic effects of pension privatization leads to the conclusion that the FF, DC system is expensive, concentrates income in the hands of the pension fund administrators, generates huge profits for the AFPs, is exclusionary, and discriminates against women and those in the lower income brackets (Borzutzky, 2002, 2008, 2011). Moreover, fiscal responsibilities resulting from the minimum pensions and Bonos de Reconocimiento have created a budget deficit that has been financed by taxes paid by all Chileans. This section develops an analysis of the impact of privatization up to 2007. The partial 2008 reform and its impact are discussed in a separate section.

High Administrative Charges. The reform promised an efficient pension market in which management charges, fees, and commissions would be determined by competition. However, this promise, like many of the others, did not materialize because the number of AFPs operating in the market declined. With only six AFPs responsible for managing workers' savings, charges have remained exceedingly high. A World Bank report estimated that pension fund administrators have retained between a quarter and a third of workers' contributions in the form of commissions, insurance, and other administrative fees since the inception of the system (Gill, Packard, & Yermo, 2004). Mesa-Lago estimated that by 2008, the AFPs retained about 27 percent of the deposit (2014, p. 9).

Privatization of pensions has led to a massive concentration of income in the hands of the AFPs (over 60 percent of GDP was controlled by the AFPs before 2007), while the profitability of the companies was estimated to be over 50 percent (Gill et al., 2004). The rate of profits of the industry has been double the rate of profit of any other industry in the country, reaching an annual rate of 53 percent in 1998 (Valdés & Marinovic, 2005). The AFPs' administrative charges are 89 percent more expensive than banks' or private stockbrokers' charges (Valdés, 1999). The question of high profits is linked to the lack of market competition and the fact that the three largest AFPs manage 86 percent of all the accounts (Mesa-Lago, 2014, p. 6). Moreover, management charges are regressive and penalize the poorest. For instance, for an insured person with an income of about $1,609, the administrative costs fluctuated between 25.6 and 37.9 percent of the deposit, whereas the cost for an insured person with an income of $13,000 fluctuated between 24.1 and 30.2 percent of the deposit (SAFP, 1998, pp. 28–32).

A comparison of management charges with those of other financial services and institutions shows that Chile has had the third highest level of charging among the Latin American DC systems (Valdés & Bateman, 1999), and if compared with Australia, Chile's have been up to 60 percent higher. Valdés and Bateman (1999) show that AFP charges were up to 67 percent higher than fees for the management of savings accounts, and professional asset management services elsewhere in the financial sector, which were less exposed to intrusive state regulation. Comparisons between the AFP charges with those of other financial institutions show that AFP charges have been up to two-thirds higher than the fees imposed by the country's banks for administering savings (Hyde, Dixon, & Drover, 2006).

Less Coverage. By 2007, about 50 percent of the population was excluded from the system, and a large portion of those who contributed were not able to save enough to obtain the equivalent to a minimum pension, forcing the state to fund the retirees through its minimum pension program. Moreover, the pension system had left out the self-employed, the unemployed, and those employed part-time. Additionally, the system discriminates against women because women live longer than men do, their salaries are about 30 percent lower than the salaries of their male counterparts, and they contribute less because of child rearing and other family responsibilities (Arenas de Mesa & Montecinos, 1996). By 2007, only 39 percent of women (vs. 61 percent of men) were actively contributing to a pension, and only 54 percent of all retirees were women as opposed to 69 percent of men (Mesa-Lago, 2014, p. 6). While the question of replacement ratios is complex and it will be addressed later, it is important to note that the replacement ratio for women is about 35 percent, whereas the replacement ratio for men is about 46 percent (Mesa-Lago, 2014, p. 6).

Investment Performance. The evidence suggests that the performance of the AFPs during the first two decades was not impressive. When returns are estimated in this way, they are "more than halved from what has been reported by the AFPs and conservative pundits" (Leiva, 2006, p. 7). According to one study (Acuña & Iglesias, 2001), the AFPs generated an average net return of 5.1 percent during the first two decades; while Kay (2003) estimates average net returns of 0.3 percent for the period 1982–1986 and 2.1 percent for 1991–1995.

This results from the fact that there is an inverse relationship between the degree of concentration in the AFP industry and its investment performance. During the first 14 years, when the number of AFPs grew substantially, monthly investment returns for all six AFPs ranged between −1.8 and 8.6 percent. During the period 1995–2000, when concentration increased, investment returns ranged between −6.4 and 6.6 percent, but between 2001 and 2004, when industry concentration was most prominent, investment returns ranged between −1.6 and 2.5 percent (Hyde & Borzutzky, 2015).

Insufficient Benefits. Contrary to the expectations created by the architects of the program, the value of the pensions offered by the FF, DC system has not changed dramatically either. In 2001, the value of an average FF pension was 12 percent higher than the value of a pension provided by the common fund system, but in the case of disability pensions, the pension provided by the common fund system was 23 percent higher than the pension provided by the FF system (SAFP, 2001, p. 199). The Instituto Libertad y Desarrollo, a right-of-center think tank, in a study that included 976,000 retirees, concluded that the AFPs pay an average old-age pension of $354, whereas the Instituto de Prevision Social, in charge of paying the pensions of those who remained in the PAYG system, pays an average old-age pension of $390. It is important to keep in mind that the AFP affiliates' payroll tax amounts to 13 percent of the wages (basic 10 percent of the wages plus additional contributions for special programs) and that the tax in the public system amounts to 20.7 percent (El Mercurio.com, July 6, 2014).

Inequality. Chile was and is a very unequal country, and both poverty and inequality increased dramatically during the Pinochet dictatorship. Because of the socioeconomic policies implemented after the transition to democracy, poverty declined from over 50 percent of the population in 1990 to 14.4 percent in 2013, but the distribution of income remains highly unequal. As a result, the Gini coefficient declined slightly from 0.53 in 1990 to 0.50 in 2013 (Encuesta Casen, 2013). Moreover, when the Gini coefficient is used to measure the distribution of pension income, a 2005 government report established that "the distribution of retirement income is much more unequal than the distribution of active life income for the same cohort. ... The same can be said for the level of minimum pension guaranteed by the state" (Reyes & Pino, 2006). Thus, the Gini index for retirement income is higher than the actual Gini index of about 0.52. A 2013 Organization of Economic Cooperation and Development (OECD) pension study reaffirms the negative redistributional impact of the pension system through its progressivity index. According to this index, a perfectly progressive system gets a score of a 100 while a system that does not have any impact on progressivity gets a 0. Chile's index is 27.9, a number well below 39, which is the average for all OECD countries, and 82, which is the average for

Anglophone countries (OECD, 2013). Thus, the OECD study confirms that the current pension system reinforces and augments Chile's skewed distribution of income.

Another way of looking at inequality is by analyzing replacement rates. In practice, the replacement ratio can be calculated either on the bases of the last wage or on the bases of the average wage received in the last 10 years. A government study looked at retirees with more than 30 years of savings and estimated that the ratio was 66 percent for men and 42 percent for women based on the wages obtained in the 10 years prior to retirement. A study done by OECD established that the net ratio—after paying taxes—was 52 percent for men and 42 percent for women (El Mercurio.com, October 20, 2014).

Fiscal Impact. Privatization did not reduce but simply changed the role of the state. In fact, the state continues to have a large number of pension responsibilities, including paying the pensions of those who stayed in the common fund system and paying the recognition bond and welfare pensions. Most importantly, the cost of paying the minimum pensions has been increasing, as more people could not save enough to have the equivalent to a minimum pension (Borzutzky, 2002, ch. 7, BVA, p. 13; Melguizo, Muñoz, Tuesta, & Vial, 2009). Therefore, the transition from the PAYG to the privatized system entailed a number of fiscal costs or transition costs that have been sizable and have evolved over time. Transition costs amounted to 7.6 percent of GDP in the early 2000s and had declined to about 5 percent in 2008 and 4.7 percent in 2010, but they were expected to remain high given the increase in the state's payment of minimum pensions.

In conclusion, because of the issues listed above, among others, by 2006 a large portion of the Chilean population was dissatisfied with the pension system because of the high administrative costs, the low pensions, the low replacement ratios, and the many inequalities embedded in the system. This dissatisfaction was confirmed by the Bravo Commission's survey conducted in 2014, which revealed that 72 percent of those polled believed that pensions would improve only if there was a total change in the AFP system. Moreover, according to the same survey, 66 percent of those polled believed that pensions were low because of the AFPs' high charges (Cambio 21).

The 2008 Reform and the Need for a Public Pillar

Presidential candidate Michelle Bachelet promised to reform pensions and shortly after her inauguration in January 2006, she established the Marcel Commission to study the pension system and propose reforms. The reform goals, as articulated by the Marcel Commission, were to universalize benefits, augment the replacement ratio from 45 to 60 percent that is the OECD average, and reduce replacement rate variability due to both gender and income level. The key component of the reform was this Public or Solidarity Pillar that aimed at reducing old-age poverty by providing a pension to that 40 percent of the population that was at that time excluded from the pension system. Additionally, the reform aimed at increasing the density of contributions of those actively contributing, developing new approaches to increase competence among the AFPs, increasing the funds' rates of return, increasing transparency in the management of the pension funds, and strengthening the voluntary pillar by providing new benefits to those who could have additional savings (Consejo Reforma Previsional, 2006, pp. 98–101). Undoubtedly, the reforms were needed because 28 years after implementation, the FF, DC scheme covered only about 60 percent of the population and had systematically excluded most of the independent workers who, given the volatilities and lack of contractual arrangements in the Chilean labor market, comprised a large portion of the population. The same labor market volatility had generated a low density of contributions (Report Comisión Marcel, p. 111).

In 2008, the Chilean Congress approved some of the proposals of the Marcel Commission (Gobierno de Chile, Law 20255), including the Public Pillar known as the basic solidarity pension (PBS) of about \$160 to all Chileans over 65 years old who had never contributed to the pension system (Gobierno de Chile, Subsecretaría de Previsión Social). The state also provides a basic disability pension to those covered by the PBS and guarantees a supplementary contribution (Aporte Previsional Solidario [APS]) to those who have insufficient contributions to finance their retirement benefits. To qualify for the state contribution, the affiliate must have made contributions to an AFP, but the value of the accumulated funds should generate a pension that is less than \$520 (Superintendencia de Pensions, Aporte Previsional Solidario de Vejez). While it is clear that the 2008 reform was much needed by those excluded from the discriminatory and exclusionary FF, DC system, it is also clear that it was designed to conceal the failure of the privatized approach and protect the AFPs' ability to accumulate large amounts of capital. It is also clear that the new fiscal responsibilities, especially the PBS designed by the state, acted to reduce old-age poverty by expanding coverage. Most favored by the PBS are workers who have been in and out of the labor market, temporary and independent workers, and especially women because about 60 percent of the solidarity pensions would benefit women.

A very interesting feature of the reform is geared to augment the value of women's pensions and mandates 18 months of state contributions per child (the state contribution is based on a minimum salary). Although the money is not deposited into the account until the woman turns 65, the contribution begins to generate interest from the moment the child is born. The logic behind the provision is that women are entitled to the same pension benefits as men, and the state is obligated to rectify inequalities produced by the labor market because of their citizenship (Comisión Marcel Report, pp. 118–120). The legislation also introduced a 10-year transitional period to integrate independent workers into the pension system. Middle-income groups benefited through the creation of a system of voluntary pension savings

(Ahorro Previsional Voluntario) that uses tax benefits to incentivize savings. The additional contribution can be deposited not only with AFPs, but also in other financial entities, including insurance companies, mutual funds, and banks (Superintendencia de Pensiones, El Sistema Chileno de Pensiones, 2014, p. 99).

Not surprisingly, the commission's recommendations that altered the capacity of the AFPs to accumulate capital were not included in the 2008 legislation due to opposition from the political right and the AFPs. Most importantly, the call for allowing banks into the pension fund administration business was rejected because it would have ended the monopolistic control that the AFPs have on the pension market and had the potential of reducing management charges. Because these problems persisted, yet another reform commission—the Bravo Commission—created by President Bachelet in early 2014, tackled them again. However, the recommendations of this commission were never implemented by the second Bachelet administration.

In brief, the many failures of the privately administered system forced a reform that included the Solidarity Pillar, or a state-financed pillar that supports pensions for the lower-income groups, young workers, and women. Financially, the 2008 reform was more expensive than any other social program created in Chile between 1990 and 2010. According to Hujo and Rally (2014), the fiscal costs associated with the reform were estimated to increase from 0.27 percent of GDP in 2009 to over 1 percent in 2025 (p. 14). The reform's costs were to be financed through the Pension Reserve Fund established in 2000. In spite of this increase in the cost, ultimately the state gained because the addition of the Solidarity Pillar reduces the fiscal costs produced by the provision of minimum pensions as shown by the estimates made by the Marcel Commission and by Carmelo Mesa-Lago (Mesa-Lago, 2014, pp. 17–20). However, the reform also protected the abusive charges and the AFPs' lack of accountability, as the right-wing legislators refused to introduce measures that would introduce more accountability and competition into the system.

The Chilean Retirement System Today

In 1973, Chile's social security system covered about 73 percent of the EAP. By 2013, the FF pension scheme covered 65 percent of the economically active population and 69.3 percent of those who were currently employed, and another 4 percent were covered by the remnants of the old PAYG system (Commission Bravo, 2015, p. 81). About 10 million Chileans are registered in one of the six AFPs, but only 4.9 million of those are active contributors. The total savings accumulated in the hands of the pension fund administrators amounted to $163,196 million, or about 69 percent of the Chilean GDP in 2013. As recently noted by José Piñera, the AFPs' success is illustrated by the fact that they have accumulated around $250 billion, or the equivalent of about 90 percent of Chile's GDP. What he did not mention is that the average monthly pension for someone who saved in an AFP for 10–15 years is only $350 and that for women it is about half of that amount. The data also show that the AFP system has provided pensions to 998,457 retirees with an average pension of about $400 monthly (El Mercurio.com, July 23, 2014).

Replacement rates range from 11 to 55 percent of the wages for men and from 8 to 40 percent for women depending on the number of years of active contributions and the consistency—or density—of contributions made into the savings account. Thus, a woman who worked all her life and never missed a deposit will get a pension equal to 40 percent of her wages, and a man in the same circumstances will get a pension equal to 55 percent of his wages. The data also show that on average, males contribute to their account for about 25 years out of a 45-year working life, whereas women are able to make only about 15 years of deposits out of a 35-year working life due to family responsibilities, which explains why the replacement rate for women is a lot smaller. The Piñera administration's Pension White Book estimated that more than half of retirees have pensions that are less than 48 percent of the average wage received in the last 10 years of active life (Jimeno Ocares, 2014). According to the Bravo Commission Report, the median replacement rate estimated from the salary obtained in the last 10 years is only 34 percent; if the PBS is added, it increases to 51 percent. The gender disparity estimated in this report is also significant since the replacement rate equals only 25 percent of the salary earned in the last 10 years and for men is 48 percent. If the PBS is included, the replacement rates increase to 31 percent for women and 60 percent for men (Commission Bravo, 2015, p. 87). By comparison, average replacement rates in OECD countries amount to 65.8 percent.

Between 1991 and 2009, the average old-age pension increased by 11 percent, but we should note that the real growth of an old-age pension was about 2 percent per year and that there was no real growth if the retiree took early retirement or retired due to disability. In the cases of widows and children, there was a 4 percent real growth of pensions. Alongside this modest performance, AFP income generated by management charges amounted to $766 million by September 2013 (El Mercurio.com, January 27, 2014). As for the Solidarity Pillar established in 2008, and fully implemented in 2012, the costs to the state were equivalent to $1,621 million per year. The basic solidarity pension amounts to about $180, and it is given to men and women over 65 years of age who are among the poorest 60 percent of the population (Jimeno Ocares, 2014).

In brief, although the 2008 reform expanded coverage, it did not substan- tially increase the value of the AFP pensions because the AFPs were not touched by the reform. As a result, in early 2014, newly reelected President Bachelet, facing popular dissatisfaction with the pension program, formed a second commission, charged with examining the nature of the system's problems and with identifying appropriate solutions. The commission experts concluded that the 10 percent contribution is inadequate and proposed to raise it to 13 percent to be able to generate a sufficient pension. Another proposal involved the establishment of a mixed contributory system that included an increase in the compulsory savings rate to about 15 percent of the wages, with the additional 5 percent deposited in a common fund that can be used by current retirees to supplement their pensions.

The AFPs for their part proposed that Chileans postpone their retirement age, which currently is 65 years for men and 60 for women. According to an estimate made by the Bravo Commission, if a woman postpones her retirement age by five years, she can increase her pension by 40 percent (Bravo Commission, 2015). To placate a very irate public that is quite critical of the management of the funds, the AFPs proposed that if the affiliate postpones retirement, the AFP would not charge management fees for the years worked beyond the statutory minimum. The pension fund administrators also favored an increase in the contributions because the current 10 percent was established when life expectancy in Chile was 40 percent lower and proposed to augment the voluntary savings and provide pension education to all Chileans (El Mercurio.com, March 27, 2014). Unfortunately, due to the weakness of the Bachelet administration, the Bravo Commission's recommendations were never implemented.

Back to the United States: Problems and Solutions

While it is clear that changes in the dependency ratio make it necessary to reform the U.S. Social Security system, what is needed is not privatization that will destroy the system, but simply financial adjustments. According to the 2018 Social Security Trustees Report, over the program's 83-year history, Social Security has collected roughly $20.9 trillion and paid out $18.0 trillion, leaving asset reserves of $2.9 trillion at the end of 2017 in its two trust funds. The trustees estimate that the combined trust funds will be depleted in 2034 and that the projected 75-year actuarial deficit for the OASDI Trust Funds is 2.84 percent of taxable payroll. This deficit amounts to 1.0 percent of GDP over the 75-year time period, or 21 percent of program non-interest income, or 17 percent of program cost. Additionally, Social Security's total cost is projected to exceed its total income (including interest) in 2018 for the first time since 1982. The cost will be financed with a combination of non-interest income, interest income, and net redemptions of trust fund asset reserves from the General Fund of the Treasury until 2034 when the OASDI reserves will be depleted. Between 2034 and 2092, the tax income is expected to pay only about three-quarters of scheduled benefits. As for the cost, Social Security amounted to 4.9 percent of GDP in 2017, and it is expected to increase to 6.1 percent of GDP by 2038, decline to 5.9 percent of GDP by 2052, and thereafter rise slowly, reaching 6.1 percent by 2092 (Social Security and Medicare Trustees Report, 2018).

Thus, the system is in need of financial adjustments, but not of privatization. In a document entitled "Twelve Reasons Why Social Security Is a Bad Idea," the Century Foundation analyzes a potential privatization and makes conclusions that are quite similar to the conclusions reached in the analysis of the Chilean system presented above. As noted in this report, depositing money in a private account will not affect the stability of the system, but in fact, it would create a revenue shortfall, and the government will be unable to use the Social Security surplus to reduce the national debt held by the public. Additionally, the administrative costs of Social Security are less than 1 percent of benefits, compared with average administrative costs of 12–14 percent for private insurers, and while the Social Security trust funds earn a modest rate of return, it does provide security because the monies are invested in U.S. government bonds (Century Foundation, 2004).

In the area of equity, it is clear that much like in the Chilean case, a potential privatization would not benefit low-income groups and would have a negative effect on both racial and gender minorities. It is quite clear that privatization will not benefit African Americans because although they have a shorter life expectancy than whites do, they also have lower average earnings than whites collect. African Americans also own fewer assets and have less extensive pension coverage than whites, so they are more likely to be highly dependent on Social Security benefits. Moreover, African Americans have a greater dependence on the life insurance and disability features of Social Security, and as such they benefit from not only these features, but also the redistributive nature of the system, which is geared to replace a larger share of past earnings for low-income versus high-income beneficiaries. African Americans receive a higher annual payoff in comparison to their past tax contributions than whites (Spriggs & Furman, 2006).

Just as in Chile, privatized accounts would reproduce and even increase existing income inequalities. Unlike the Social Security system, which replaces a larger proportion of the income of low-wage than high-wage workers, there would be no redistribution of income to low-wage workers in a privatized system. As noted in the Century Foundation report (2004), "In 2002, 40% of American families earned total incomes of less than $35,000, and 12.1% of all Americans—34.6 million people—lived below the poverty line. Low-income people are thus unable to save enough to finance a privatized plan and administrative expenses would consume a disproportionate amount of their savings." Ultimately, they would become dependent on a welfare system, if one were devised for the elderly poor.

Additionally, as the Century Foundation report (2004) argues, if male and female workers invested 5 percent of their payroll taxes in private accounts for 40 years, the current gender gap between men's and women's benefits would actually widen because of the gender pay gap and women's interrupted careers. And, because women invest more conservatively than men, another study estimates that after 35 years in a retirement plan, the value of the average male's investment portfolio would be 16 percent greater than the average woman's. Moreover, Social Security guarantees the same earnings-based benefits for life, regardless of life expectancy, and benefits women through the cost-of-living adjustment policy; Social Security guarantees a retired woman who has been married for 10 or more years her own working benefit or half the amount her husband (or ex-husband) receives, whichever is larger. Many privatization proposals would reduce or eliminate this benefit (Century

Foundation, 2004). We assume that other minorities, especially Hispanics and Native Americans, would experience the same kind of negative effects.

Although there is little research on the impact that privatization could have on other gender minorities, it is clear that privatization will be detrimental for the LGBT community because it will cut guaranteed retirement benefits by hundreds of thousands of dollars while introducing up to $15 trillion in new debt that will burden future generations of Americans. Because LGBT families do not have the full recognition and support of the law, because LGBT workers in 34 states can be legally fired, and because LGBT people earn less, on average, than their heterosexual counterparts, Social Security is a crucial and stable form of support in a society rife with anti-LGBT discrimination (Hu, 2005).

Instead of privatization, which effectively destroys the system and increases our ever-widening inequality, policymakers should opt for one or several of the many solutions proposed by a variety of experts and reports. These solutions include increasing the retirement age, increasing the Social Security tax, eliminating the maximum taxable wage, or at least increasing the maximum substantially, eliminating or reducing the COLA, and increasing the IRA tax benefits (Aaron, 2018). For instance, a study done by the Center on Budget and Policy Priorities shows that increasing or eliminating Social Security's cap on taxable wages, now $118,500 a year, would help mitigate the erosion of Social Security's payroll tax base caused by rising wage inequality. In fact, this policy alone "could close roughly a quarter to nearly nine-tenths of Social Security's solvency gap, depending on how they were structured" (Romig, 2016). Moreover, "increasing tax rates alone could close the entire solvency gap; even a modest change, such as a gradual increase of 0.3 percentage points each for employees and employers (or less than $3 per week for an average earner), could close about one-fifth of the gap" (Romig, 2016).

Conclusions

Privatization in Chile and proposals to privatize in the United States have not resulted from the need to overhaul the system, but from ideological positions sustained by a group of market-based economists whose entire foundation resides in the need to reduce or eliminate critical government functions and support the activities of private actors such as investment firms. In both Chile and the United States, these efforts have been accompanied by a concerted effort geared to undermine the very nature of publicly provided pensions. As noted by Max Skidmore, "this has led to the demonization of the welfare state, an enormous increase in income inequality, a concentration of wealth upward, a significant effort aimed at largely withdrawing the government from the provision of health care..." (Skidmore, 2018). This demonization has been generously financed by powerful interest groups and involved repeating a message arguing that only the wealthy are paying a fair share and the young are subsidizing the old. As James Buchanan puts it, "Those who seek to undermine the support of the system would do well to propose increases in the retirement age and increases in the payroll taxes" so as to irritate recipients at all income levels (MacLean, 2017, pp. 179–180). As noted by MacLean, "the right was not against putting away for their retirement. To the contrary, they wanted people to save.... They just wanted those savings taken out of the Federal Government and put in the hands of capitalists, just as it was done in Chile. And to end employers' contributions as Chile had" (MacLean, 2017, p. 180).

In brief, it is clear that if privatization were to take place in the United States, it would not only have a negative effect on women, racial and gender minorities, and those in the lower income bracket, but it would also eliminate the universality and solidarity characteristics that are essential to any social security system and effectively destroy a policy that has benefited millions of Americans since the 1930s.

References

Aaron, H. (2018). "How to keep Social Security secure: Here's a plan that eliminates the long-term shortfall in its finances and updates the system for the 21st century." *The American Prospect.* http://prospect.org/article/how-keep-social-security-secure

Acuña, R., & A. Iglesias. (2001). *Chile's pension reform after 20 years.* Working paper 0129. Washington, DC: World Bank.

AcusaChileAFP. http://acusachile.blogspot.com/2011/11/nace-acusa-afp-chile.html

Arenas de Mesa, A., & V. Montecinos. (1996). "The privatization of social security and women's welfare: Gender effects of the Chilean reform." *Latin American Research Review*, 34, 37–38.

Biggs, A., & M. Tanner. (2001). *Still good to privatize social security.* CATO Institute. https://www.cato.org/publications/commentary/still-good-privatize-social-security

Borzutzky, S. (2002). *Vital connections: Politics, social security, and inequality in Chile.* Notre Dame, IN: Notre Dame University Press.

Borzutzky, S. (2008). "Social security privatization and economic growth." In J. Midgley & K. Tang (Eds.), *Social security, the economy and development* (pp. 111–136). Hampshire: Palgrave-McMillan.

Borzutzky, S. (2010). "Pension market failure in Chile: Foundations, analysis and policy reforms." In M. Hyde & J. Dixon (Eds.), *Comparing how various nations administer retirement income: Essays on social security, privatization, and inter-generational covenants* (pp. 197–216). Lewiston, NY: Edwin Mellen Press.

Borzutzky, S. (2011). "Reforming the reform: Attempting solidarity and equity in Chile's privatized social security system." *Journal of Policy and Practice*, 11, 77–91.

Century Foundation. (2004). *Twelve reasons why privatizing Social Security is a bad idea.* https://tcf.org/content/commentary/twelve-reasons-why-privatizing-social-security-is-a-badidea/

Comisión Asesora Presidencial sobre el Sistema de Pensiones (Comisión Bravo). (2015, September). Informe final. www.comision-pensiones.cl/Documentos/GetInforme

Consejo Reforma Previsional, Comisión Marcel. (2006). Informe final. https://www.previsionsocial.gob.cl/sps/download/estudios-previsionales/comisionpensiones/documentos-interes-general/informe-consejo-asesor-presidencial-reforma-del-sistema-previsional-comision-marcel-2006.pdf

Dayaratna, K., R. Greszler, & P. Tyrrell. "Is social security worth its cost?" *Backgrounder.* https://www.heritage.org/sites/default/files/2018-07/BG3324_0.pdf

Delgado, L. (2007, January 9). "Trabajadores debatieron en torno a la reforma y daño previsional en la UACH." Noticias UACH. http://noticias.uach.cl/principal.php?pag=noticiaexterno&cod=8777

Dreyfus, R. (1996). "The biggest deal: Lobbying to take social security private," *The American Prospect.* http://prospect.org/article/biggest-deal-lobbying-take-social-security-private

El Mercurio.com. (2014, January 27). *Diferencias sobre $300 mil al año hay entre AFP más barata y la más cara.* http://www.economiaynegocios.cl/movil/iphone.asp?id=1165611

El Mercurio.com. (2014, March 27). *Las AFP no fuimos suficientemente categóricas para alertar los cambios que venían.* http://www.economiaynegocios.cl/noticias/noticias.asp?id=118241

El Mercurio.com. (2014, April 19). *Los argumentos a favor y en contra para la creacion de una AFP estatal.* http://impresa.elmercurio.com/pages/LUNHomepage.aspx?BodyID¹⁄₄2&dt¹⁄₄2014-4-19

El Mercurio.com. (2014, June 20). *Las AFP proponen veinte ideas para mejorar pensiones e incentivar postergación de retiros.* http://www.economiaynegocios.cl/noticias/noticias.asp?id=120715

El Mercurio.com. (2014, June 24). *Chile es el país donde las empresas hacen el menor aporte a la pensión de sus trabajadores.* http://www.economiaynegocios.cl/noticias/noticias.asp?id=120802

El Mercurio.com. (2014, July 6). *700 mil personas siguen recibiendo su jubilación del IPS: Pensiones del sistema antiguo son 45% más bajas que las que entregan las AFP.*

El Mercurio.com. (2014, July 23). *Número de nuevos pensionados por año crecerá más Del doble entre 2015 y 2020.* http://www.economiaynegocios.cl/noticias/noticias.asp?id=121652

El Mercurio.com. (2014, October 7). *Salvador Valdés plantea crear AFPs sin fines de lucro y permitir retiros de dinero a afiliados.* https://politicaspublicas.uc.cl/prensa/salvador-valdes-plantea-crear-afps-sin-fines-de-lucro-y-permitir-retiros-de-dinero-a-afiliados/

El Mercurio.com. (2014, October 20). *Definición de la tasa de reemplazo de las pensiones sería un tema clave en primer informe.* http://www.economiaynegocios.cl/noticias/noticias.asp?id=124100

El Mercurio.com. (2018, June 15). *José Piñera defiende rentabilidad del sistema de pensiones y dice que Chile ya es desarrollado.* http://www.economiaynegocios.cl/noticias/noticias.asp?id=478518

Encuesta Casen. (2013). *Ministerio de desarrollo Social, Gobierno de Chile.* http://www.ministerio desarrollosocial.gob.cl/resultados-encuesta-casen-2013/

Ferrara, P. (1997, April 30). *A plan for privatizing social security.* Cato Institute Social Security Choice Paper No. 8. https://object.cato.org/sites/cato.org/files/pubs/pdf/ssp8.pdf

Galston, W. (2007, September 21).*Why the 2005 social security initiative failed, and what it means for the future.* Brookings Institution. https://www.brookings.edu/research/why-the-2005-social-security-initiative-failed-and-what-it-means-for-the-future/

Gill, I., T. Packard, & J. Yermo. (2004). *Keeping the promise of old age income security in Latin America: A regional study of social security reform.* Washington, DC: World Bank. https://openknowledge.worldbank.org/handle/10986/7391

Gobierno de Chile. Decree Law 3500. http://www.leychile.cl/Navegar?idNorma=7147

Gobierno de Chile. Law 20255. http://www.leychile.cl/Navegar?idNorma=269892

Gobierno de Chile. Subsecretaría de Previsión Social, Pensión Básica Solidaria. http://www.previsionsocial.gob.cl/subprev/?page_id=7430

Gobierno de Chile. Superintendencia de Pensiones, Aporte Previsional Solidario de Vejez. http://www.spensiones.cl/portal/orientacion/580/w3-article-5786.html

Gobierno de Chile. Reforma Previsional Gobierno de Chile. http://www.spensiones.cl/portal/prensa/579/w3-article-4193.html

Gobierno de, C. (2014). Superintendencia de Pensiones, El Sistema Chileno de Pensiones. https://www.spensiones.cl/portal/institucional/594/articles-7206_libroVIIedicion.pdf

Heritage Foundation. (1997, April). *Creating a better Social Security system for America.* https://www.heritage.org/social-security/report/creating-better-social-security-system-america

Heritage Foundation. (2004, October). *Social Security personal accounts? Yes!* https://www.heritage.org/social-security/commentary/social-security-personal-accounts-yes

Hu, M. (2005). *Selling us short: How Social Security privatization will affect lesbian, gay, bisexual and transgender Americans.* http://www.thetaskforce.org/static_html/downloads/reports/reports/SellingUsShort.pdf

Hujo, K., & M. Ralli. (2014). *The political economy of pension re-reform: Toward more inclusive protection.* United Nations Research Institute for Social Development, Social Policy and Development (2000-2009). http://www.unrisd.org/80256B3C005BCCF9/search/13C947C84CC4FAFFC1257CAF0 04697A0? OpenDocument

Hyde, M., & S. Borzutzky. (2015). "Chile's 'neoliberal' retirement system? Concentration, competition and economic predation in 'private' pensions." *Poverty & Public Policy, 7*(2), 123–157.

Hyde, M., & J. Dixon. (2009). "Individual and collective responsibility: Mandated private pensions in comparative perspective." *Journal of Comparative Social Welfare, 25*(2), 119–128.

Hyde, M., J. Dixon, & G. Drover. (2006). *The privatization of mandatory retirement income protection: International perspectives.* Lewiston, NY: Edwin Mellen Press.

International Monetary Fund. (2014, July). IMF Country report 14/219, Chile. Selected issues paper. Washington, DC: Author. https://www.imf.org/external/.../cr14219.pdf

Jimeno Ocares, P. (2014, October 26). "Pensiones: Los cambios que estudia La Comisión Bravo." *La Tercera, Santiago.* http://www2.latercera.com/noticia/pensiones-los-cambios-que-estudia-la-com ision-bravo/

Kay, S. J. (2003, March). "State capacity and pensions." Paper presented at the LASA XXIV International Congress, Dallas.

Leiva, F. (2006, May/June). "Chile's privatized social security system: Behind the free market hype, a scam." *Connections,* 1–13. https://fleiva.files.wordpress.com/2009/10/leiva-socialsecurity.pdf

MacLean, N. (2017). *Democracy in chains: The deep history of the radical right stealth plan for America.* New York: Scribe.

Madrick, J. (2015, March 5). "The rocky road to taking it easy." *The New York review of books.* https://www.nybooks.com/articles/2015/03/05/rocky-road-taking-it-easy/

Melguizo, A., A. Muñoz, D. Tuesta, & J. Vial. (2009). *Pension reforms and fiscal policy: Some lessons from Chile.* BBVA Working Papers. Economic Research Department, No 0915.

Mesa-Lago, C. (1976). *Social security in Latin America: Pressure groups, stratification and inequality.* Pittsburgh: University of Pittsburgh Press.

Mesa-Lago, C. (2014). *Reversing pension privatization: The experience of Argentina, Bolivia, Chile and Hungary.* ESS Working Paper 44. International Labor Office, Geneva. https://ideas.repec.org/p/ilo/ilowps/994848943402676.html

Organization of Economic Cooperation and Development. (2013). *Pensions at a glance: OECD and G20 indicators.* https://doi.org/10.1787/pension_glance-2013-en

Reyes, G., & F. Pino. (2006). *Income inequality in an individual capitalization pension system: The case of Chile.* https://scholar.google.com/scholar?hl=en&as_sdt=0,39&cluster=4275999287603283397

Romig, K. (2016, September 27). "Increasing payroll taxes would strengthen Social Security." Center on Budget and Public Policy Priorities. https://www.cbpp.org/research/social-security/increasing-payroll-taxes-would-strengthen-social-security

Schieber, S., & J. Shoven. (1999). *The real deal: The history and future of social security.* New Haven, CT: Yale University Press.

Skidmore, M. (2018). *Considering structural and ideological barriers to anti-poverty programs in the United States: An uninhibited, unconventional analysis.* Paper presented at the Annual Meeting of the American Political Science Association, Boston.

Smith, B. (2017, December 22). "The tax cuts ignore this impact on Social Security's finances." MarketWatch. https://www.marketwatch.com/story/the-tax-cuts-ignore-this-impact-on-social-securitys-finances-2017-12-21

Social Security and Medicare Trustees Report. 2018, https://www.pgpf.org/analysis/socialsecurity-medicare-trustees-reports

Spriggs, W., & J. Furman. (2006). "African Americans and Social Security: The implications of reform proposals," Center on Budget and Policy Priorities. https://www.cbpp.org/research/african-americans-and-social-security-the-implications-of-reform-proposals

Superintendencia de Administradoras de Fondos de Pensiones. (1998). Boletín Estadístico Mensual (Vol. 148, pp. 28-32). Santiago.

Superintendencia de Administradoras de Fondos de Pensiones. (2001). Boletín Estadístico Mensual (Vol. 199). Santiago.

Superintendencia de Administradoras de Fondos de Pensiones. (2003). Estadísticas Principales. Santiago.

Tankersley, J. (2018, July 25). "How the Trump tax cut is helping to push the federal deficit to $1 trillion." *The New York Times.* https://www.nytimes.com/2018/07/25/business/trump-corporate-tax-cut-deficit.html

The New York Times, "How the Trump Tax Cut Is Helping to Push the Federal Deficit to $1 Trillion." https://www. nytimes.com/2018 /07/25/business/trump-corporate-tax-cut-d.

Valdés, S. (1995). *Vendedores de AFP: Producto del Mercado o de Regulaciones Ineficientes?* Working Document No. 178. Institute of Economics, Catholic University of Chile, Santiago. http://economia.uc.cl/publicacion/vendedores-de-afp-producto-del-mercado-o-de-regulaciones-ineficientes/.

Valdés, S. (1999). "Las Comisiones de las AFPs son caras o baratas?" *Estudios Públicos*, 73, 255–291. Santiago. https://www.cepchile.cl/cep/site/artic/20160303/asocfile/20160303184509/rev73_valdes.pdf

Valdés, S., & H. Bateman. (1999, April). *The mandatory old age income schemes of Australia and Chile: A comparison.* Paper presented at the Second Regional Reform of APEC on Reforms to Pensions Systems, Catholic University of Chile, Santiago.

Valdés, S., & I. Marinovic. (2005). "Contabilidad regulatoria para las AFP 1993–2003." Documento de Trabajo (no. 279). Instituto de Economía Universidad Católica, Santiago.

Implementation of Medicaid-Funded Long-Term Care: The Impact of Prior History on the Development of the Nursing Home Industry

David E. Kingsley

Department of Health Policy and Management, Kansas University Medical Center, Kansas City, Kansas

Growth of the "nursing home" industry was enhanced considerably by passage of Medicare and Medicaid in 1965 (Public Law 89–97, Titles XVIII and XIX of amendment to the Social Security Act). Injection of federal funds into Medicare for extended-care nursing (ETC) and into Medicaid for means-tested, long-term care (LTC) spurred the growth of for-profit and nonprofit enterprises. Prior to 1965, the effects of vendor payments for Medicare and Medicaid and federal low-interest real estate loans for facility construction resulted in the initial development of a specialty real estate industry that was to become an important substrate in extended- and long-term medical care. Although the LTC industry has evolved over the decades, the basic structure and function of the industry had been established prior to passage of the 1965 Social Security Amendments. The power and influence of Southern Democrats, the American Medical Association, and ultraconservative Republicans were major factors in development of a nursing home system designed for welfare medicine, state control, and industrialization. No vision of care for a looming precipitous growth in an elderly population needing long-term care in skilled-nursing facilities guided congressional debate during the enactment of Medicaid. The Medical Assistance for the Aged Act (MAA or "Kerr-Mills") and other legislation preceding the passage of Medicaid established precedent for vendor payments, spend downs, and, consequently, means-testing. Kerr-Mills codified elderly individuals too poor to pay for medical care but not poor enough to qualify for Old Age Assistance into a new category of U.S. resident: "the medically indigent." This categorization through legislation of poor Americans needing care would have far-reaching consequences in the U.S. medical care system. By legislating a categorical, means-tested, industrialized, long-term care system into existence, Congress ensured that the nursing home system would be characterized by the "total institution" as opposed to maximum support for community and home-based systems. Excessive institutionalization of the frail elderly and disabled in institutions based on profitability and, hence, economy and efficiency, has been responsible for an industry with revenues approaching a half trillion dollars. From the view of Southern Democrats and their allies, Medicaid-funded, long-term care has been well implemented. Advocates for patients and most scholars believe that it has failed the patients whom it was intended to serve.

KEY WORDS: Medicaid, long-term care, welfare medicine

1965年通过的养老医疗保险计划和贫穷医疗补助计划极大促进了"疗养院"行业的发展（"公共法"第89‐97号，"社会保障法"修正案第十八和第十九章）。联邦资金注入医疗保险用于延伸护理(ETC)，注入医疗补助用于经过收入调查的长期护理(LTC)，刺激了营利性和非营利性企业的增长。1965年以前，受供应商支付医疗保险和医疗补助以及用于设施建设的联邦低息房地产贷款的影响，特殊的房地产行业得以初步发展，并将成为延长医疗保健和长期医疗救助的重要基础。虽然LTC行业发展已有数十年，但在1965年"社会保障修正案"通过之前，该行业的基本结构和功能已经确立。南方民主党人、美国医学会和极端保守的共和党人的权力和影响力是发展为福利医疗、国家管制和工业化需求而设计的疗养院系统的主要因素。面对需要在成熟护理机构接受长期护理的老年人即将出现的急剧增长，没有一种愿景能够引导国会在制定医疗补助计划时进行辩论。"老年人医疗援助法"(MAA或"Kerr‐Mills")和在通过医疗补助之前的其他立法已经为供应商付款、支出下降以及因此而进行的收入调查开了先河。Kerr‐Mills将那些因贫困而无法支付医疗费用但尚未贫穷到领取老年援助的老年人纳入了一种新的美国居民类别："医疗贫困者"。根据立法对需要照顾的美国穷人进行分类，将对美国医疗系统中产生深远的影响。国会通过制定一项经过经济状况检验、工业化的长期护理体系，确保疗养院制度的特点是"完全制度"，而不是最大限度地支持社区和家庭系统。以盈利能力为基础的机构将体弱的老年人和残疾人过度送进机构，以及其所带来的经济和效率促使该行业收益接近五万亿美元。从南方民主党及其盟友的角度来看，医疗补助资助的长期护理已经得到了很好的实施。为病人发声的倡导人士和大多数学者认为，它辜负了它打算为之服务的病人。

关键词：长期护理，护理，医疗保险，医疗补助，延伸护理

El crecimiento de la industria de los "hogares de ancianos" se mejoró considerablemente con la aprobación de Medicare y Medicaid en 1965 (Ley Pública 89-97, títulos XVIII y XIX de la enmienda a la Ley de Seguridad Social). La inyección de fondos federales en Medicare para enfermería de atención prolongada (ETC) y en Medicaid para atención médica a largo plazo (LTC), estimuló el crecimiento de empresas con fines de lucro y sin fines de lucro. Antes de 1965, los efectos de los pagos a proveedores por Medicare y Medicaid y los préstamos federales a bajo interés de bienes raíces para la construcción de instalaciones dieron lugar al desarrollo inicial de una industria de bienes raíces especializada que se convertiría en un importante sustrato en la atención médica a largo y largo plazo. Aunque la industria de la LTC ha evolucionado a lo largo de las décadas, la estructura básica y la función de la industria se habían establecido antes de la aprobación de las Enmiendas de la Seguridad Social de 1965. El poder y la influencia de los demócratas del sur, la Asociación Médica Americana y los republicanos ultraconservadores fueron factores importantes en el desarrollo de un sistema de hogares de ancianos diseñados para la medicina social, el control estatal y la industrialización. No hay visión de la atención para un crecimiento precipitado inminente en una población anciana que necesita atención a largo plazo en centros de enfermería especializada guiados por el debate en el Congreso durante la promulgación de Medicaid. La Ley de Asistencia Médica para los Ancianos (MAA o "Kerr-Mills") y otra legislación anterior al paso de Medicaid establecieron un precedente para los pagos de los proveedores, las reducciones de gastos y, en consecuencia, las pruebas de recursos. Kerr-Mills codificó a las personas de edad avanzada que son demasiado pobres para pagar la atención médica, pero no lo suficientemente pobres como para calificar para la Asistencia a la vejez en una nueva categoría de residentes en los EE. UU .: "los indigentes de medicina". Consecuencias en el sistema de atención médica de Estados Unidos. Al legislar la existencia de un sistema de atención a largo plazo categórico, mediado por los medios, industrializado, el Congreso aseguró que el sistema de hogares de ancianos se caracterizaría por la "institución total" en lugar del apoyo máximo para los sistemas comunitarios y basados en el hogar. La institucionalización excesiva de los ancianos y discapacitados frágiles en instituciones basadas en la rentabilidad y, por lo tanto, en la economía y la eficiencia, ha sido responsable de una industria con ingresos que se aproximan a medio billón de dólares. Desde el punto de vista de los demócratas del sur y sus aliados, la atención a largo plazo financiada por Medicaid se ha implementado adecuadamente. Los defensores de los pacientes y la mayoría de los eruditos creen que les ha fallado a los pacientes a quienes estaba destinado a servir.

PALABRAS CLAVES: cuidados a largo plazo, enfermería, Medicare, Medicaid, enfermería de cuidados prolongados

Introduction

What is meant by implementation of anti-poverty programs in general and welfare medicine in particular? This article addresses this question by focusing on Medicaid-funded, long-term care (LTC)—an antipoverty, welfare medicine, program. In the following discussion, the hypothesis that the philosophy and design of the current nursing home system was set in place well before passage of Public Law 89–97 (Medicare and Medicaid) in 1965 will be posited. Indeed, long-term care evolved from the "total institution,"[1] of the ignominious alms-house system,[2] as that system was modified by legislation preceding the enactment of Medicaid by a decade and a half.

It will further be argued that legislation laying the groundwork for means-tested medicine[3] solidified the "needy," or "indigent elderly," category of medical patient. As a major innovation in the United States, the ideal of medical care as an equal right in accordance with the general welfare clause of the U.S. Constitution[4] and as a public good was foreclosed by categorization of citizens as "deserving" and "undeserving" of what in many cases could be lifesaving medicine.

Although the focus of this article is directed toward the implementation of Medicaid LTC, it must be mentioned that the contemporary nursing home system reflects centuries of racial, religious, and economic characteristics of American culture and society. These factors have been conducive to the dehumanizing, privatized "nursing home" system that is increasingly dominated by large chains of skilled nursing facilities.

Although the impacts of the New Deal and Lyndon Johnson's Great Society are typically highlighted by historians in explaining the end of the disgraceful almshouse system and the beginning of today's LTC system, the anti-government and racial animus of the Southern Democrats, American Medical Association, and ultraconservative Republicans—as a coalition—in the design of Medicaid are, for the most part, ignored.[5] For Southern Democrats, medical justice was a threat to strict racial hierarchies, undermining of brutalizing apartheid, and the rights of states to insulate themselves from federal policy. The abominable racism perpetrated by legislators from the South was for the most part based on white voter demands and their own bigotry. Nevertheless, economic elites had a vested interest in fomenting and supporting Jim Crow culture, which placed African Americans not only in a subclass of human but also in a subclass of laborer.

Plantation capitalists dominated the Democratic Party of the South and were dependent on subjugated—in many cases, re-enslaved—laborers for increased return on their investment (Blackmon, 2009; Domhoff & Webber, 2011).

In addition to the desire of most members of the American Medical Association (AMA) to preserve the organization's traditional and pervasive racist practices,[6] they abhorred the notion that its control over U.S. medical policy, exercised through state politics, would be diluted. Right-wing Republicans in the North and South were more than willing to ally themselves with the Southern Democrats to prevent what they saw as federal encroachment and potential regulation (Domhoff & Webber, 2011).

The history of politics of Southern states, the AMA, and the conservative wealthy and corporations, as a coalition, is a history of fighting for devolution of federal programs and power to the states. On the right wing of U.S. politics, especially in the South, an incessant effort has been underway from time throughout history to undermine the duties and obligations of federal government.[7] This effort has been accompanied by bogus claims of what the founders intended. The truth of the matter is that the framers had a jaundiced view of states and the types of factions and corruption generated in these smaller units of government.[8] As will be discussed below, the Medicaid LTC system set in place by the coalition mentioned above exhibits the consequences of ignoring the wisdom of the framers.

Corporations—both profit and nonprofit—their trade associations, immense amounts of money for lobbying and campaigns, sympathetic politicians (recipients of campaign funds), and a plethora of influencers in so-called think tanks within the Washington, DC, beltway have been instrumental in shielding nursing home businesses from the type of federal oversight that would lead to humane, ethical, competent medical care of the frail elderly and disabled needing medical care on a daily basis. That is, appreciation of and sensitivity to the needs of such vulnerable patients in the medical system has not historically been and is not currently the primary goal of the nursing home system. In the initial stages of the proprietary nursing home business, scandals in the form of abuses, neglect cases, and corruption were beyond the pale of what could possibly be tolerated. Hearings were intermittently held to expose and condemn widespread, intolerable cruelty and exploitation visited by the industry upon medically fragile elderly and disabled patients.[9] However, over time, the industry and its political patrons have been successful in resisting the type of major reforms that would lead to a humane and medically suitable form of care.

Although a significant piece of federal legislation designed to regulate the industry was passed in 1987 (Morford, 1988), the industry continues to operate with a "bottom line" modus operandi and modus vivendi. As a result of industry resistance to reform and regulation, the nursing home system is rife with horrendous cases of abuse and neglect. Advocates, attempting to protect and improve conditions for patients, are met with industry representatives' pleas of hardship before state legislatures.

The industry and its trade associations[10] are involved far more with regulators at the state level than at the federal level. These trade groups are well financed and operate through affiliates in all 50 states. In the states, advocates for patients are usually volunteers with no funding or pay. Hence, the power relationship between the advocates and the industry is asymmetrical. The passage of Medicaid propelled the industry into existence. Over the past three quarters of a century, the nursing home business has become increasingly complexified, become concentrated in large chains, developed a correlative massive real estate component, and become adept at hiding ownership through networks of LLCs.

The public has been conditioned to disdain welfare; those who receive it are denigrated as inferior. Widespread racism and conflation of welfare and African Americans have evoked revulsion from those—especially whites—who have not suffered the misfortunes of poverty and consider welfare a drain on their "hard-earned money."[11]

It is well established that care in Medicaid-funded, skilled nursing facilities is qualitatively less desirable than care provided to self-pay patients in the skilled nursing facilities associated with CCRCs or in community- and home-based care. The lowering of quality for patient care reimbursed by Medicaid is compounded when facilities are in inner-city, African American neighborhoods (Grabowski & McGuire, 2009).

Racial and class disparities aside, the idea of ending life in a "nursing home" horrifies most everyone in the United States. The industry is characterized by an ignominious history of poor care and widespread tales of despicable acts committed against patients by poorly supervised staff. Therefore, from the perspective of patients and their families and the public in general, barriers to implementation of means-tested LTC as an anti-poverty program have been considerable and have prevented the care of patients most everyone would considerable suitable.

From the perspective of state-rightists, proponents of privatization of government services, real estate investors, and other businesses billing Medicaid, the implementation of Medicaid LTC has gone quite well. Industry revenues could have possibly reached a half trillion dollars; private equity firms are undertaking leveraged buyouts of the largest chains; the network nursing home trade association affiliates have significant control over regulation at the state level while they are able to employ an army of lobbyists inside the DC beltway and make large contributions to campaigns.

In any given nursing home, on any given day, one will find a dearth of physicians, registered nurses, and experts with time to adequately care for patients with serious chronic conditions such as dementia and Alzheimer's disease. As celebrity physician Atul Gawande (2014) wrote in his marvelous book, *Being Mortal*: "Nursing home priorities are matters like avoiding bed sores and maintaining residents' weight—important medical goals to be sure—but they are means, not ends." This work is carried out by unskilled, low-paid staff. Good geriatric medicine is not a high priority.

It is often said that many of the U.S. systems vital to a well-functioning, democratic society are in dire need of reform. For instance, one hears that the prison system is "broken." Given the widespread disdain for nursing homes, it would seem that the nursing home system is broken. But as an elderly African

American activist has said, these systems are not broken; rather, they are working just as they were intended to work. It will be argued in the following pages that this is true of the government-funded, privatized long-term care system.

An ominous set of circumstances is now threatening gains made in oversight of the industry over the past few decades, such as they are. With an administration in Washington bending to the will of deregulations forces, CMS has substantially weakened the advances in oversight set in place by the Obama administration. Nursing home trade associations for both the so-called nonprofit segment and the for-profit segment, LeadingAge and the Health Care Association of America, respectively, have immense amounts of money to spend on political action and lobbying.[12]

Leading academic work on the topic of nursing homes uniformly suggests that treatment and life in a long-term care facility are woefully inadequate. However, people in general have no concept of what an alternative would be. Models of humane care in long-term care do exist. A small circle of scholars and activists are aware of them. For instance, the Eden Alternative and Greenhouse models are homes providing intense skilled nursing for patients unable to live independently. These models provide patients with a life free of the rigid and dependency-inducing characteristics of the total institution.[13]

Nevertheless, the U.S. political-governmental realm, along with the society and culture encompassing it, has no vision about how medically fragile, dependent members of society are to be treated in skilled nursing facilities. The vision of legislators with the greatest influence in the design and enactment of Medicaid was weak federal control, low-tier medicine, privatization, and a strong role for states. This vision was not aimed at the most humane care for future nursing home patients.

Cultural, Political, and Economic Background

During the 1950s, when the industrialization of nursing home care was set in place through a variety of legislative enactments, there was no overt philosophical or bioethical vision guiding public discourse over how our society would care for the medically fragile elderly and disabled. Rather than come to grips with the meaning of quality of care and quality of life in Medicaid-funded "nursing homes," politically powerful groups with other agendas maneuvered the current system into place.

The juggernaut of Southern Democrats, the AMA, and conservative Northern Republicans succeeded in preventing a federally administered, universal, single-payer (by federal income tax) medical care system. Although the AMA deserves plenty of the blame for this tragedy and is typically credited with blocking Roosevelt's and Truman's plans for medical care for all citizens as a right, they were not as effective in the endeavor as were the Southern Democrats who constituted a powerful, solid block of votes and controlled key committees.

The coalition undermining liberal attempts to legislate medical care justice incorporated traditional American cultural themes into their legislative goals.

First, medical care is, in the conservative view, a privilege when it is provided to those who cannot pay for it and/or do not receive it through their workplace. Therefore, medicine for the poor or unfortunate is best provided through charitable, Christian good works in eleemosynary institutions. It is not expected that such care would meet the standards of medicine provided to the affluent who can pay for it themselves. In other words, it should be a lower tier of medicine lest the poor be encouraged in their lazy and indolent ways.[14]

Second, medical care, controlled and funded at the federal level, and which suggested the same rights and benefits to all races and classes, directly threatened rigid racial and class hierarchies of the Jim Crow South. White supremacy and the treatment of African Americans as subhuman were deeply ingrained in Southern and much of Northern culture. This attitude was no doubt strongly held and intensely expressed politically, religiously, educationally, and in practically every other way in day-to-day life. The dehumanization and brutalization of African Americans served as an economic function for plantation capitalists, the economic elites of the South, who controlled the region's politics and determined the destiny of politicians in their domain—the Southern Democrats. The racial caste system kept hardscrabble poor whites near the bottom, but they always knew that blacks would be beneath them. Threatening that hierarchy would further threaten the hold of the economic elites over the Southern economy, which relied on cheap labor. Playing off poor whites against even poorer, subjugated blacks was an effective mechanism for maintenance of cheap labor and preventing the likelihood that poor blacks and poor whites would team up to challenge the planter oligarchy.

Third, nothing threatened the Southern oligarchy, the racist and segregationist views of the American Medical Association, and reactionary Northern Republicans like federal power per se. A program as significant and impactful as the right to equal medical treatment for every U.S. citizen would require an immense federal bureaucracy. Furthermore, such a right would open the door to leveling society racially and economically. It would inject the federal government into the affairs of Southern states to an extent not seen since Reconstruction. The conservative and privileged position of the AMA would be threatened if federal power were to be exerted over the medical labor market and education of physicians. Reactionary Republicans, already horrified by labor organization and the New Deal, feared enhanced federal power in the realm of taxation, regulation, civil rights, and further liberalization of society.

The current nursing home system has its roots in the drive by the three major factors explicated above. The coalition driving the effort to undermine medicine as a right was solidified in the 1940s by challenges generated during the New Deal (Rutkow, 2010). The biggest challenge was recognition by the Roosevelt administration and the liberals in Congress that the federal government had an important role to play in assisting people who fall into the lowest economic strata. Among those were the elderly who had no economic choice but to seek shelter in what were the obvious subhuman conditions of an almshouse.

The federal Old Age Assistance (OAA) grant program to the states provided cash assistance to poor elderly for purchasing room and board and thereby avoid the degradation of the ignominious almshouse system.[15] OAA as a federal categorical aid program of cash assistance to poor elderly Americans was buttressed by passage of Social Security in 1935, which provided some security in old age as an "earned right." The impact of these programs for the elderly along with the plethora of other New Deal programs, enacted as a necessary means of rescuing capitalism from its radical laissez-faire past, cannot be underestimated in what was a historical shift in power from the states to the federal level of government.

In the process of enacting legislation providing cash assistance to the poor, Congress was influenced by the sordid history of almshouses and ensured that no federal dollars would support any residual elements of that system. Hence, federal assistance through OAA funds paid directly to institutions in which poor elderly Americans were housed was prohibited. The spirit of this law was to ensure that institutional "snake pits" represented by almshouses, and many orphanages and mental institutions of the time, would not be supported and maintained in existence by legislation designed to provide the most basic needs of poor Americans.

Hence, there was not much in major 1940s medical care legislation that would propel a long-term care industry into existence. The highly significant Hill-Burton Act for hospital construction, passed in 1946, did not include funding for long-term care facilities (Olson, 2003). The federal government overlooked continuing segregation of hospitals funded under Hill-Burton. Furthermore, the entities owning the facilities were not forced to provide much care to indigent patients (Rutkow, 2010).

Lack of Hill-Burton funding for long-term care facilities, cash assistance to the elderly, and prohibition on providing payments to institutional settings resulted in the growth of mom-and-pop enterprises—mostly boarding homes with perhaps a small amount of nursing care in some. Realtors and would-be operators did not see much opportunity in building and running nursing homes.

The 1950s and the Beginnings of the Proprietary Nursing Home as a Major New Industry

With the passage of the Social Security Act in 1935, the federal government made its debut into programs for addressing poverty incurred by elderly Americans. However, the conscious attempt to eliminate the degrading and reviled almshouse system driving the design of cash assistance to the poor left the need for long-term, institutional care for frail elderly patients unaddressed. The passage of amendments to the Social Security Act in the 1950s opened the door to what would become a powerful industry and major segment of the U.S. medical care system, that is, the nursing home system.

The 1950s amendments authorized payments from the states to vendors such as nursing homes, physicians, and other medical goods and services. With the allowance of vendor payments, these amendments became the primordial roots to privatization of, and considerable state power over, government-funded medical care for the poor. Old Age Security, Aid to the Blind and Disabled, and Aid to Families with Dependent Children as categorical aid programs provided cash assistance to recipients with funding shared by the states and the federal government, but no provision in the enabling legislation provided for reimbursement to providers of medical services.

Vendor payments per se are not contrary to the best interests of the public and patients. In fact, no health care systems in technologically advanced and democratic governments of the world function without purchasing goods and services from private industry. Indeed, purchase of manufactured goods such as pharmaceuticals and medical devices is a necessity in all medical systems. In capitalistic systems, governments do not generally manufacture products that can be manufactured in the private sector.

Privatization of an entire medical care system, however, extends far beyond purchase of medical products that are not ordinarily manufactured by governments. When corporations own facilities such as hospitals, nursing homes, clinics, and the land on which they sit, and when they employ all professional and non-professional labor, privatization is far beyond what is necessary for obtaining supplies such as hospital sets, needles, beds, and so forth. Indeed, decisions made early in the development of Medicaid and Medicare set the United States on a path toward industrialization of medicine.

Today, practically three-fourths of the $5 trillion U.S. medical system is owned and operated by private enterprise. Furthermore, three-fourths of the long-term care segment of the U.S. medical system is fully privatized. The one-fourth of LTC that is considered nonprofit is comprised of entities that run their enterprises as bottom-line, revenue-wealth-generation operations.

The daily rates are nearly as high in 501(c)(3), faith-based, long-term care institutions as in private, for-profit facilities. The same spend-down requirements exist for placement in the "medically indigent" category and, consequently, eligibility for Medicaid reimbursement to the institution for their care.[16]

A new industry, euphemistically labeled "the nursing home industry," was on the horizon after the 1950s Social Security amendments. Following those amendments, Congress approved low-interest Small Business Administration (SBA) and Federal Housing Administration (FHA) financing for construction of facilities needed by proprietary nursing home operators. Congress also approved Hill-Burton funds for construction of facilities owned by nonprofit entities. The writing was on the wall: medical technology would be advancing, people would be living longer, and the number of elderly patients needing long-term care would increase precipitously (Vladeck, 1980).

To fully appreciate the impact of Social Security legislation from the New Deal forward and, consequently, the funding that began to flow to proprietary long-term care corporations in the 1950s, one must take the devolution of power and responsibility from the federal government to the states into account. Traditionally, welfare was the responsibility of communities, counties, and other local entities of government. Although federal funding and minimal requirements for administration of OAA were innovative aspects of government involvement in welfare, considerable power and responsibility over the program was passed to the states. Therefore, the culture of each state would come to play a critical role in the welfare milieu and the posture of the bureaucracy toward recipients.[17]

In a country of the massive size and heterogeneity of the United States, localizing the administration of welfare medicine has led to a wide variety of approaches to and beliefs about applicants for assistance. For instance, Northeastern states and California have carried out welfare programs, federally funded in part, with a display of enlightenment and respect for applicants and recipients. Conversely, some states, especially Southern states where a large African American population resides, have taken great pains to stigmatize welfare and have attempted to frustrate applicants through draconian reductions in benefits and humiliating requirements.[18]

Matching funding and regulatory responsibilities passed to the states also laid the groundwork for the development of dispersed corporate nursing home power centers in each state. Although the for-profit and nonprofit nursing home trade associations (AHCA and LeadingAge, respectively) exert considerable weight within the Washington, DC, beltway, they are, through their state affiliates, effective in protecting operators from effective regulations in all 50 states. The point here is that the initial conditions for domination of long-term care and less than desirable conditions so widespread in the industry as it has evolved can be traced to what was certainly a pragmatic move on the part of the New Dealers to allow states to set standards and determine the philosophy underpinning treatment of the poor.

As suggested by recent scientific theory (Crossman, 2017), all stages of nonlinear, complex systems exhibit sensitive dependence on initial conditions. As systems, such as the nursing home system, develop through time, seemingly minor early-stage characteristics become increasingly potent and play an increasingly greater role in driving the overall system. Like the U.S. medical care system in general, the nursing home system began with small, charitable, or small-business entities for which federal funding was, for the most part, unavailable. Furthermore, federal control and regulation were practically nonexistent.

Initially, the federal government played a minor role, at best, in designing and regulating facilities and practices within them. Federal funds began to trickle through small federal matching programs to states to pass along to nursing home operators. Payment to vendors were allowed after a decade and a half of prohibition under New Deal cash assistance programs. A small stream of funding for real estate financing began to flow in the form of low-interest SBA and FHA loans. Hill-Burton funding was made available to nonprofits for facility construction.

Industry trade associations were in their initial stages in the 1950s. Wall Street, looking for return on investment, and corporations needing to expand were taking notice of possibilities likely to accompany an aging population, medical advancements, and the potential for an injection of public funds into care for the elderly.

If legislation of the 1950s served as the headwaters of federal funds flowing through state agencies to for-profit and nonprofit nursing homes, a major downstream project was engineered by two Southern legislators: U.S. Senator Robert Kerr of Oklahoma and Congressman Wilbur Mills of Arkansas. These gentlemen, who represented their Southern brethren in the House and Senate, would provide the infrastructure for turning the initial trickle into a raging river. The Medical Assistance for the Aged (MAA) program, otherwise known as "Kerr-Mills," set a framework in place for what would become Medicaid and the diverting of massive amounts of federal medical care funds into state-administered medicine for the poor—including the poor in nursing homes.

With vendor payments, spend downs, and a considerable amount of state control, LTC would mature into a marketized/financialized medical care system in which markets would continually become concentrated through mergers and acquisitions. Small businesses would struggle and disappear. Care of patients would be carried out by low-wage, unskilled labor. Patients would become commoditized and dehumanized.[19]

Over time, entrepreneurial-oriented businessmen and women with a bent toward exploiting government funding saw the possibilities for state-controlled long-term care with federal financing for construction and real estate. It could be said that the industry came to represent the type of faction James Madison warned about in *Federalist No. 10*. Given human nature, a powerful, self-serving industry could and should be expected most potently in states prone to bending to the will of corporate wealth and power.

The U.S. Supreme Court has clearly recognized the *Federalist Papers* as the fundamental authority regarding the intent of the framers (i.e., the Federalists).[20] A careful analysis of the writing of Jay, Madison, and Hamilton reveals a rather jaundiced view of the states. Indeed, these deep-thinking and brilliant men appeared to be warning against a federal system with a federal government too weak to dominate and control the states.[21] In the past few decades, their wisdom has become less and less salient in U.S. policy.

Unfortunately, contrary to the intentions of the framers of the Constitution to protect citizens from factions able to exert their will in opposition to the interests of the public, corporate and plutocratic wealth has, with the blessing of a conservative Supreme Court and the U.S. Congress, come to dominate public policy. The *Citizens United*[22] case opened the floodgates of vast wealth flowing into the political system on behalf of the wealthy elite.

Kerr-Mills: A Framework for Medicaid and the Future of U.S. Medicine

There is no doubt that powerful factions, interested mostly in perpetuating their privileged status, have captured a significant share of government and are bending it to their will. Publicly funded medicine has come to be dominated by wealthy industries wielding vast amounts of money for lobbying, payoffs, and campaign contributions. The roots of this medical-industrial complex are deeper than most people realize. And it did not come about simply because of *Citizens United*, the "Reagan Revolution," or the free-market frenzy and anti-government zeitgeist of the 1980s and 1990s.

Furthermore, it is widely believed that welfare medicine, including means-tested long-term care, in the United States as we know it began with the passage of Medicaid in 1965. That is far from correct. Arkansas Congressman Wilbur Mills, powerful chairman of the Ways and Means Committee, and Oklahoma

Senator Robert Kerr nurtured legislation providing for means-tested medical care for the elderly through Congress to passage in 1960. Most importantly, this legislation, Medical Assistance for the Aged (MMA, popularly known as Kerr-Mills), codified the elderly poor into a new category of U.S. resident: the "medically indigent."[23]

The medically indigent under Kerr-Mills were the elderly who were not poor enough to qualify for OAA but were too poor to afford necessary medical care. This expanded the concept of the deserving-poor-elderly somewhat. The determination of the "privilege" as a poor older person—but not simply as a human being—to receive medical assistance would still be made by welfare bureaucrats rather than medical professionals. Patients would still be required to prove that they should be granted the privilege of medical care through revealing their financial worth. In other words, it ingrained means-testing into U.S. medicine in a way that has become a hallmark of U.S. medical care.

Along with the medically indigent category as an innovation, Kerr-Mills expanded the right of proprietors to seek reimbursement for care with real estate costs such as depreciation and mortgage interest rolled in. The real intentions of Senator Kerr and Congressman Mills were to thwart efforts to pass federally funded and administered medical care for the elderly, which would be available to citizens as a "right" when they reached old age—however "old age" would be defined. Reading histories of long-term care, one might presume that Kerr-Mills failed badly and merely disappeared into medical history's dumpster because ultimately it was not a roadblock to Medicare. That would be an unjustified presumption. With the exception of Medicare[24] and the Veterans Administration, the law became the model for most government-provided medical care.

From the enactment of Medicaid through passage of the Affordable Care Act, a special category of poor persons for the purposes of eligibility to receive publicly funded medical care has been woven into the fabric of the U.S. medical care system. Throughout U.S. history, people too poor to pay for medical care have been assisted through charity—either by charitable physicians and nurses or in eleemosynary institutions. However, with Kerr-Mills, the "medically indigent" became a legal category that would come to define U.S. health care as unique in contradistinction to the health care programs of all other governments in the advanced industrial world.

The Kerr-Mills program was innovative and highly significant in the U.S. medical care system for reasons that must be appreciated by those who wonder how current government medical care policy came to be what it is currently:

1. Concepts of the "medically indigent," "welfare medicine," and "means-testing" were introduced into the development of federally funded medical care. These concepts would provide the framework for Medicaid.

2. Welfare departments and other nonmedical bureaucracies rather than medical personnel became the gatekeepers of access to the medical care system. Income, rather than medical need, became an important criterion in the determination of who would receive care.

3. Had the U.S. Congress and the Johnson administration rejected the Kerr-Mills framework as the basis for Medicaid, government-funded medical care would reflect the human rights tradition enveloped in the U.S. Constitution from the *Declaration of the Rights of Man and of the Citizen*, coauthored by Thomas Jefferson and passed by the French Assembly in 1789. Instead, Congressman Mills, as the chairman of the Ways and Means Committee and a powerful member of Congress, stood as a barrier to Medicare and insisted on inclusion of a welfare component for the poor, which reflected the Kerr-Mills philosophy. In the United States, medical care is not treated as a public good, made available in accordance with the "general welfare clause" of the Constitution, such as is the case with emergency services in disasters, police and fire protection, and elementary and secondary education. There is no equal right to reasonable, customary, and medically necessary medical services.
4. The primary responsibility of the new category of the "medically indigent" was devolved to the states. Within flexible federal guidelines, eligibility determination, regulation, and levels of support were passed to the 50 different governmental entities. By burdening states with a large share of the funding, the quality of care would be allowed to vary from state to state, as would the treatment of those deemed eligible or ineligible for medical services.

The significance of Kerr-Mills is not that it appears to have failed because most states provided only tepid to absolutely no funds to support it; rather, its significance is in the innovations included in the legislation. The basic framework for means-tested welfare medicine was introduced into the American medical care system by the law. The importance of the concept of the "medically indigent" cannot be overestimated.

Proof of one's poverty is not just a qualifying feature of much of the government-funded medical care. Rather, it reflects a philosophy of human merit in the medical care system. The affluent and the fortunate are accorded dignity and respect while the poor and unfortunate can be denied treatment, or, at the very least, suffer degradation at the hands of welfare bureaucrats who typically have no medical training or credentials.

Contrary to medical ethics, international law, and basic human decency, the poor can be denied healing services and technology—necessary for alleviating suffering or saving lives—as punishment for not sufficiently proving worthiness to a nonmedical bureaucrat. For instance, not proving to state officials that one is not energetically pursuing work or failure to prove that one is not violating some other middle-class moral standard can be grounds for denial of medical care. The glaring irrationality—even insanity—of such a medical system in the wealthiest, most highly developed country on the planet becomes even more apparent when one considers that even the most hardened, incorrigible, and dangerous incarcerated criminals receive medical care as a right.

The traditional deserving poor, frail elderly and disabled patients, are not denied LTC. However, the quality of that care depends upon race and class. Impoverished elderly and disabled patients needing LTC are welfare patients and as such are typically placed in a lower tier of medical care. Nursing homes taking Medicaid patients are visibly of less quality. Not only do LTC patients suffer the indignity of care in a total institutional setting, but also they are required to assume membership in the "medically indigent" category.

If the value of patients' assets exceeds the level for qualification as "medically indigent," they are forced to "spend down"—liquidate their assets to pay the nursing home corporation—until they are sufficiently impoverished. Investors in the nursing home business are recipients of what would be passed to their children or other heirs. An even more despicable facet of the spend-down process is the passage from self-sufficient human being to dependent welfare recipient.

The state and local tax codes supporting state revenue funding for LTC for the medically indigent are tilted in favor of the wealthiest citizens. The burden of sales and property taxes falls heaviest on the poor. Over the past few decades, corporate and income taxes have been reduced and replaced with sales taxes at the state level. Some states, such as Texas, have no income taxes whatsoever. In a large number of states, taxes have been eliminated for "pass-through" income, which is income accruing to an LLC. Hence, some very wealthy people incorporate themselves as LLCs and escape responsibility for their fair share of taxes. So, while states burden the poor with a disproportionate share of government funding, they force them into the degrading category of medically indigent.

Shameful classifications placed on citizens have an origin and a purpose. Vladeck, in his excellent history of the nursing home system to the 1980s, summarized the impact of legislation of the 1950s and Kerr-Mills on welfare medicine, and a long-term care industry:

> By the time Medicare was enacted in 1965, ... public funds *under a welfare program* were paying a large, and rapidly increasing, share of the costs of a rapidly expanding nursing home industry, especially in those few states with the largest vendor-payment programs—and the largest number of nursing homes. In the debates over the new legislation, almost no attention was paid to this phenomenon. Instead, in 1965, the welfare-based nursing home system was incorporated, willy-nilly, into new programs designed to finance health services. They didn't fit comfortably then and still don't. (Vladeck, 1980, p. 48)

With President Kennedy's push to pass legislation providing medical care for the elderly, he was positioning the federal government to enter medical care in a large way. Proposals offered by more liberal Democrats included an adjustment to the Social Security payroll tax for the purpose of funding hospitalization. Consequently, the proposed legislation would be a quasi-universal—all 65+ who earned benefits through working a sufficient number of quarters would qualify for hospital benefits as a "right." Furthermore, by connecting it to Social Security through the payroll tax, control over and administration of the program would occur at the federal level without devolution of either funding or administrative responsibility to the states.

Americans are conditioned to abhor welfare of any type—including welfare medicine. "Being on the dole" is subject to denigration and avoided by most of the public at all costs. Historically, a large share of U.S. politicians and government administrators of welfare programs have had a propensity to view themselves as guardians of the public purse and believe their role was to erect barriers to qualification and, consequently, to benefits. Their attempts at frustrating and blocking applicants are humiliating and dehumanizing and have no place in ethical medical care. Indeed, Kerr-Mills included draconian and cruel features in its means tests.

Not only were applicants forced to prove they were sufficiently poor for assistance under Kerr-Mills, but they were also required to submit a list of all close relatives, such as children, who would also be liable for liens on their property (U.S. Senate, Subcommittee on Health of the Elderly, 1963). Although this draconian measure of involving one's relative in one's means-tested welfare is no longer part of welfare medicine, the humiliation of applicants for Medicaid has been a common feature of state-controlled Medicaid programs throughout the decades. As a Senate committee noted in 1963:

Stringent eligibility tests, "lien type" recovery provisions, and responsible relative provisions have severely limited participation in those jurisdictions where the program is in operation. In July of 1963, only 148,000 people received MAA—or less than 1 percent of the Nation's older citizens. (U.S. Senate, Subcommittee on Health of the Elderly, 1963, p. 1)

The impoverishment of citizens as a means to qualify them for needed medical services is a unique U.S. phenomenon. No doubt, the provision requiring the exposure of relatives' assets reveals the distrust and disrespect necessarily accompanying a medical care program in which patients must prove they belong to the correct demographic category, and are worthy, honest, and poor enough to deserve medical care.

Although initial legislation provided for matching funds to voluntary state programs for aiding the poor elderly in obtaining medical care, states were reluctant to take advantage of it. Whatever the level that state funding would reach was at the discretion of the states. Most either funded an insignificant amount or none at all (Olson, 2003). Nevertheless, hospitalization, physician services, and drugs benefits for the elderly were eventually covered by a payroll-funded Medicare program.[25] These benefits included extended care for a specific number of days following hospitalization, but patients needing long-term stays in a skilled nursing facility must either pay for it out of pocket or qualify for Medicaid.

When Medicare passed, it was intended to be a program only for the elderly. Nevertheless, in the lead-up to its passage, Southern Democrats knew that it would be a giant step toward a single-payer, universal health care system as a right for all U.S. citizens. They were well aware of the clamor among Democrats for including ever younger age groups in the years ahead. Lyndon Johnson needed the powerful Wilbur Mills to help move his Medicare legislation through Congress. Mills helped him but convinced Johnson to include a welfare component, which would include long-term care. Although Mills is given considerable credit for the passage of Medicare and Medicaid, his accomplishment was not so much in enacting government-provided medical care to the elderly and the poor. Rather, in what he called his "three-layer cake," he was able to erect barriers to any future attempts by Congress to enact a federally administered, single-payer medical care program to which all U.S. residents would have access as a right (Blumenthal & Morone, 2009).

The Southern Democrats and their allies among the AMA and Northern Republicans moved to forestall federally administered medical care for the poor —including nursing home care. They had been successful in maneuvering legislation through Congress that provided matching funds to states for long-term care. Allowance of vendor payments directly to nursing home operators had become an established feature of welfare medicine and a huge deal.

Welfare medicine is an entrenched part of the U.S. medical care system and will not easily be transformed into a "medicine as a right" program. The federal portion of Medicaid expenditures alone has grown to hundreds of billions of dollars.[26] Powerful constituencies have evolved with an interest in keeping control over management of the program at the state level. Liberal advocacy groups have developed and are now lobbying to expand it under Obamacare. It will still be means tested and will still be welfare medicine.

Industrialization

The nursing home industry developed after 1965 in a rapidly shifting economic environment. Innovations in global shipping provided a path to low-wage labor markets in Asia and other parts of the world. Manufacturing was transferred from U.S. factories to plants in undeveloped countries. With decline in investment in plant and equipment in the United States, the commercial real estate industry looked to other opportunities for return on investors' capital.

The vendor payment system arising incrementally from Social Security Act amendments and other developments during the 1950s and early 1960s was well established by passage of Medicaid. Because reimbursements were designed for owners of real estate as well as for providers of the care taking place in their properties, an enormous opportunity for investment of surplus capital was opened. U.-S. monetary and fiscal policy beginning in the Nixon administration had resulted in an excess capacity and liquidity problem; therefore, capital flows increased at a high rate, and speculative investments were vigorously pursued by the financial services industry (Wall Street and Finance, Insurance, and Real Estate [FIRE]).

Furthermore, corporations looking to expand moved into the burgeoning medical care system, of which hospitals and nursing homes were part. For instance, the Holiday Inn Corporation and a few other enterprises from the hospitality industry, seeking to enhance revenues, attempted to enter the nursing home business. Those types of enterprises did not last long in the business of caring for frail, dependent elderly and other disabled patients.

Nevertheless, the real estate industry and investors in general saw potential return on investment (ROI) and gave little to no thought to a philosophy of caring for patients with severe disabilities and geriatric-related issues—including Alzheimer's disease and dementia. Vendor payments—reimbursements—for service included initially, and still includes to this day, mortgage interest and depreciation on property in addition to the costs of caring daily for some of the most fragile and dependent patients in the medical care system.

It was readily apparent to investors that a guaranteed stream of revenue would be available from Medicare and Medicaid funds and that these funds were likely to be available in perpetuity and grow over time. The elderly population was predicted to grow precipitously from 10 percent of the population in the early 1970s to 21 percent by 2030. Because Americans could be expected to approach their natural life span of 85 years (on average) by the time the last "baby boomer" retires, the 65+ population was slated to reach between 75 and 80 million.

What the industry has never recognized and has not been forced to recognize is the optimum needs of the types of patients treated in nursing homes. The needs of patients were never really seriously considered in the design of Medicaid. Long-term care for a rapidly increasing number of frail elderly in what was traditionally thought of as "convalescent homes" was included in Medicaid as an afterthought without much theorizing about humane and medically appropriate design (Vladeck, 1980). In the best of possible worlds, a nursing home system, owned and operated by the government or nonprofit institutions, and based on a well-thought-out gerontological view of the elderly, would have been incorporated into Medicaid. That was not to be the case.

The foresight of experts in aging and disabilities would have most certainly led to a system driven less by the needs of a real estate, for-profit industry and more by the needs of patients. There would have been far fewer inmates of what are generally undesirable long-term care facilities, and patients would have been served longer in their own homes at much less than the cost of institutionalization. Without the discussion that should have taken place, the nursing home system muddled forward through the next decades following enactment of Medicaid with a sub-rosa belief among physicians, politicians, and the public in general that the nursing home was a place to go to die. The growth of the industry was driven more by capital markets than ethically appropriate medical care.

The failure in the design and subsequent implementation with the needs of industry rather than patients as the highest priority was unfortunate. The 1970s and 1980s, when capitalism was shifting rapidly from a manufacturing domination to a financial services sector, was a time of the "perfect storm" for elderly Americans. The 65+ population was growing rapidly due to better medicine and medical care while at the same time the usefulness of the elderly, as a zeitgeist, practically disappeared. Excess people with no perceived contribution to the survival of a society became a problem—a burden, so to speak. A large number of 55+ people were pushed out of the labor market. Younger workers are less of a burden on labor costs.

Furthermore, unneeded subpopulations in a capitalist-dominated society are vulnerable to abuse and exploitation. Throughout most of the history of Western civilization and in most cultures of the world, the elderly have been viewed as important and useful leaders and guides to the management of families, communities, and nations. But by 1950, a mature, highly technological, capitalistic system dominated American culture. The economy had reached a stage in which the need for the elderly was greatly diminished.

As the elderly employees lost their utility in the economic system, striving for an ever-greater standard of living became the goal of families. Moving "up" to a better neighborhood, "keeping up with the Joneses," and buying all those consumer products that suggested economic success replaced mere survival of the family, for which grandparents had historically been crucial support. With a need to invest a growing amount of excess capital, banks began to issue amounts of consumer credit unforeseen in the economic system. Taking advantage of credit and taking on large amounts of debt (increasing faster than wages) required two incomes—that is, dad's and mom's. Furthermore, the expectation that children would "do better" than their parents became a central cultural value. Parents, especially those experiencing the devastating impact of the Great Depression, wanted their children to have what they didn't have; to not experience the grinding and horrifying poverty they experienced; and to move to a higher economic station in life.

Children were not necessary for survival of the family as they had been traditionally, nor were grandma and granddad. As the elderly were shunted aside, children were doted on and finding increasing opportunities for extracurricular activities. They had goals to go to college, and looked to achieve a higher standard of living than their mom and dad. In the middle class, it was all about them. American families were on the go and had no time to care for aging parents who were living longer, and suffering an increasing number of chronic illnesses. A larger proportion of the U.S. population was becoming increasingly dependent on others for daily care. A proliferation of long-term care facilities occurred in the 1970s and provided a convenient place for parents needing assistance with daily living and medical care.

The care was far too often scandalously bad, and the owners and operators had little interest in cutting-edge gerontology. The elderly and disabled were seen more as commodities than patients with specific needs. In 1974, nearly a decade after passage of Medicaid, the Subcommittee on Long-Term Care of the Senate Special Committee on Aging began a report on federally funded long-term care with the statement that "federal support of long-term care for the elderly has, within a decade, climbed from millions to billions of dollars." The question posed by the committee was, "What is the nation receiving for this money?" The conclusion was that the nation had received a failed program for older Americans. The authors declared the following:

> Today's entire population of the elderly, *and their offspring* [italics in the report], suffer severe emotional damage because of dread and despair associated with nursing home care in the United States today.

This policy, or lack thereof, may not be solely responsible for producing such anxiety. Deep-rooted attitudes toward aging and death also play major roles.

But the actions of Congress and of States, as expressed through the Medicare and Medicaid programs, have in many ways intensified old problems and have created new ones.

Efforts have been made to deal with the most severe of those problems. Laws have been passed; national commitments have been made; declarations of high purpose have been uttered at national conferences and by representatives of the nursing home industry.

But for all of that, long-term care for older Americans stands today as the most troubled, and troublesome, components of our entire health care system. (U.S. Senate, Special Committee on Aging, Subcommittee on Long-Term Care, 1974, p. III)

The report proceeded to decry the increasingly costly nature of long-term care paid for with public funds and warned that the number of long-term care beds had exceeded the number of hospital beds but would continue to grow as the U.S. elderly population grew. The committee reported that "nursing home care is associated with scandal and abuse," and had "grown very rapidly in just a few decades—and most markedly since 1965, when Medicare and Medicaid were enacted" (U.S. Senate, Special Committee on Aging, Subcommittee on Long-Term Care, 1974, p. III).

One surmises from the text of the preface to the Subcommittee Report that a considerable amount of public outrage had been visited on Congress because of the appalling state of care received in proprietary nursing homes into which a large amount of public funds was channeled.

The Apotheosis of Industrialization

The nursing home industry is a subsystem of a larger medical system (the "medical-industrial complex").[27] In addition to facilities owned by a variety of corporations, the system includes medical professionals, wage labor, social work, ancillary services, federal and state regulations, public attitudes, and patients. More importantly, the business subsystem developed within a historical context—a much longer history than is conventionally considered in nursing home histories.

As suggested above, that context includes a culture that had been centuries in development. The constellation of thousands of nursing homes, the design of these of brick-and-mortar facilities, the patients within, and all other aspects of day-to-day activities of skilled nursing care reflect the same history as all other means-tested welfare, such as Temporary Aid to Needy Families (TANF), Supplemental Nutrition Assistance Program (SNAP or food stamps), or Section 8 Housing Assistance.

Most nursing home care is funded by Medicaid—as welfare medicine—and Medicaid is stigmatized as a handout to people who either cannot take care of themselves or have not been responsible citizens and thereby made themselves a burden to the rest of society. Poverty has always been stigmatized in U.S. history.

The contemporary nursing home system has carried forward a weltanschauung that has characterized much of American society and culture since the North American continent was settled by religious refugees from Europe and the first slave ship dropped anchor off the coast of Virginia. This worldview includes several themes that characterize welfare programs to this very day. First, the poor are often dichotomized into the deserving and undeserving—not equally, since undeserving is most likely the characterization.

Second, minimal care as opposed to appropriate and adequate care of impoverished individuals suggests Christian duty to lesser types. Third, a potent belief in the idea that individuals are responsible for their own survival and cooperative, governmental efforts at amelioration of poverty are denigrated in defense of individualism. And, finally, social Darwinism, predestination, and biological determinism have been combined with 400 years of the most brutalizing slavery, apartheid (Jim Crow), and institutionalized bigotry and racism.

The association of welfare with human inferiority based on race and class cannot be ignored in writing the history of what is now often merely referred to as "the nursing home industry." Welfare medicine, like any tangible item or service provided as welfare, is treated as inferior to medicine provided through one's work, earned through a payroll tax, or purchased in some manner by those who have the resources to purchase it.

Juxtaposed to the deeply ingrained myths about race and class are fantasies about the virtues of American treatment of the "needy" and the "less fortunate." Americans like to think of themselves as good to the "downtrodden." In a sort of Manichean philosophical and political ideal, it is widely believed that something is religiously virtuous about charitable work, whereas harnessing the capabilities of government is inherently undesirable. However, when it comes to people with black skin, Christian "do-goodism" has historically placed them below the level of deserving, no matter what their circumstances happen to be.

As was the case with the almshouse system, in which the federal government was only a bystander, state and local governments play a dominant role in nursing home licensing and regulation. The federal government does match state funding and has, from time to time, enacted some significant reforms, but power over the industry is divided among 50 states and a powerful industry. And as will be discussed in more detail below, business entities in the nursing home business have become increasingly effective at influencing government at the state and federal level. Furthermore, the nursing home market is becoming increasingly concentrated.

No doubt, the industry developed through a series of phases after the almshouse system ended. Boarding houses paid for their services directly by residents began with New Deal programs providing cash assistance to the elderly. A major boost to industrialization came with legislative approval of vendor payments to proprietors. The Kerr-Mills program solidified state and local control over welfare medicine and, finally, passage of Medicaid.

If the efficient market hypothesis, that is, that a competitive market will determine which corporations will have the best outcomes, is the summum bonum, then it follows that profitability, shareholder value, and corporate growth are measures of success (the most bang for the buck for taxpayers and the greatest return on investment for investors). Conversely, if the most compassionate and humanistic care possible is the summum bonum, it follows that profitability, shareholder values, and corporate growth will be incompatible with the ends toward which operations are directed. Indeed, it is a well-established economic principle of capitalism that a manager's duty is first and foremost to shareholders. Therefore, it is a truism that care is worse when quality of care is traded for return to shareholders.[28]

Therefore, when it came to institutionalizing the poor for the purposes of providing long-term care, institutions were designed for instrumentalism rather than humanism. Control, effectiveness, and efficiency of business organizations were copied by proprietary and charitable institutions alike. The best long-term inpatient situation possible had to be sacrificed for the sake of profitability.

Basic human needs for privacy, independence, autonomy in setting routines, and other facets of living life outside of a regimented institution are eliminated in the life of people placed in a nursing home. The environment of typical long-term care facilities is suited for the capitalistic, profit-seeking nature of the corporations operating and owning them.

As profit-making, capitalistic enterprises operating in a competitive market, long-term care facilities operate on the principles of economy and efficiency—the least amount of input with the greatest amount of output. Rather than care for patients needing extensive care, they process people at the lowest possible cost. Hence, their modus operandi is to employ as much low-wage, low-skilled labor as they can get by with in caring for highly fragile and vulnerable patients.

The design of facilities and the operating processes are designed around a production modus operandi and a modus vivendi of uniformity and control. But the standard structures and functions of the contemporary nursing home were in place long before the takeoff growth of the industry with the passage of Medicaid. The treatment of inmates in mental hospitals, prisons, and almshouses was indicative of the total institution.

Renowned sociologist Erving Goffman, in his classic work *Asylums: Essays on the Social Situation of Mental Patients and Other Inmates*, defined a total institution "as a place of residence and work where a large number of like-situated individuals, cut off from the wider society for an appreciable period of time, together lead an enclosed, formally administered round of life (1961, p. xiii).

The total institution, as Goffman, describes it, is characterized by separation from the community in which one's sense of self is nurtured. Isolation, segregation, and loss of connection to family, friends, routines, creature comforts, pets, the food one likes, entertainment, and so many aspects of one's life space are suddenly introduced upon admission to a skilled nursing facility. The private space so cherished by most people is suddenly gone. One finds oneself sharing a room with a stranger (Goffman, 1961, pp. 4–13).

Every patient enters a long-term, skilled nursing facility with a presenting culture and a self, developed out of an infinite number of life experiences and years of living. In a world presenting opportunities for joy, pleasantries, and little escapes from drudgery, insults, and threats, the self (the mind's self) discovers and invents means for taking advantage of the things making life worth living. Those are left behind as one becomes a "resident" in the typical skilled nursing facility.

> The recruit comes into the establishment with a conception of himself made possible by certain stable social arrangements in his home world. Upon entrance, he is immediately stripped of the support provided by these arrangements. In the accurate language of some of our oldest total institutions, he begins a series of abasements, degradations, humiliations, and profanations of the self. His self is systematically, if often unintentionally, mortified. He begins radical shifts in his *moral career*, a career composed of the progressive changes that occur in the beliefs that he has concerning himself and significant others. (Goffman, 1961, p. 14)

The organizational roles and processes of a nursing home are conducive to the economies and efficiencies typical of the instrumental rationality required of profit-seeking entities. Goffman describes the following characteristics in the functioning of the total institution. All aspects of life are conducted in the same place and under a single authority, with determination of privacy and independence a prerogative of administrators.

Each patient's daily activities are often carried on "in the immediate company" of a large batch of other patients. As much as possible, all patients "are treated alike."

Schedules are arranged by staff with a set of actions at preset times over which the patient has little control. These schedules and daily activities are generally arranged to meet the needs of management and not the needs of patients (Goffman, 1961, p. 6).

It is unfortunate that the psychological trauma of stripping individuals of their dignity and humanity for the sake of economy and efficiency has not been a larger focus of scholarship among gerontologists and others with an interest in elderly issues in today's world of changing demographics—especially the demographics of the elderly. Economists and other social scientists collecting data and producing models in which a few independent variables impact outcomes within the system as it is are missing the point of how minor shifts in organizational behavior fail to impact the underlying structure of the system. This type of research unwittingly reinforces a system that cannot be reformed.

As an example of what scholars generally miss in their research, Goffman explained how the enduring aspects of the total institution damage the psyches of inmates:

> When people are moved in blocks, they can be supervised by personnel whose chief activity is not guidance or periodic inspection (as in many

employer-employee relations) but rather **surveillance—a seeing to it that everyone does what he has been clearly told is required of him, under conditions where one person's infraction is likely to stand out in relief against the visible, constantly examined compliance of the others.** Which comes first, the large blocks of managed people, or the small supervisory staff, is not here at issue; the point is that each is made for the other.

In total institutions there is a basic split between a large managed group, conveniently called inmates, and a small supervisory staff. Inmates typically live in the institution and have restricted contact with the world outside the walls; staff often operate on an eight-hour day and are socially integrated into the outside world. Each grouping tends to conceive of the other in terms of narrow hostile stereotypes, staff often seeing inmates as bitter, secretive, and untrustworthy, while inmates often see staff as condescending, highhanded, and mean. Staff tends to feel superior and righteous; inmates tend, in some ways at least, to feel inferior, weak, blameworthy, and guilty.

Social mobility between the two strata is grossly restricted; social distance is typically great and often formally prescribed. Even talk across boundaries may be conducted in a special tone of voice, as illustrated in a fictionalized record of an actual sojourn in a mental hospital.

Just as talk across the boundary is restricted, so, too, is the passage of information, especially information about the staff's plans for inmates. Characteristically, the inmate is excluded from knowledge of the decisions taken regarding his fate. Whether the official grounds are military, as in concealing travel destination from enlisted men, or medical, as in concealing diagnosis, plan of treatment, and approximate length of stay from tuberculosis patients, such exclusion gives staff a special basis of distance from and control over inmates. (Goffman, 1961, pp. 9–14)

The Industry Today

The processes of care in skilled nursing facilities reflect the total institution and welfare medicine values that had been set in place by 1965 and incorporated into Medicaid-funded nursing home care. The cultural facets of welfare from the time of initial settlement of the North American continent by religiously persecuted Europeans and the beginning of slavery were combined with state control and privatization of services as the post-1965 phase commenced. The total institution as explained by Goffman had emerged from early American alms-houses, prisons, and mental institutions. In 2018, the typical nursing home still operates on the same principles he described in his classic 1950s study.

Over the following decades, industry operations have been a reflection of what had gone on before, but its financial and business practices evolved in sync with U.S. and global macro-economic trends. Globalization normalized stagnant and low wages. The nursing home industry benefited greatly from a massive, low-wage pool conducive to keeping costs low and profits high as corporations sought greater economies and efficiencies in a chase for return on investment.

Government deregulation and radical, neoliberal economics have weakened government and increased the power of the finance, insurance, and real estate segment of the U.S. economy. As manufacturing and the production of tangible goods have been moved to cheap labor markets, speculative finance has become the major economic activity in advanced economies. The nursing home industry is increasingly characterized by this trend.

Nine of the top 10 for-profit nursing home chains have been taken over by private equity (PE) firms (United States Government Accountability Office [GAO], 2010). For instance, the Carlyle Group purchased the closely held nursing home chain HCR ManorCare—operator of the second largest chain of skilled nursing facilities. PE firms take over companies through leveraged buyouts (LBOs), which means that they use a small amount of their own capital and saddle companies they take over with a large amount of debt. It is not uncommon for the PE firms to drain purchased firms of resources and place them in a precarious financial position.

PE firms are known for reorganizing the companies they take over. The goal of reorganization is to cut costs and increase profits. Because skilled nursing care is labor intensive, cost cutting is directed primarily toward higher-skilled and higher-cost labor. Analysis of staffing and deficiencies indicates a significantly lower level of staffing and a higher level of deficiencies. Indeed, the metrics pertaining to quality of care suggest that economies of scale do not lead to better care. But it does lead to more financialization.

In addition to PE firms, buying and selling corporations operating skilled nursing facilities as a speculative activity, real estate investment trusts (REITs) moved strongly into the business of buying real estate undergirding the operation, that is, the buildings known as nursing homes. REITs have many advantages for investors seeking a high return on their investment or a tax shelter. Returns of 18–25 percent are not uncommon for REITs, which is much better than fixed income investments. Furthermore, the real estate industry in general and REITs in particular are advantaged more than any other industry by U.S. tax codes.

As the industry matured and large chains began to emerge, a real estate segment emerged with them. Some chains sold their properties to large real estate firms such as Welltower or to REITs and leased them back for their operations. Some chains set up their own LLCs to which the properties were transferred and then leased back by them.

It would be too simplistic, however, to say that the industry is comprised of an operating segment and a real estate segment. The industry has been intentionally structured for opaqueness. A single facility in a small town in a rural state could involve four or five LLCs without a clear indication of the responsible owner when a lawsuit might brought by a patient or the patient's family when abuse and neglect occurs in a facility.

So, if a nursing home operator in a small Kansas community is operated by one LLC with a headquarters listed in the state of Maryland, which is owned by another LLC, which is owned by another LLC owned by an REIT in Chicago, it would be difficult for a lawyer for a party harmed by the operation to identify the responsible party.

A realistic view of the nursing home industry is this: it is impossible to fully understand it because so much of the financial and ownership information has been skillfully hidden from the public and regulators. The opaque nature of the nursing home industry was the subject of a United States Government Accountability Office study completed in 2010. Utilizing data in the "Provider Enrollment, Chain, & Ownership System" (PECOS), the GAO examined the role of private investment (PI; or private equity) firms in the nursing home industry and determined the following:

1. A total of 1,876 unique nursing homes were acquired by PI firms from 1998 through 2008.
2. While some of the acquisitions involved entire nursing home chains, which included operations and any owned real estate, other acquisitions involved only real estate.
3. Sometimes the same nursing homes were acquired more than once.
4. Ten PI firms accounted for 89 percent of the 1,876 unique nursing homes acquired by PI firms during this period.
5. Of the six PI firms from which data were acquired, firms buying both operations and real estate reported being more involved in operations than firms buying only the real estate. These firms had representatives on the nursing home chain's board of directors, but they generally characterized their involvement as related to the chain's strategic direction rather than day-to-day operations.
6. PI firms that acquired real estate only had no representatives on the boards of the operating companies, but officials at one PI firm observed that some leasing arrangements have the potential to affect operations.
7. PECOS provided a confusing picture of the complex ownership structures and chain affiliations of the six PI-owned nursing home chains the GAO reviewed. The database did not provide any indication of the hierarchy or relationships among the numerous organizational owners listed for PI-owned nursing homes.
8. PI ownership was often not readily apparent in the data, which could be the result of (1) PI firms' not being required to be reported because of how they structured their acquisitions, (2) provider confusion about the reporting requirements, or (3) related entities that were reported but were not easily identifiable with the PI firms.
9. PECOS chain information was not straightforward and was sometimes incomplete, making it difficult to link all the homes in a chain.

10. Compounding these shortcomings, CMS's ability to determine the accuracy and completeness of the reported ownership data is limited.
11. HHS has made limited use of PECOS ownership data. The only CMS division with routine access to PECOS data has been largely focused on populating the database and has not developed any standardized reports on nursing home ownership that it could share with interested parties.
12. Some states collect their own ownership information, but it can be limited to owners that operate in their state. As a result, tracking compliance problems among commonly owned homes or multistate chains can be ad hoc.
13. State officials and others expressed interest in nationwide ownership data, such as PECOS, to improve nursing home oversight.
14. Recognizing the growing interest in PECOS data, CMS has established a workgroup to consider how to accommodate the PECOS interests of other groups within the agency and is considering whether and how to provide access to external parties such as states.
15. The implementation of the Patient Protection and Affordable Care Act provides CMS with an opportunity to address shortcomings in the current PECOS database and to make ownership information available to states and consumers in a more intelligible way.

The GAO recommended that CMS and HHS require owners to make their ownership structures transparent. If ownership of nursing home corporations is undiscernible, the public, political representatives, and scholars cannot undertake activities that protect patients.

The formation of oligopolies is a natural phenomenon in capitalistic industries. The nursing home industry is no exception to this rule of free markets. It must be said, however, that the nursing home industry has been fueled to an overwhelming degree by taxpayer funding through welfare medicine. Much of the capital funneled into the industry is from U.S. taxpayers. The big players are accumulating billions in assets and billions in revenue gratis the government.

Small operators are typically not capitalized sufficiently to compete with Wall Street–backed PE firms and major real estate corporations. Mergers and acquisitions (M&A) have become commonplace as the natural market forces of capitalism move the bigger companies to swallow up smaller companies or merge with entities providing an advantage in their quest for growth and market domination.

This normal capitalistic modus operandi is not confined to the so-called private corporations. The 501(c)(3), nonprofit, Evangelical Lutheran Good Samaritan (ELGSS) system is the seventh largest chain in number of facilities and eleventh in number of beds,[29] has reported a billion in revenues, and operates as much as a 501(c)(3) can operate like a for-profit entity. The auditor's report in 2015 was revealing in that it recommended strengthening M&A capability by adding staff with a background in this area of finance. Apparently, ELGSS had been on an M&A growth pattern but had handled the transactions incompetently due to a lack of expertise in that realm of finance.

It is also interesting to note how a faith-based organization emerging out of religious good works during the Great Depression has grown into a major profit-seeking corporation that has little to do with charity. The ELGSS operates 14 nursing homes in the state of Kansas. It would appear, based on inspection data, that their facilities range from very bad to very good with an average, however, below the state overall. Out of the 344 licensed facilities in Kansas in 2017, one of the most notoriously bad facilities was operated by the ELGSS—it ranked in the top two in deficiencies. An incident occurred in the facility that calls into question the organization's capability to treat and care for patients with Alzheimer's disease. The behavior of a patient with the disease was too difficult for the staff in the facility at the time, and the police were called. The police, no more capable of dealing with Alzheimer's disease than the nursing home staff, used a Taser gun to subdue the elderly man.

As hard as it is to believe, the incident was widely reported in the press and immediately became a horrifying legend that will most certainly live on in the nursing home lore of Kansas. The question is, "what should we make of this treatment in a nursing home of all places?" This was not the only severe case of abuse and neglect occurring in an ELGSS facility.

Although the current nursing home system has it roots in a history of genuine care for the poor, Christian morality inherent in the earliest stages of serving the impoverished elderly was lost as privatization and financialization grew to permeate all aspects of the industry. One fourth of the companies currently operating nursing homes are classified as nonprofit. Practically all of the nonprofits are classified as faith-based, which means they are owned and/or operated by Christian-affiliated organizations such the Evangelical Lutheran, Presbyterian, and Catholic long-term care facilities.

The ELGSS Lutheran experience is mirrored by the Catholic, Presbyterian, and other religiously affiliated LTC chains. The faith-based operators and owners have exchanged their religious faith for faith in the market, which became exceedingly popular in American culture during the 1980s.

Contemporary nursing home enterprises have incorporated the underlying characteristics of America's attitude toward and treatment of the poor. In addition to the total institution design of facilities and processes, nursing home care is based on what can be minimally dispensed to the deserving poor. The Eden Alternative and the Greenhouse models would require expenditures that profit-making entities would not be willing to make. They would not see it in their financial interests to provide the kind of humanizing care indicative of these more humane and civilized models.

One might think that the perception that welfare is bad because it goes to black people is an anachronism that has been left in the dust bin of history. Or that contempt for government carried out at the federal level lessened as the South began to reflect some of the more liberal attitudes of the North in metropolises such as Atlanta and in high-tech corridors around Winston-Salem, North Carolina. But it was in the not too distant past that President Reagan denigrated government ("government doesn't solve problems—it is the problem") and overtly expressed racist attitudes toward welfare recipients by describing them as "welfare queens driving their Cadillacs to the welfare office," or as "big black bucks getting food stamps to buy steak."

The Reagan administration's attack on government and poor people was continued by the so-called "New Democrats" and organizations ancillary to the Democratic Party, such as the Democratic Leadership Council and the Third Way. Under President Clinton, scapegoating of the poor, the elderly, and African Americans was coded as "triangulation," which could justifiably be interpreted as a compromise with the same reactionary forces that had historically abused and denigrated the poor—and abused and denigrated African Americans in one of the most brutal slavery/apartheid systems in the known history of the human species. He declared that "the era of big government is over," worked to reduce welfare assistance to poor families with children, and led the way to a draconian criminal justice system that has devastated a large part of the African American community.

The anti-government, racist, classist views of the 1980s and 1990s grew in tandem with a radical, laissez-faire, so-called free market craze. Widespread in the population of the United States as it entered the twenty-first century, were some of the traditional attitudes toward race, class, and poverty that have existed since the initial settlement of the North American continent. Although complexified and updated somewhat, these attitudes are characterized by the view that the poor are inferior to the affluent and that African American poor are lazy, dependent, and largely responsible for welfare expenditures.

There is nothing consistent in the outlook regarding welfare as a bad thing. Some whites think that welfare medicine is a diversion of their hard-earned money through taxes to the lazy poor. However, most of the same people believing this are facing the prospect of nursing home care that will require them to "spend down" all of their assets until they reach penury and qualify for Medicaid.

Conclusion

How one views barriers to implementation of Medicaid-funded long-term care depends upon how one's interests are served by the program. Patients and their advocates do not generally think the implementation as it has proceeded over the past half century has been very beneficial to them. The outcomes they expect pertain to quality of life and quality of care—however, those can be clearly delineated and measured.

Unfortunately, existence in a total institution is dehumanizing and undermining to the sense of self that is so necessary for mentally healthy living. The naturalness of life in a community, among family and friends, in one's life space of daily pleasures such as entertainment, favored foods, private places for meditation and security, pets, and other aspects of day-to-day life are all eliminated when one enters the total institution. What this means is that a nursing home system organized on such principles cannot be reformed or tweaked to make quality of life remotely meaningful in its facilities.

Activities aimed at reducing cases of abuse and neglect throughout the system keep advocates immersed in ongoing fights in state and federal legislatures and regulatory agencies. These fights are costly in terms of personal energy and whatever funding nonprofit groups can raise to counter lobbyists funded by trade associations with millions to spend on furthering their interests. More importantly, engaging the industry on the grounds that nursing homes can be improved reinforces a tacit assumption that the system that is, is the only system that can be.

Indeed, the Panglossian view that "this is the best there is in the best of all possible worlds" has led to a widespread public view that it is normal to be condemned to the misery of the dreaded nursing home when frailty leads to such a loss of independence that the family—if a family is available—can no longer provide assistance in daily living to a frail elderly loved one.

Like a fish must certainly take water for granted, humans tend to take systems that have grown up around them as normal and natural. "It is what it is." "Whata ya gona do?" These pessimistic attitudes have been reinforced by a potent stream of macro-economic propaganda coming from reactionary political forces—adopted eventually by more moderate Democrats. The economics of conservatives would have one believe that "the market knows best," "leave it to the market, and keep the government out of it." They claim that government spending on the poor is counter to good economic policy and poor fiscal policy.

Lack of knowledge about economic and budgetary principles on the part of the public has served corporations now profiting from taxpayer dollars through Medicaid and misguided, anti-government, racist politicians keeping the government out of the business of states. So, from the perspective of the for-profit world and anti-government, racialist political forces, the nursing home system is working as it was intended to work. Free market myths combined with racism, states' rights, and do-goodism in ameliorating poverty have reduced the power of the federal government to effect meaningful change in the nursing home industry.

It is widely believed that the efforts of Southern Democrats to prevent passage of Medicare through maneuvers such as the Kerr-Mills legislation were abject failures. That would be wrong. Medicare was going to happen eventually —the usual reactionary coalition of Southern Democrats, the AMA, and Northern Republican extremists were not able to muster enough public support to stop it. What could be stopped, however, was the spread of Medicare to the entire U.S. population. What Wilbur Mills accomplished with his "three-layer cake" was keeping all but eligible elderly Medicare beneficiaries in means-tested, lower-tier medicine for whom only a select group of poor could qualify.

The poorest of the poor with children, perhaps people with serious disabilities, and elderly meeting poverty requirements for nursing home care could qualify. Everyone else needed luck or money to find their way into access to suitable medical care. Obamacare was designed to spread coverage to all

Americans. No longer could preexisting conditions, lifetime maximums, and worthless insurance policies keep people from medical care and/or bankruptcy.

Besides not working out too well due to a total privatization under the existing insurance industry, Obamacare did not address the means-tested nursing home business. It remains the same lower-tier, privatized, state-controlled system that existed prior to passage of the Affordable Care Act.

From the perspective of advocates, barriers to implementation as they would like it to happen are overwhelmingly and frustratingly intractable. From the perspective of the representatives of the nursing home industry, implementation is working out quite well. The AHCA and LeadingAge are dominated by the "players" in the nursing home industry. The largest chains with the largest number of facilities and beds also have the capital to influence legislation and lobbying. Government capture will proceed apace. Over time, the thousands of small operators will be gobbled up by the behemoths emerging out of a half century of Medicaid funding and extraordinarily generous federal tax support for the underlying real estate component.

If the current trajectory continues, state control will be strengthened, federal control weakened, and unacceptably poor conditions in total institutions will wax and wane as politics fluctuate between more or less liberalism or, conversely, more or less conservatism. Decent, humane treatment of the elderly in nursing homes is not on the horizon. The total institutional nature of the system will be tweaked now and then, but systems now in place to protect it are too strong for opponents to eliminate it and replace it with what could be.

Notes

1. For a definition of a "total institution," see Goffman (1961), discussed in depth later in this article.
2. Almshouses were total institutions in which the poor elderly became inmates throughout U.S. history preceding legislation of the New Deal, which provided some subsistence through the Old Age Security grant program to the states and Social Security for qualified beneficiaries. Conditions in the almshouse were despicable. See Katz (1996).
3. Means-tested medicine is a unique characteristic of U.S. government–sponsored medical care in which patients must provide proof that they meet income qualifications for approval of benefits available in a program. In the United States, practically all medical care is either means-tested or must, like Medicare, be earned through a sufficient amount of contribution through a payroll tax. Even the "universal" nature of the Affordable Care Act (ACA or "Obamacare") includes many elements of means-testing. Under the ACA, the levels of subsidization of programs purchased through private insurance underwriters are determined by proof of income. States were, under the act, required to expand Medicaid to include the poor as a condition for continuation of federal matching funds. The Supreme Court has held that states cannot be forced to expand Medicaid as a condition of federal matching funds. Long-term care (LTC) is a major portion of Medicaid expenditures. As will be discussed in this article, patients receiving Medicaid LTC assistance must prove that their assets do not exceed the amount allowable for qualification. If their assets exceed the qualifying level, patients must "spend down" to indigency.
4. See the U.S. Constitution, Preamble, Article I, Section 8. For the extant interpretation of the "general welfare" clause by the U.S. Supreme Court, see *New York v. United States et al.*, 505 U.S. 144 (1992).
5. The excellent histories of welfare medicine in general and long-term care in particular include Olson (2003, 2010), Stevens and Stevens (2004), and Vladeck (1980).

6. It was not until 2008 that an apology to the African American community was offered by the AMA. See Harriet A. Washington, "Apology Shines Light on Racial Schism in Medicine," *New York Times*, July 7, 2008, https://nytimes.com/2008/07/29/health/views/29essa.html. According to Washington's article, "By 1938, the situation [of lack of medical care] had grown so dire that Dr. Louis T. Wright of Harlem Hospital declared, 'The A.M.A. has demonstrated as much interest in the health of the Negro as Hitler has in the health of the Jew'." See also Newkirk II, "The Fight for Health Care Has Always Been about Civil Rights," 2017, https://www.theatlantic.com/politics/archive/2017/06/the-fight-for-health-care-is-really-all-about-civil-rights/531855/.

7. This article focuses most attention on the influence of Congressman Wilbur Mills, a quintessential Southern Democrat who was able to gain a considerable amount of seniority and become the powerful chair of the House Ways and Means Committee. However, Southern Democrats in general had achieved power far exceeding their sphere of representation by the time the Great Depression hit the United States, and thereby they were able to steer legislation in a direction that would lessen federal power, keep control over medical care at the state level, and determine how the medical care system would evolve over the following decades. For a discussion of the Harry Byrd machine in Virginia and its disdain for and intense fight against federal programs and civil rights, see MacLean (2017).

8. See, for example, Hamilton, Madison, and Jay (1982).

9. See, for example: United States Senate, Special Committee on Aging, Subcommittee on Long-Term Care (1974), and United States Senate, Special Committee on Aging (1987).

10. The American Health Care Association (AHCA) is a trade association for the for-profit segment of the industry and LeadingAge is the trade association for the so-called nonprofit segment of the industry. Both of these association exhibit the same posture toward legislators and regulators through a "knee-jerk" reaction to legislative attempts to strengthen inspections and enact suitable punitive measures for poor quality of care, to say nothing of poor quality of life for long-term patients. The representatives of these trade associations have an adversarial relationship with advocates for better care.

11. Racism's being intertwined with welfare has resulted from the vicious dehumanization of African Americans ingrained in the American psyche since the beginning of slavery. While welfare recipients are denigrated, religious good works, Christian duty, and noblesse oblige have characterized assistance to those whose misfortune has obviated their share of capitalist production for meeting the basic necessities of life. Generally, acceptable welfare programs are intended for those deemed by society as the "deserving poor." The elderly and disabled served by Medicaid-funded nursing care are two groups that have been among the "most deserving."

12. The Trump administration has taken a radical deregulation approach to Washington and has shown an ardent intent to disassemble progress made in making industry accountable in many areas, including in Medicaid- and Medicare-funded long-term care. The nursing home industry has been all too willing to jump aboard the deregulation movement. As an example, LeadingAge Kansas forwarded a letter dated November 20, 2017, to Congressman Kevin Yoder decrying financial penalties members of the association were receiving for severe abuse and neglect cases. Congressman Yoder forwarded a letter on November 27, 2017, to Seema Verma, CMS administrator, with complaints related to what LeadingAge considered excessive. It became apparent that CMS was moving to undo the belated efforts of the federal government under the Obama administration to impose meaningful penalties for neglect and abuse of nursing home patients. On February 14, 2018, 10 Democratic U.S. senators requested that standards not be weakened.

13. For a discussion of the Eden Alternative and Greenhouse models, see Baker (2007) and Gawande (2014).

14. The deserving poor and undeserving poor dichotomy played a religious role as much as it played a political role. One's Christian duty could be expressed through aid to those seen to be less fortunate and not morally responsible for their plight. It is OK if the almshouse or the poorhouse (as in today's homeless shelters) provided care through cruel, unhealthy, dehumanizing conditions. Humanity is depraved, and suffering is God's plan for us before we reach that better place in the afterlife. Through Christian do-goodism and noblesse oblige, the poor can be helped even in despicable charitable institutions.

15. See https://socialwelfare.library.vcu.edu/public-welfare/aid-for-the-aged/. Created by Title I of the Social Security Act of 1935, Old Age Assistance cash grants to impoverished elderly Americans are significant for several enduring features of U.S. governmental programs for addressing poverty: (1) recipients were required to prove that they met income requirements to qualify for

assistance; (2) the federal government entered the realm of welfare, which had previously and traditionally been a local governmental responsibility but left substantial funding, power, and control with the states; and (3) no portion of the grants were allocated to medical care. The philosophy of the means-tested, welfare-oriented qualifications for OAA failed to address the flaws in a capitalistic system responsible for inadequate wages, technological causes of job loss, and the vicissitudes of economic cycles (from robust growth to recession) inherent in a capitalistic system. Rather than placing the burden for under- and unemployment, inadequate pension and health benefits, and an evolving capitalistic system on corporations and wealthy elites, through a basic, guaranteed income, the burden was placed on labor, the members of which would be forced to go "hat in hand" to a welfare agency and suffer all of the degradations of "the dole."

16. "Spend down" typically involves the transference of patients' wealth that they might hold in liquid assets such as savings, stocks and bonds, CDs, real property, or other form of investment to for-profit and nonprofit nursing home corporations. They are required to liquidate these assets for the purpose of paying for their institutional care until all, except a few protect assets, have been exhausted. Nursing home spend down is a form of wealth transfer from the middle class to higher income levels. Investors and executives are often richly rewarded through appreciation of real estate, dividends, and salaries in the millions of dollars per year. In essence, middle-class wealth is turned over to long-term care corporations until the patient is impoverished, at which time Medicaid reimbursement becomes the source of payment for care.

17. A decision by the state of Arkansas to eliminate the right of 4,350 Medicaid recipients from the program because of a perceived failure to seek work is a very recent example of how states are allowed to exercise their power and deny medical care to poor citizens: Reported by Robert Pear (Pear, 2018).

18. As this article is being written, the state of Arkansas has implemented a program of denying Medicaid benefits to individuals who have not displayed sufficient effort to find employment. Nothing better illustrates the stigmata of welfare medicine and abuse of citizens' rights to a fundamental, biological necessity. Withholding medical care as punishment for even felonious behavior, not to mention, bureaucratic perceptions of laziness and profligacy, is a violation of international human rights law, contrary to medical ethics, and out of step with U.S. moral development.

19. Over the decades after passage of Medicaid, hearings were regularly held for the purpose of addressing poor conditions in nursing homes supported with federal funds. The most scandalous abuses abated somewhat but are still widespread. For decades, patients were restrained with poseys—straps for tying them in wheelchairs. Those abominable practices continued into the 1980s and were only eliminated by the determination of advocates who pressed for stronger regulations. However, methods for restraining patients by tying them to a wheelchair or bed were replaced by chemical restraints. In the past few years, efforts have been made to eliminate the foisting of unnecessary psychotropic drugs on patients with dementia—a technique widespread in nursing homes for the purpose of managing patients in the lowest-cost manner possible.

20. *New York v. United States et al.*, 505 U.S. 144 (1992).

21. See, for example, Jay, *Federalist No. 3*: "As to those just causes of war which proceed from direct and unlawful violence, it appears equally clear to me, that one good national government affords vastly more security against dangers of that sort, than can be derived from any other quarter. Because such violences are more frequently caused by passions and interests of a part than of the whole, of one or two states than of the Union. Not a single Indian war has yet been occasioned by aggressions of the present Federal Government, feeble as it is, but there are several instances of Indian hostilities having been provoked by the improper conduct of individual States, who either unable or unwilling to restrain or punish offences, have given occasion to the slaughter of many innocent inhabitants."

22. *Citizens United v. Federal Election Commission*, 588 U.S. 310 (2010).

23. The "medically indigent" as a legal category for the purposes of eligibility to welfare medicine is still very much with us but has been changed to "medically needy." The Children's Health Insurance Program (CHIP) is for the children of "medically needy" families who are not poor enough to qualify for TANF but too poor to provide their children with necessary medical care.

24. It is not entirely true that Medicare has none of the "welfare medicine" characteristics of Kerr-Mills. Some means-testing is applied to beneficiaries not able to afford the out-of-pocket costs of Medicare. These individuals can prove through provision of their income and finances that they are poor enough to supplement their Medicare with Medicaid benefits that pay for unaffordable

charges not covered by traditional Medicare. These individuals are insensitively labeled "dual eligible."

25. A required 1.45 percent employer tax and 1.45 percent employee payroll tax fund Medicare Part A, which is hospitalization. Part B, physician services, is a voluntary program for the elderly who pay a premium deducted from beneficiaries, Social Security checks. Part D is a drug benefit, also voluntary, for which the beneficiaries pay a premium to an underwriter such as United Health Care. Failure to voluntarily enroll in Parts B and D at age 65 will result in penalties that increase for each year a qualified beneficiary remains unenrolled. In lieu of enrolling in Parts A, B, and D, beneficiaries can elect to enroll in Part C, Medicare Advantage, which is a privatized version of Medicare. All components of Medicare include out-of-pocket costs through premiums, copays, and co-insurance. Supplemental insurance can be purchased for covering these OPCs. Long-term care is not included in Medicare. Extended care for a specific number of days after hospitalization is covered. Long-term care is provided to the frail and dependent elderly and disabled patients who qualify for Medicaid.

26. See Senior Housing News, https://seniorhousingnews.com/.

27. The term "medical-industrial complex" entered the lexicon of health policy in 1980 due to an article by Arnold Relman, MD, entitled "The New Medical Industrial Complex." Dr. Relman included proprietary nursing homes among the major segments of the medical care industry. He conjectured the following: "In 1977 there were nearly 19,000 nursing-home facilities of all types, and 77 percent were proprietary. Some, like the proprietary hospitals, are woned by big corporations, but most (I could not find out exactly how many) are owned by small investors, many of them physicians" (1980, p. 967).

28. The duty and obligation of management to shareholders is not a mere philosophical principle of management—it is settled law. In 1919, in *Dodge v. Ford Motor Co.*, the Supreme Court held that "business corporation is organized and carried on primarily for the profit of the stockholders." The Dodge brothers (later inventors of the Dodge automobile) were minor shareholders of the company. When Henry Ford decided to reinvest profits in expansion of the company rather than pay dividends, the Dodges sued, claiming that investors were entitled to the profits in the form of dividends. The Supreme Court found in the brothers' favor.

29. See Senior Housing News, https://seniorhousingnews.com/.

References

Baker, B. (2007). *Old age in a new age: The promise of transformative nursing homes*. Nashville, TN: Vanderbilt University Press.

Blackmon, D. (2009). *Slavery by another name*. New York: Anchor Books.

Blumenthal, D., & J. Morone. (2009). *The heart of power: Health and politics in the oval office*. Los Angeles: University of California Press.

Crossman, A. (2017). *Chaos theory*. ThoughtCo. Retrieved from thoughtco.com/chaos-theory-3026621

Domhoff, G. W., & M. J. Webber. (2011). *Class and power in the New Deal: Corporate moderates, Southern Democrats, and the liberal-labor coalition*. Stanford, CA: Stanford University Press.

Gawande, A. (2014). *Being mortal: Medicine and what matters in the end*. New York: Metropolitan Books.

Goffman, E. (1961). *Asylums: Essays on the social situation of mental patients and other inmates*. New York: Anchor Books.

Grabowski, D., & T. McGuire. (2009). "Black-white disparities in care in nursing homes." *Atlantic Economic Journal*, 37(3), 299–314.

Hamilton, A., J. Madison, & J. Jay. (1982). *The federalist papers*. New York: Bantam-Dell.

Katz, M. (1996). *In the shadow of the poorhouse: A social history of welfare in America*. New York: Basic Books.

MacLean, N. (2017). *Democracy in chains: The deep history of the radical right's stealth plan for America*. New York: Penguin Books.

Morford, T. (1988). "Nursing home regulation: History and expectations." *Health Care Financing Review*, 1988(Annual Supplement), 129–132.

Olson, L. (2003). *The not-so-golden years: Caregiving, the frail elderly, and the long-term care establishment.* New York: Rowman & Littlefield.

Olson, L. (2010). *The politics of Medicaid.* New York: Columbia University Press.

Pear, R. (2018). "Advisors sound an alarm after thousands are dropped from Medicaid." *New York Times,* September 15, p. A15.

Relman, A. (1980). "The new medical industrial complex." *New England Journal of Medicine,* 303, 963–970.

Rutkow, I. (2010). *Seeking the cure: A history of medicine in America.* New York: Scribner.

Stevens, R., & R. Stevens. (2004). *Welfare medicine in America: A case study of Medicaid.* New Brunswick, NJ: Transaction.

United States Government Accountability Office. (2010). *Nursing homes: Complexity of private investment purchases demonstrate need for CMS to improve the usability and completeness of ownership data.* Retrieved from https://www.gao.gov/new.items/d10710.pdf.

United States Senate, Special Committee on Aging, Subcommittee on Long-Term Care. (1974). *Nursing home care in the United States: Failure in public policy.* Washington, DC: Author.

United States Senate, Special Committee on Aging. (1987). *Developments in aging: The long-term care challenge.* Washington, DC: Author.

Vladeck, B. (1980). *Unloving care: The nursing home tragedy.* New York: Basic Books.

Weber, M. (1958). *The Protestant ethic and the spirit of capitalism: The relationships between religion and the economic and social life in modern culture.* New York: Charles Scribner's Sons.

Economic Inequality and the Violation Economy

Biko Koenig

Franklin & Marshall College, Lancaster, Pennsylvania

The rise of the service economy, low-wage jobs, and precarious employment practices are often noted as the core drivers of contemporary inequality. This article argues that the new economy should be understood alongside a policy regime that provides tremendous leeway for employers to routinely flout labor regulations, and some of the fissuring of the labor market is due to the ability of employers to engage in illegal activity. This article describes four policy areas to explore how employer violations impact the economics of employment: (1) union violations and the National Labor Relations Act; (2) wage theft and the Fair Labor Standards Act; (3) the categorization of temporary workers and independent contractors; (4) and workplace safety violations under the Occupational Safety and Health Administration.

KEY WORDS: inequality, labor unions, wage theft, misclassification, OSHA

经济不平等与违法经济

崛起的服务经济、低酬劳工作和不稳定就业往往被认为是当代不平等的核心驱动因素。本文笔者认为，要理解新经济，需要理解一种政策机制，它为雇主例行公事地藐视劳动法规提供了巨大的空间。由于雇主能够从事非法活动，劳动市场出现了一些裂痕。本文描述了以下四个政策领域，以探讨雇主违规行为如何影响就业经济学：(1)违反工会和"国家劳动关系法"；(2)工资盗窃和"公平劳动标准法"；(3)临时工人和独立承包商的分类；(4)职业安全和健康管理局规定的工作场所安全违规行为。

Desigualdad económica y la economía de la violación

El auge de la economía de servicios, los empleos de bajos salarios y las prácticas de empleo precario a menudo se consideran como los motores centrales de la desigualdad contemporánea. Este documento sostiene que la nueva economía debe entenderse junto con un régimen de política que ofrece un tremendo margen de maniobra para que los empleadores burlen rutinariamente las regulaciones laborales, y algunas de las fisuras del mercado laboral se deben a la capacidad de los empleadores para participar en actividades ilegales. Este documento describe cuatro áreas de políticas para explorar cómo las violaciones de los empleadores afectan la economía del empleo: (1) las violaciones sindicales y la Ley Nacional de Relaciones Laborales; (2) el robo de salarios y la Ley de normas laborales justas; (3) la categorización de trabajadores temporales y contratistas independientes; (4) y

169

violaciones de seguridad en el lugar de trabajo bajo la Administración de Seguridad y Salud Ocupacional.

PALABRAS CLAVES: Desigualdad, sindicatos, robo de salarios, clasificación errónea, OSHA

Introduction

How do labor protections function in an increasingly neoliberal political economy? The postwar model—characterized by long-term employment, union density, and rising wages—has mostly disappeared. Nonetheless, much of today's U.S. labor policy is based on this earlier structure, as both the laws that govern labor protections as well as the legal foundations for unionization are based on increasingly outmoded ways of working. In place of this older economic model we see a dynamic, globalized economy increasingly characterized by inequality, income polarization, and precarious work structures. Actors across the economy have struggled to adapt to these changes with limited success as changes to the political landscape have magnified economic issues. For example, the decline of unions is a reflection, in part, of the ability of employers to disregard union protections, while worker centers often run campaigns that simply look to enforce those labor policies already on the books but routinely ignored. Thus, the twin phenomena of economic inequality and pro-business political structures are co-constituted. Given the background of an increasingly low-wage and neoliberal political economy, how well have labor protections adapted to changing times, and how well are they enforced?

To answer this question, I begin by examining changes to the modern political economy in the United States. The landscape of employment that workers see today is characterized by large gaps in wage inequality, steadily increasing wealth transfers to the wealthy, and the continual disappearance of the middle class as low-wage jobs steadily become the norm. Given these qualities, I next examine the state of labor policy: perhaps if workers make relatively lower wages, strong protections and labor rights could serve as a societal bulwark against inequity. Looking across four major themes of labor policy—wage regulations, union protections, employee classification, and health and safety—I find that the current regulatory regime is best characterized as a "violation economy," where rampant abuses by employers are the norm. To the extent that labor policy is intended to protect and empower workers, the current structure leaves much to be desired. Given the relationship between class and political inequality, it comes as no surprise that an era of increased economic inequality would be characterized by an employer-centric labor regime.

The evolution of the economy and the political landscape are crucial factors that structure the enforcement of labor policy. Since the 1970s, globalization, deindustrialization, and the changing nature of employment have dramatically changed the structure of work, and public policy either has remained stagnant or has been adjusted in ways that mainly benefit employers. The dream of long-term employment and middle-class wages has given way to a polarization of income; today, high-wage professionals and low-wage service workers define the major contours of the labor market. While the start of this phenomenon can be charted in the 1970s, economic inequality continues to rapidly increase—middle-class jobs saw the largest losses during the 2008 recession, whereas the majority of job growth since then has been in low-wage sectors (Bernhardt, 2012). These changes impact how political actors mobilize and organize workers as precarious, temporary, and low-wage employment grows. By and large, traditional unions have struggled to keep up with the changing economy, and the legal foundation of the union model remains largely reflective of an earlier era of stable jobs and large-scale employers.

The story of a changing economy occurs alongside a policy landscape increasingly defined by a political structure that weakens the regulatory appara-tus of the state, introduces aggressive economic liberalization, and values employer profit over wages as the engine of the economy. As such, here I examine two interrelated topics: increasing economic inequality and the ability of labor policy to protect workers. The rise of a globalized economy alongside a neoliberal political state has significantly altered the landscape of employment in the United States. Changes to the political and economic structures have led to an increasingly unequal economic landscape, with wealth concentrated among the rich. This, in turn, concentrates political power among the same group. Unions and other civil society actors have seen their own power wane as the legal frameworks that undergird their standing in the political arena have been reduced, undercut, or ignored. Such changes have led the Democratic Party and other political actors to slowly shift their programs away from explicitly material and working-class issues. As such, issues of labor protections and inequality have lost their traditional political homes and, in turn, have left the mainstream political debate.

The empirical data on economic inequality are clear, though its causes remain complex and interrelated. In particular, research shows that a political system increasingly dominated by the economic elite will adjust policies to act in line with their interests (Gilens & Page, 2014). Within this context, I look toward policies designed to protect workers and grant them rights in a variety of employment settings, from the right to unionize, to laws governing wages, to policies that define employees and give them protections as such. Much of these policies seem commonsense and straightforward: workers should be entitled to their pay for their work, and employers should pay payroll taxes on their workers. This research instead finds significant problems with the current regime of labor policy, one better characterized by consistent violations on the part of the employers and a lack of effective enforcement on the part of federal regulators.

This violation economy fits into the current political culture of economic redistribution to the wealthy. When companies flout union regulations to stop organizing drives, they perceive this as an action to increase profits. The reduction or absence of health and safety procedures is considered a cheaper alternative to paid training and equipment. Misclassifying employees as independent contractors shifts the tax burden to those workers while removing them from the purview of most labor protections. Many of these problems are concentrated among low-wage workers, who are less likely to have the resources to combat illegal practices or easy choices to work in other sectors. Thus, these issues are interrelated and will continue to be so in an economy that continues to add low-wage jobs.

The Changing Economy

This section discusses how this new economy has important implications for workers and the groups that seek to organize them and has placed a new emphasis on the importance of the enforcement of basic labor protections for labor organizations.

Historical Shifts and Economic Inequality

The dominant narrative about the evolution of the modern U.S. economic system begins in the 1970s, when shifts toward the globalization of production spurred domestic deindustrialization. In an increasingly competitive landscape, so the story goes, companies moved production facilities abroad, causing well-paid (and often unionized) employment to disappear. While such changes have led to dramatic changes in American society, they have nonetheless enabled the continual growth of our economy and ensured that the United States remains a global economic leader. This restructuring, as such, is posited as good for all in the general prosperity that accompanies these shifts. Proponents of this viewpoint look to steady increases in GDP, strong stock markets, relatively low unemployment rates, and rising levels of economic productivity (U.S. Bureau of Economic Analysis, 2017; U.S. Bureau of Labor Statistics, 2017a). Perhaps the challenges faced by workers in specific industries could be justified if the overall situation for workers had improved during these changes, as some commentators believed would happen (Block, 1990).

Instead, these changes have laid the foundation for an increasingly unequal economy: working-class wages have remained stagnant since the 1970s, whereas business profits and the income shares of the wealthy have risen to levels not seen since the 1920s (Kimball & Mishel, 2015). This divergence has occurred alongside increases in worker productivity: between 1973 and 2014, worker productivity rose by 72 percent, while hourly wages only increased 8 percent (Bivens & Mishel, 2015). And this is not a historical footnote, as worker productivity grew 21 percent between 2000 and 2014 alone, while only translating into less than a 2 percent increase in real wages. So, what happens to the wealth generated by more productive workers? The answer is higher compensation for the professional class: in the same period, the real wages of the top of the income distribution rose by almost 10 percent (Bivens & Mishel, 2015). In 2012 alone, the top 10 percent of the income bracket took in 47.8 percent of income, the highest figure since 1917. The U.S. economy continues to grow, but less and less of that growth ends up in the pockets of regular workers: in 2014, over 40 percent of all workers earned under $15 per hour, with 70 percent of that group earning wages below $12 per hour (Tung, Sonn, & Lathrop, 2015). The Economic Policy Institute concludes that increasing economic inequality drives roughly 80 percent of the divergence between wages and productivity (Bivens & Mishel, 2015).

Rising wage inequality mirrors the polarized employment landscape, within which post-recession job growth occurred mainly for low-wage service workers and high-wage professionals while middle-class employment continued to disappear (Piketty, Saez, & Zucman, 2016). In response, the two sides presented of the inequality story—deindustrialization and globalization—provide the rhetorical logic behind calls for "Make America Great Again" trade policies that promise a return to widespread factory employment and middle-class careers. Given the strength of President Trump's populist rhetoric on global trade and employment, it is ironic that the policies delivered under his presidency have mainly been geared toward increased liberalization.

Beyond Offshoring

The narrative of deindustrialization and globalization only partially explains the structural changes behind growing inequality, as place-bound industries that did not suffer the fate of globalized offshoring or the slow death of deindustrialization also saw across-the-board deunionization and stagnant wage growth. For example, food retail workers in grocery stores, a job category one would imagine is safe from being moved overseas, saw their union density drop from 24.5 to 8.0 percent between 1985 and 2016, and real wages for cashiers dropped 10 percent between 1997 and 2017 (U.S. Bureau of Labor Statistics, 2017a).[1] Dramatic structural changes in some industries have negatively affected workers even as they have generally increased profits and production. The prime example is factory-based manufacturing, where the loss of 5 million jobs since 1980 stands in contrast to the 131 percent increase in output between 1982 and 2007: while many believe American factory work is dead, manufacturing as a profit-making industry remains quite healthy (Baily & Bosworth, 2014; Moody, 2016). Rather, it is the abundance of stable, full-time, and well-paid blue-collar jobs that has disappeared (Baily & Bosworth, 2014).

The characteristics of modern low-wage jobs are worth noting. While whites, as the largest demographic, hold the majority of low-wage jobs, immigrants, people of color, and women are overrepresented in lower-income jobs (Berube, 2016; Capps, Fix, Passel, Ost, & Perez-Lopez, 2003; Entmacher, Frohlich, Robbins, Martin, & Watson, 2014; Martin, 2015). The qualities of these jobs are significant in their challenges: high turnover; poor legal protection; higher instances of wage theft, harassment, and discrimination; and higher rates of injury (Cascio, 2006; Cooper & Kroeger, 2017; Frye, 2017; Garcia, 2009; Leigh, 2011). Many of these workers also have limited access to traditional forms of political representation, due either to their status as immigrants or the usual roadblocks that the poor face in securing a voice in the political arena (Bartels, 2016).

173

Further, the current prevalence of low-wage employment is not simply a blip but predicted to expand at a high pace. The Bureau of Labor Statistics projects that through 2024 over 80 percent of all new nonmanagerial, nonprofessional jobs will pay roughly $15 per hour or lower, while a third of those jobs will offer just over $10 per hour (2015).[2] For the majority of workers who are not doctors, lawyers, or financiers, this means poverty-level wages are predicted to increasingly be the norm through the next decade.

Wages and income shares alone do not tell the whole story, as these numbers may imply full-time, year-round work. The structural changes to employment suggest that jobs that once offered long-term, stable positions will continue to shift toward contingent work arrangements. This rise of contingent and precarious employment is driven by flexible employment practices typically framed as necessary to keep companies competitive (Standing, 2014). In practice, this competition comes from the transfer of profits away from labor and toward capital. Precarious work is defined by qualities that were historically typical of the secondary labor market, namely, exclusion from legal protections, a lack of employment security, and the overall fragmentation of the traditional relationship between worker and employer. Practices such as part-time employment, temporary work structures, independent contracting, short-term work contracts, non-compete agreements, franchising, third-party employer models, freelancing, and subcontracting all increase competition and profitability while shifting economic risk onto the backs of smaller firms and the workers themselves (Weil, 2011).

The Political Context and Policy Drift

While low wages, precarious work, and the disappearing middle class offer a set of challenges for many workers, these structures remain largely within a legal economic framework. In the free market, employers are not required to pay more than minimum wages, to offer comfortable work, or to provide opportunities for advancement to their employees. However, even legal minimum standards have not kept pace with a changing economy. Such conditions set the stage for a range of illegal practices made possible by economic competition and a policy agenda that reduces the ability of regulators to enforce laws. The scope of unforced illegal workplace practices is such that it is the main terrain of conflict for many worker centers and other groups that organize low-wage workers. As one organizer in the restaurant industry put it to me, "if employers just followed the law, I would be out of a job."

Two theoretical frames, both drawn from Hacker's work on social policy retrenchment, can help us understand problems with labor policy enforcement (2004). The first, policy drift, explains how the efficacy of a given policy can change dramatically over time through changes to the policy context rather than the policy itself (Hacker, 2004). Thus, if the resources and capabilities of the Department of Labor's Wage and Hour Division remain stagnant, their ability to enforce wage laws will decrease over time as the economy grows and becomes more complicated. Further, if employer strategies to circumvent laws grow in sophistication, the sheer lack of updates by policymakers will reduce the ability of regulators to address modern violations of policy. Federal union rules offer another example of this, in that they privilege the employment structure of traditional manufacturing: full-time, long-term work with a single, large employer.

Policy conversion offers a second way to frame these changes (Hacker, 2004). While pro-business interests have sought to explicitly remove union protections from workers via legislation, their efforts have also focused on adjusting how current legislation is enforced. Thus, the recent U.S. Supreme Court decision in *Epic Systems Court v. Lewis* regarding arbitration clauses removes the ability of workers to use class action lawsuits against employers, even involving cases of labor policy enforcement. Similarly, the ability of presidents to influence the decisions and process of the National Labor Relations Board (NLRB) offers pathways to significantly undercut protections for workers (Storm, 2018). In both cases, protections for workers are undercut without needing to pass new legislation or repeal standing laws through Congress.

These problems intersect at numerous points. When regulators are unable to enforce workplace standards due to a lack of resources or standing, employers have an incentive to flout labor laws to reduce costs and enhance profits and routinely do so. This is especially true if the chances of being caught are low, or if violations do not carry serious punishments (Galvin, 2016). Further, these problems are more prevalent with a low-wage workforce, where employers can easily replace workers. When workers are low-wage and come from vulnerable populations, the fear of losing one's job means that they tend not to report violations (Azaroff, Lax, Levenstein, & Wegman, 2004). As union density continues its decline, the ability of workers to have a protected, unified voice on the job is also reduced, removing what could be an important check on illegal practices.

The following sections describe the current state of policy enforcement across four issues: union protections, wages, employer classification, and health and safety. Across the board, there is evidence of significant problems of employer violations. There are some bright spots in enforcement procedures, especially at the state level. With the ability of political actors to pressure state-level agencies and legislators to update enforcement efforts, without significant changes to federal law, a state-by-state approach means that some workers will continue to face an employment landscape beset by rampant violations.

Union Rights and Employer Resistance

Unions loom large in this entire discussion. As a historical vehicle for higher wages, collective voice among employers, and political influence in elections, unions have the potential to offer workers power in public and private settings. Indeed, research indicates that levels of unionization have strong effects on wage inequality (Fortin & Lemieux, 1997; Western & Rosenfeld, 2011). In the United States, unions maintain a center of gravity for the political left due to their historical weight, continued presence in political action on all levels of policy, membership numbers that remain in the millions, and significant resources of money and people. For better or for worse, this blend of history, numbers, and resources also gives unions stature on the left more broadly, both in specific terms of support for the Democratic Party as well as a general anchor for left-based social movements (Warren, 2010). There simply is not a larger network of people and resources on the left outside of the Democratic Party.

Nonetheless, union decline has been the story of the modern U.S. labor movement since its peak in 1954, when union density stood at 28.3 percent of all workers (Mayer, 2004, p. 11). While density declined through the postwar era, the overall number of union workers reached its highest in 1979 at 21 million workers as the workforce expanded (Mayer, 2004, p. 10). Since then it has been consistently downhill. Regardless of whether one looks at union density or overall membership, 2016 marked the lowest figures since before the passage of the National Labor Relations Act (NLRA), at 10.7 percent and 14.6 million, respectively (U.S. Bureau of Labor Statistics, 2018a). In 2017, the numbers edged up slightly to 10.7 percent and 14.8 million (U.S. Bureau of Labor Statistics, 2018b). However, these figures include a substantial proportion of public sector employees, who face political and economic structures that are distinct from that of private employees in that their employers are governments and elected officials. As government employees, it is typically easier for public sector unions to pressure politicians and win contracts, though some states are rolling back laws that enable these strategies. Regardless, the union density of the public sector stood at 34.4 percent in 2017, making up a sizable portion of all unionized workers. In the same year, private sector union density on its own stood at its lowest recorded level at 6.5 percent with 7.6 million workers (U.S. Bureau of Labor Statistics, 2018a). Completing the downward spiral, the reduction of union workplace power led to the collapse of union legitimacy in the eyes of some workers, who saw them as willful conspirators in the deindustrialization of their jobs through years of givebacks (Lopez, 2004). The causes of this decline are attributed to an interrelated mix of factors.

In addition to their role in changing employment writ large, globalization and deindustrialization have often been implicated in declining rates of unionization. As noted earlier, as U.S. manufacturing faced competition abroad, technological and transportation advancements allowed for cheaper international production while the mobility of capital incentivized employers to move production abroad to capture lower labor costs and higher profit margins (Slaughter, 2007). Unions in manufacturing, such as auto and steelworkers, made the decision to defend what membership they had at any cost, typically through employer "givebacks" of wages, benefits, and membership numbers. The resulting erosion of union strength in manufacturing reversed earlier trends in employment, where non-union companies would offer union-level wages and benefits to act as a hedge against labor mobilization—the "rising tide lifts all boats" adage of how widespread union density helps all workers (Greenhouse, 2008).

In today's economy, the situation is reversed. The competition of *non-union* employers puts downward pressure on wages for the remaining union firms, a problem magnified when this competition is understood from a global perspective. But while globalization is certainly part of the story, it cannot explain why union density has decreased in place-bound sectors such as construction, hospitals, and food processing. Further, some sectors, such as clothing manufacturing, that have seen major offshoring of employment and deunionization have nonetheless experienced domestic employment growth in the same period (Milkman, 2006, pp. 88–89). Such data indicate that other factors are at work in this decline, namely, the political shifts against union rights. Most unions, constructed to fight contract wars on battlefields defined by large employers, industrial specialization, and long-term employment, are poorly equipped to organize the low-wage precariat of the modern globalized economy. Given that union models are bound up in the legal rights provided by the NLRA, we might expect that a changing economic context would lead to policy adjustments to give unions a fighting chance in a changing economy.

The crux of neoliberalism is the deregulation and privatization of the economy, both globally and on national levels. As both a political process and an ideology, the backers of neoliberal projects have explicitly sought to eliminate unions, weaken labor laws, and challenge the legitimacy of collective action to impact economic processes (Robinson, 2000; Vachon, Wallace, & Hyde, 2016). In the United States, these goals have been largely successful and help to partially explain deunionization across the board. While the deregulation of industry has impacted place-bound service sectors, the recent rollback of labor laws in states like Wisconsin and Indiana have put pressure on the strongholds of public sector unions as well. Union decline is both a cause of and an effect of the rise of economic liberalization, as the declining strength of labor in the United States removed an organized voice from the national political arena while also making room for growing economic inequality.

Unions have been a specific target of the neoliberal agenda, particularly the federal protections offered under the NLRA that allow workers to organize unions without interference from their employers. In practice, these rights have significantly deteriorated since the 1970s. While the legal rights of workers to unionize remain clear on paper, the combined weakness and slow pace of the National Labor Relation Board to act on employer violations means that union drives can wait months or years to have an employer disciplined, by which time the energy behind a campaign is often stalled. These delays are particularly challenging when they involve workers illegally fired for their role as union leaders, a strategy that can easily defeat a campaign. The data on violations are telling: a sixfold increase in employer violations between 1950 and 1990, a precipitous drop in the success rate of first-time campaigns from 86 percent in 1960 to as low as 44 percent in 2008, and research that shows a worker has a 20 percent chance of illegal termination during a union campaign (Dunlop Commission, 1994; Ferguson, 2008; Schmitt & Zipperer, 2008). While many expected the Obama administration to usher in a new age of union policy, the hoped-for

Employee Free Choice Act never passed Congress, and union density declined 10 percent during Obama's eight years (Dirnbach, 2017; Warren, 2010).

As part of a wider strategy, employer violations and delays are crucial tactics in stopping a union from winning representation or bargaining for a contract. When the NLRB does address a violation, the legal remedies involve only posting notices about the nature of violations or rehiring and paying lost wages of illegally fired workers. For an employee illegally fired for union activity, current statute does not allow damages or civil suits, and in the months or years it can take to process the violation, workers move on to other jobs. Even after a successful election, if a company refuses to bargain with a union, the power of the NLRB is limited to ordering them to bargain more. As Schiffer (2005) puts it, such remedies "don't sound like much because they aren't that much" (p. 5). Aggressive employer strategies are backed by a booming industry of anti-union consultants ready and willing to mount countercampaigns. In such an environment, companies have profitable incentives to flout labor laws that have no real teeth to avoid a collective bargaining agreement (Logan, 2006). This again shows the power of policy drift, as union opponents have effectively reduced the power of policy to protect workers by doing nothing more than just not passing updated policies that address the dramatic increase of employer violations. Taken together, these changes show that decreased unionization—and the accompanying increased inequality—are the products of political choices as much as changes to the economy.

Wage Enforcement

While the context of employment for most Americans has changed significantly, the NLRA of 1936 and the Fair Labor Standards Act (FLSA) of 1937 remain the last major pieces of federal legislation that provide rights and protections for workers. On such a timeline, by not updating the policies governing work and workplaces as those contexts change over time, Congress leaves employees in a weaker position. Minimum wage laws and overtime regulations are a clear example of policy drift, both of which are set through individual legislation and rule changes rather than automatically adjusted over time. If the minimum wage was pegged to inflation, it would currently be set somewhere between $9.22 and $10.52 rather than $7.25.[3] If it instead reflected gains in worker productivity, the range would be $12.25 to $21.72 (Schmitt, 2012). Thus, while minimum wages are intended to provide a fair wage floor, their effectiveness over time decreases.

However, problems of wage policy can take a more nefarious turn. Watered-down regulations, rules that do not address the new structures of the economy, and limited support for enforcement set the stage for employers to engage in illegal and questionable practices. For example, the fractured employment relationships of temporary work and subcontracting have been linked to much higher rates of workplace injury as regulators struggle to adapt to a new economy without updated mandates from Congress (Boden, Spieler, & Wagner, 2015). Problems of wage theft—when employers fail to pay workers the full amount they have earned—are emblematic of the modern, low-wage economy and provide a sharp example of policy failures around work issues. Wage theft is illegal under the Fair Labor Standards Act, which includes mechanisms for enforcement and punishment. Nonetheless, employers routinely steal their employees' wages with limited concerns about government enforcement. The scale of the problem is vast—in 2012, employees recovered over $933 million through wage theft cases, and this only involves amounts that have been reported and recovered in only 44 states. Galvin puts this number in perspective, in that it is "more than the total amount lost in all bank, residential, convenience store, gas station, and street robberies put together" (2016, p. 327). While the full extent of violations is unknown, national estimates put the overall figure at $50 billion in stolen wages per year (Galvin, 2016; Meixell & Eisenbrey, 2014).

While wage theft violations of overtime pay involve larger amounts, minimum wage noncompliance is particularly egregious in that low-wage workers can least afford to be underpaid. This practice is not on the margins of employment but is prevalent across low-wage work. A survey of low-wage workers in New York City, Los Angeles, and Chicago indicates that in a typical week, two-thirds of respondents experienced at least one pay violation, for a yearly average of $2,634 in lost wages out of $17,616 in annual earnings (Bernhardt et al., 2009). Given that wage theft is illegal, the inability of regulators to enforce laws is a critical reason wage theft practices are so prevalent. The Fair Labor Standards Act was passed in 1937 to deal with these very problems by creating minimum wage and overtime policy complete with investigators to enforce the laws. Yet Congress has not adjusted the provisions of the act to keep pace with a growing and changing economy. While the number of workers who fall under the protection of the Fair Labor Standards Act has grown sixfold since 1948, the number of investigators in the Wage and Hour Division only increased by 10 percent in the same time (Galvin, 2016, p. 325). While some individual states have passed laws to pick up the slack, policies have varied widely in their effectiveness (Galvin, 2016). In such a policy vacuum, it is no surprise that issues like wage theft run rampant, as it hinges on a practical incentive: more money for the employer.

Employee Misclassification

Most workers in the United States are classified as employees: they fill out a W-2 form for payroll, receive a paycheck with tax deductions, and are covered by a host of policies from minimum wage and overtime to union rights and workers compensation law. Some workers are instead classified as independent contractors, a category that indicates the worker is self-employed rather than a direct employee of the company who hired them. Workers who control their own work even when hired by a company—such as plumbers, attorneys, IT consultants, and landscapers—are considered self-contained entities rather than directly hired employees. Independent contractors exist in a dramatically different policy landscape than regular employees. Most labor laws do not apply to independent contractors, including minimum wage laws, overtime, and unionization rights. Further, they exist outside of unemployment insurance and workers compensation laws. While employers cover half of all payroll taxes for standard employees, independent contractors are responsible for the entire burden. This includes Social Security, Medicare, unemployment insurance, and workers compensation insurance. If an employer offers benefits to their regular employees, independent contractors do not typically have access to those benefits, including medical insurance and retirement accounts.

The intent of this classification is to make space for workers who are legitimately self-contained actors, such as single-employee small businesses and contract workers. And for some, especially those on the higher end of the wage scale, the independence offered by independent contracting is a desirable benefit. However, data indicate that independent contractors hold health insurance plans at lower rates; in 2014, only 75 percent had health insurance compared with 87 percent of regular wage earners. The same is true for retirement, with only 8 percent of self-employed workers making a 2014 contribution to a retirement account compared with 42 percent of traditional employees (Jackson, Looney, & Ramnath, 2017).

These issues aside, the core problem of this system is the ability for employers to intentionally misclassify employees as independent contractors, especially in on-demand sectors, and among low-wage workers. In these circumstances, workers miss out on important workplace protections while employers reap the benefits of lower burdens on taxes, benefits, and insurance. As one interviewee put it, such a decision might be better classified as payroll fraud rather than misclassification. Regardless of the label, the misclassification of employees as independent contractors presents unique challenges for both researchers and government actors.

While independent contractors make up a relatively small portion of the overall workforce, they make up millions of workers and represent a significant tax base. In May 2017, there were 10.6 million independent contractors in the United States, making up 6.9 percent of overall employment (Bureau of Labor Statistics, 2018b). Another 6–8 percent of workers have jobs as independent contractors in addition to standard employment (Jackson, Looney, & Ramnath, 2017). The largest occupations of independent contractors in 2018 are management, professional, and related activities (43 percent), which account for much of the high-wage consultant and professional occupations of the classification (Bureau of Labor Statistics, 2018b). Of the remainder, 16 percent of independent contractors were in sales, 12 percent in construction, and 5 percent in transportation.

Data on misclassification is challenging to gather for a number of reasons. In the first instance, illegal practices are hard to measure with surveys and audits of tax data, as offenders are unlikely to indicate that they are engaged in such practices. Further, many state-level studies involve audits of companies and industries where suspected misclassification exists. As an enforcement strategy, such an approach is logical for targeting problematic sectors, but from a research perspective, it offers data that skew the prevalence of misclassification. Finally, much of the research conducted on the state level begins with audits of unemployment insurance programs, meaning that employers who fail to report their payments to workers will be missed (Leberstein, 2012). Nonetheless, the data show that it is a widespread problem, and interviews with state officials indicate that it is getting worse over time (U.S. Government Accountability Office, 2009).

Even with small portions of the workforce acting as independent contractors, the impacts of misclassification can be significant. Unfortunately, there are few national studies on misclassification, so much of what we know is from historical data and state-level studies. In 1984, the IRS conducted the only comprehensive analysis of misclassification and found over 3.4 million workers had been misclassified and estimated the tax revenue losses to be $1.6 billion in 1984 dollars (U.S. Government Accountability Office, 2009). In 2000, a DOL study of audits from nine states noted that 10–30 percent of all employers misclassified at least a single employee (de Silva et al., 2000). This same study noted that unemployment trust funds would lose roughly $200 million each year for every percentage point of misclassified workers. Using estimates from the 1984 IRS data set and state-level audits, a 2009 GAO study estimated that misclassification cost the federal government $2.7 billion in 2006.

Misclassification leads to reduced tax revenues through a few methods. In the first instance, unemployment and workers compensation insurance are simply not usually paid by independent contractors. If a misclassified worker is able to successfully contest their categorization in order to receive workers compensation or unemployment, those funds are drawn from state trusts directly rather than charged back to the original employer. For federal payroll taxes, independent contractors are required to pay the entire tax burden. In practice, these workers end up underpaying taxes and underreporting their income by large amounts. The GAO found that self-employed workers underreported 32 percent of their income, and those who were paid in cash underreported 81 percent of their income (Carré, 2015). For low-wage workers, underreporting and taking cash payments can be a crucial survival strategy.

Targeted state-level audits show that while misclassification rates vary across the economy, employers that engage in the activity do so at relatively higher rates:

> For example, in Massachusetts, from 2001 to 2003, 13–19 percent of employers overall misclassified at least one worker but, among these employers, 25–39 percent of the workforce was misclassified. In construction, the situation was worse: 14–24 percent of employers misclassified, and among these, 40–48 percent of workers were misclassified (Carré & Wilson, 2004). An analysis of Michigan audit data for 2003–2004 found that 30 percent of employers misclassified and that 24 percent of workers in these employers' workforces were misclassified (Belman & Block, 2009, p. 14). The Michigan study used audits from construction, trucking, and security guard industries. (Carré, 2015)

The construction industry seems to have particular challenges with misclassification. Surveys of construction workers in southern states found that 32 percent of workers were misclassified (Theodore, Boggess, Cornejo, & Timm, 2017). The concentration of these practices in certain industries is connected to the relative incentive employers have to misclassify. In general, the reduction in tax burden and protections transfers more revenues toward profits. In construction-related and other potentially high-risk jobs, workers compensation insurance can run as high as 50 percent of payroll, creating an incentive for employers to misclassify.

No single department is responsible for the enforcement of classification issues, and misclassification itself is not illegal. Instead, various federal and state-level departments oversee different aspects of the problem. The Wage and Hour Division of the U.S. Department of Labor enforces policies around record keeping and wage payments, which may be violated by misclassification. Similarly, the IRS deals with challenges of tax evasion and underreporting of income and wages.

On paper, the power of the IRS to assess penalties and back taxes on violators seems the strongest tool in the enforcement playbook. However, Section 530 of the Revenue Act of 1978 offers a "safe harbor" loophole which allows employers to continue to misclassify workers without penalty and continue to do so even after an IRS audit so long as they meet certain criteria. The criteria for legal misclassification under Section 530 are vague, and a company can simply argue on a "reasonable basis" that it is necessary, or that it is standard practice in the industry regardless of legality. While Section 530 was intended to be a short-term measure while Congress developed a long-term fix, it remains the law to this day.

Workplace Safety

The Occupational Safety and Health Administration (OSHA), brought into being by a 1970 law signed by President Nixon, is unique in that it does not come out of the host of New Deal and postwar policies described above. OSHA covers almost all workers in the economy, with the important exception of self-employed independent contractors.[4] Regulations contain various components of health and safety, including employee training, worksite safety, and reporting procedures. Historically, OSHA regulations seem to be a resounding success, as the number of workplace injuries and fatalities has declined significantly since the 1970s. Nonetheless, problems remain in the current policy structure. In considering issues of enforcement of regulations, two issues rise to the fore: processes for carrying out inspections, and penalties associated with violations.

Inspections and investigations are the main tactic for enforcement. Given the breadth of its responsibilities, OSHA has a relatively small staff. As they note in their own statistics: "with our state partners we have approximately 2,100 inspectors responsible for the health and safety of 130 million workers, employed at more than 8 million worksites around the nation — which translates to about one compliance officer for every 59,000 workers" (OSHA, 2018a). In 2017, this translated into 77,947 workplace inspections by OSHA and state-level regulators in an economy that had 6.75 million employers in 2015 (OSHA, 2018a, U.S. Census Bureau, 2015a). Given the capacity to inspect on a fraction of worksites, OSHA both targets industries with high rates of injuries (such as construction) and relies on workers to submit reports for inspections.

Unfortunately, relying on worker reporting does more to illustrate the power dynamics of worksites than to help regulate unsafe working conditions, as under-reporting is the norm.

In 2016, there were roughly 3 million serious workplace injuries and over 5,000 deaths (Bureau of Labor Statistics, 2017a, 2017b; OSHA, 2018a,b). While these numbers may appear high, a review of reporting mechanisms and practices indicates that "many, and perhaps the majority" of injuries are not reported by employers (OSHA, 2015). Workers tend not to file for a number of reasons: fear of retribution from employers, worries about losing their job, challenges with the language, or not knowing about their workplace rights or how to file a complaint (OSHA, 2015). These barriers are particularly challenging for low-wage workers, immigrants, and workers in areas with few job prospects.

Of course, some employers see incentives in having unsafe working conditions and not filing claims, as they are strategies to reduce costs and to avoid OSHA fines, and research supports this finding. As the operating margins of employers decrease, they are more likely to engage in serious health and safety violations (Filer & Golbe, 2003). In general, some employers avoid reporting injuries specifically to avoid paying fines (Boden, Spieler, & Wagner, 2016). And on paper, these fines can appear serious, including $12,934 per day when problems are not solved, and a maximum of $129,336 for "willful or repeated" violations (OSHA, 2018b).

While these fines may be significant on paper, they require an inspection in the first place. An enforcement regime that utilizes a small number of inspectors and requires low-wage workers to file reports allows for employers to control the field of conflict. Even with inspections, OHSA has a troubled history of not uniformly applying regulations, including a *New York Times* expose that noted they did not seek prosecution and actively worked to protect employers in 93 percent of all workplace fatalities between 1982 and 2002 (Barstow, 2003). Further, employers routinely seek to reduce and contest fines, with an average penalty reduction of 49 percent for those who entered into negotiations in 2012 (Kramer, 2014). When employers took cases to an administrative law hearing in the same year, those who settled received an average of 58 percent in penalties, with another 17 percent having their cases dropped (Kramer, 2014). For those who continued on through the entire process, one-third had their citations (Kramer, 2014) dismissed.

As the U.S. Senate Committee on Health, Education, Labor and Pensions put it:

> Data indicates that OSHA routinely buckles under the threat of litigation, reducing penalties in settlement more than they would absent a

contest. Clearly, this strategy sends exactly the wrong message to employers—that fighting regulators has concrete financial rewards. (2008)

Conclusion

Rising levels of economic inequality are driven by political and economic processes. An economy that continues to produce low-wage jobs at higher rates will push income polarization to higher levels over time. Low-wage workers have less power in both economic and political contexts: they are less able to control employment markets while elected officials and party structures respond to high-wage and wealthy voters. In such a context, it makes sense that workplace policies function in ways that benefit employers over workers. In a context where workers have little political power as workers, updating and strengthening labor policy is an uphill battle. And when these same structural changes both reduce the power of the labor movement while encouraging the Democratic Party to focus on elite social issues, historical spaces of worker power disappear.

Thus, on the ground, we see a violation economy in which employers face incentives to flout labor law in order to lower costs, and a policy regime that is ill equipped to adequately match the ability of employers to do so. The problems are legion and interrelated: low numbers of inspectors, the lack of political will at higher levels of the administration, and legislators who are actively seeking methods to reduce protections and weaken regulations.

Notes

1. Inflation calculated using Consumer Price Index.
2. Jobs that were nonmanagerial and nonprofessional accounted for 83 percent of the economy in 2016 (U.S. Bureau of Labor Statistics, 2018a). Assuming current trends, this means that by 2024, two-thirds off all new jobs across the entire economy will pay $15 per hour or lower.
3. The federal minimum wage for tipped employees is $2.13.
4. Some farm workers as well as workers covered by other acts are also outside of OSHA's purview.

References

Azaroff, L. S., M. B. Lax, C. Levenstein, & D. H. Wegman. (2004). "Wounding the messenger: The new economy makes occupational health indicators too good to be true." *International Journal of Health Services*, 34(2), 271–303.

Baily, M. N., & B. P. Bosworth. (2014). "US manufacturing: Understanding its past and its potential future." *Journal of Economic Perspectives*, 28(1), 3–26.

Barstow, D. (2003). U.S. rarely seeks charges for deaths in workplace. *The New York Times*. Retrieved from https://www.nytimes.com/2003/12/22/us/us-rarely-seeks-charges-for-deaths-in-workplace.html

Bartels, L. (2016). *Unequal democracy: The political economy of the new Gilded Age*. Princeton, NJ: Princeton University Press.

Belman, D. L., & R. Block. (2009) *Informing the Debate: The Social and Economic Costs of Misclassification in the Michigan Construction Industry.* East Lansing, MO: Institute for Public Policy and Social Research, Michigan State University.

Bernhardt, A. (2012). *The low-wage recovery and growing inequality.* Washington, DC: National Employment Law Project.

Bernhardt, A., R. Milkman, N. Theodore, D. Heckathorn, M. Auer, J. DeFilippis, … M. Spiller. (2009). *Broken laws, unprotected workers: Violations of employment and labor laws in America's cities.* Center for Urban Economic Development, National Employment Law Project, UCLA Institute for Research on Labor and Employment, New York.

Berube, A. (2016, August). *Job shifts may help explain why earnings are declining for black Americans.* The Brookings Institute. Retrieved from https://www.brookings.edu/blog/the-avenue/2016/08/29/job-shifts-may-help-explain-why-earnings-are-declining-for-black-americans/

Bivens, J., & L. Mishel. (2015). *Understanding the historic divergence between productivity and a typical worker's pay.* Washington, DC: Economic Policy Institute.

Block, F. L. (1990). *Postindustrial possibilities: A critique of economic discourse.* Oakland: University of California Press.

Boden, L. I., E. A. Spieler, & G. R. Wagner. (2015). *The changing structure of work: Implications for workplace health and safety in the US.* Washington, DC: U. S. Department of Labor.

Boden, L. I., E. A. Spieler, & G. R. Wagner. (2016). "The changing structure of work: Implications for workplace health and safety in the US." *Future of Work Symposium.* Washington, DC: U.S. Department of Labor.

Capps, R., M. E. Fix, J. S. Passel, J. Ost, & D. Perez-Lopez. (2003). *A profile of the low-wage immigrant workforce.* Washington, DC: Urban Institute.

Carré, F. (2015). *(In)dependent contractor misclassification.* Washington, DC: Economic Policy Institute.

Carré, F., & R. Wilson. (2004) *The Social and Economic Costs of Employee Misclassification in Construction.* Cambridge, MA: Report of the Construction Policy Research Center, Labor and Worklife Program at Harvard Law School, and Harvard School of Public Health.

Cascio, W. F. (2006, December). "The high cost of low wages." *Harvard Business Review.* Retrieved from https://hbr.org/2006/12/the-high-cost-of-low-wages

Cooper, D., & T. Kroeger. (2017). *Employers steal billions from workers' paychecks each year.* Washington, DC: Economic Policy Institute.

de Silva, L. et al (2000) *Independent Contractors: Prevalence and Implications for Unemployment Insurance Programs.* Washington, DC: Report of Planmatics, Inc., for U.S. Department of Labor Employment and Training Administration.

Dirnbach, E. (January 31). *Solidarity forever? Union membership continues its long decline.* Retrieved from https://medium.com/@ericdirnbach/solidarity-forever-union-membership-continues-its-long-decline-43d348b37b12

Entmacher, J., L. Frohlich, G. K. Robbins, E. Martin, & L. Watson. (2014). *Underpaid & overloaded: Women in low-wage jobs.* Washington, DC: National Women's Law Center.

Ferguson, J.-P. (2008) "The Eyes of the Needes: A Sequential Model of Union Organizing Drives, 1999-2004." *Industrial and Labor Relations Review,* 62(1), 3–21.

Filer, R., & D. Golbe. (2003). "Debt, operating margin, and investment in workplace safety." *The Journal of Industrial Economics,* 51, 359–381.

Fortin, N. M., & T. Lemieux. (1997). "Institutional changes and rising wage inequality: Is there a linkage?" *Journal of Economic Perspectives,* 11(2), 75–96.

Frye, J. (2017, November 20). "Not just the rich and famous." Center for American Progress. Retrieved from https://www.americanprogress.org/issues/women/news/2017/11/20/443139/not-just-rich-famous/

Galvin, D. J. (2016). "Deterring wage theft: Alt-labor, state politics, and the policy determinants of minimum wage compliance." *Perspectives on Politics,* 14(2), 324–350.

Garcia, R. J. (2009). "Toward fundamental change for the protection of low-wage workers: The workers' rights are human rights' debate in the Obama Era." *University of Chicago Legal Forum*, 1, 421–457.

Gilens, M., & B. I. Page. (2014). "Testing theories of american politics: Elites, interest groups, and average citizens." *Perspectives on Politics*, 12(3), 564–581.

Greenhouse, S. (2008). *The big squeeze: Tough times for the American worker*. New York: Anchor Books.

Hacker J. S. (2004). Privatizing risk without privatizing the welfare state: The hidden politics of social policy retrenchment in the United States. *American Political Science Review*, 98(2), 243–260.

Jackson, E., A. Looney, & S. Ramnath. (2017). *The rise of alternative work arrangements: Evidence and implications for tax filing and benefit coverage*. Washington, DC: The Department of the Treasury, Office of Tax Analysis.

Kimball, W., & L. Mishel. (2015, February 3). *Unions' decline and the rise of the top 10 percent's share of income*. Economic Policy Institute. Retrieved from http://www.epi.org/publication/unions-decline-and-the-rise-of-the-top-10-percents-share-of-income/

Kramer, W. (2014). "Is it a safe bet to challenge OSHA?" *Risk Management*, 61(1), 32–36.

Leberstein, S. (2012). *Independent contractor misclassification imposes huge costs on workers and federal and state treasuries*. Washington, DC: National Employment Law Project.

Leigh, J. P. (2011). "Economic burden of occupational injury and illness in the United States." *The Milibank Quarterly*, 89(4), 724–772.

Logan, J. (2006). "The union avoidance industry in the United States." *British Journal of Industrial Relations*, 44(4), 651–675.

Lopez, S. H. (2004). *Reorganizing the rust belt: An inside study of the American labor movement*. Berkeley: Univeristy of California Press.

Martin, L. L. (2015). "Low-wage workers and the myth of post-racialism." *Loyola Journal of Public Interest Law*, 16, 47–62.

Mayer, G. (2004). *Union membership trends in the United States*. Washington, DC: Congressional Research Service.

Meixell, B., & R. Eisenbrey. (2014). *An epidemic of wage theft is costing workers hundreds of millions of dollars a year*. Washington, DC: Economic Policy Institute.

Milkman, R. (2006). *L.A. story: Immigrant workers and the future of the U.S. labor movement*. New York: Russel Sage Foundation.

Moody, K. (2016, June 20). *The state of American labor*. Jacobin. Retrieved from https://www.jacobinmag.com/2016/06/precariat-labor-us-workers-uber-walmart-gig-economy/

OSHA. (2015). *Adding inequality to injury: The costs of failing to protect workers on the job*. Washington, DC: U.S. Department of Labor.

OSHA. (2018a). *Commonly used statistics*. U.S. Department of Labor, Occupational Health and Safety Administration. Retrieved from https://www.osha.gov/oshstats/commonstats.html

OSHA. (2018b). *OSHA penalties*. U.S. Department of Labor, Occupational Health and Safety Administration. Retrieved from https://www.osha.gov/penalties/

Piketty, T., Saez, E., & Zucman, G. (2016, December). *Distributional national accounts: Methods and estimates for the United States*. NBER Working Paper No. 22945.

Robinson, I. (2000). "Neoliberal restrucruting and U.S. unions: Toward social movement unionism?" *Critical Sociology*, 26(1–2), 109–138.

Schiffer, N. (2005). *Whither vs. wither: How the NLRA has failed contingent workers*. Paper presented at the annual meeting of the American Bar Association, Chicago.

Schmitt, J. (2012). *The minimum wage is too damn low*. Washington, DC: Center for Economic and Policy Research.

Schmitt, J., & B. Zipperer. (2008) *The Decline in African-American Representation in Unions and Manufacturing, 1979-2007*. Washington, DC: Center for Economic and Policy Research.

Slaughter, M. J. (2007). "Globalizaiton and declining unionization in the United States." *Industrial Relations*, 46(2), 329–346.

Standing, G. (2014). *The precariat: The new dangerous class.* London: Bloomsbury.

Storm, A. (2018, August 31). *At Trump's NLRB, workers don't even get a hearing.* OnLabor: Workers, Unions, Politics. Retrieved from https://onlabor.org/at-trumps-nlrb-workers-dont-even-get-a-hearing/

The Dunlop Commission on the Future of Worker-Management Relations (1994) Washington, D.C.: Cornell University Press.

Theodore, N., B. Boggess, J. Cornejo, & E. Timm. (2017). *Build a Better South: Construction working conditions in the southern U.S.* Austin, TX: Workers Defense Project.

Tung, I., P. Sonn, & Y. Lathrop. (2015). *The growing movement for $15.* Washington, DC: The National Employment Law Project.

U.S. Bureau of Economic Analysis. (2017, December 21). *National income and product accounts.* Retrieved from https://bea.gov/newsreleases/national/GDP/GDPnewsrelease.htm

U.S. Bureau of Labor Statistics. (2017a, December 7). *Labor productivity and costs.* Retrieved from https://www.bls.gov/lpc/prodybar.htm

U.S. Bureau of Labor Statistics. (2017b, Janurary 26). *Union members summary.* Retrieved from https://www.bls.gov/news.release/union2.nr0.htm

U.S. Bureau of Labor Statistics. (2018a). *Economic news release: Union members summary.* Retrieved Janurary 2018, from U.S. Department of Labor https://www.bls.gov/news.release/union2.nr0.htm

U.S. Bureau of Labor Statistics. (2018b, Janurary 10). *Employed persons by detailed occupation, sex, race, and Hispanic or Latino ethnicity.* Labor Force Statistics from the Current Population Survey. Retrieved from https://www.bls.gov/cps/cpsaat11.htm

U.S. Census Bureau. (2015). *2014–2015 SUSB employment change data tables.* Retrieved from https://www.census.gov/data/tables/2015/econ/susb/2015-susb-employment.html

US. Department of Labor. (2017). *Foreign-born workers: Labor force characteristics summary.* Retrieved from https://www.bls.gov/news.release/forbrn.nr0.htm

U.S. Government Accountability Office. (2009). *Employee misclassification: Improved coordination, outreach, and targeting could better ensure detection and prevention.* Washington, DC: Author.

U.S. Senate Committee on Health, Education, Labor and Pensions. (2008). *Discounting death: OSHA's failure to punish safety violations that kill workers.* Washington, DC: U.S. Senate.

Vachon, T. E., M. Wallace, & A. Hyde. (2016). "Union decline in a neoliberal age: Globalization, financialization, European integration, and union density in 18 affluent democracies." *Socius: Sociological Research for a Dynamic World*, 2, 1–22.

Warren, D. (2010). "The American Labor Movement in the Age of Obama: The challenges and opportunities of a racialized political economy." *Persepctives on Politics*, 8(3), 847–860.

Weil, D. (2011). "Enforcing labour standards in fissured workplaces: The U.S. experience." *Economic and Labour Relations Review*, 22(2), 33–54.

Western, B., & J. Rosenfeld. (2011). "Unions, norms, and the rise in U.S. wage inequality." *American Sociological Review*, 76(4), 513–537.

Considering Structural and Ideological Barriers to Anti-Poverty Programs in the United States: An Uninhibited, and Unconventional, Analysis

Max J. Skidmore

Department of Political Science, University of Missouri–Kansas City, Kansas City, MO

Historical circumstances and ideological factors combine to obscure the presence and severity of poverty in the United States. Moreover, in recent years, America's two-party system has become increasingly nonsymmetrical, with a significant segment of the political system devoted to privatization, deferring to demands from religious fundamentalists, and draining power and authority from the government (with the notable exception of police and military powers). The result is continual pressure to shrink government, minimize taxes, reduce or eliminate regulation, enhance the power of private commercial interests, and rely upon citizens to care for themselves without assistance. This has led to a demonization of the "welfare state," an enormous increase in income inequality, a concentration of wealth upward, a significant effort aimed at largely withdrawing government from the provision of health care, and the retreat of a major political party from acceptance of any obligation to promote the general welfare.

KEY WORDS: poverty, structural barriers to legislation, ideological barriers to legislation, language and politics, fundamentalism

考量美国扶贫方案的结构性和意识形态障碍：种不受约束的非常规分析

历史环境和意识形态因素结合在一起，掩盖了美国贫困的存在和严重程度。此外，美国近几年来的两党制越来越偏离正常的轨道，相当一部分的政治体系致力于私有化，服从宗教原教旨主义者的要求，削弱政府的权力和权威(警察和军事权力除外)。其结果是不断施加压力削减政府规模，减少税收，放宽或取消管制，增强私人商业利益的权力，并依靠公民在没有得到援助的情况下接济政府。"福利国家"因此走向妖魔化，收入不平等差距加大，财富向上集中，政府很大程度上停止提供医疗保险，主要政党拒绝承担任何促进全民福利的义务。

关键词：两党制，私有化，医疗保健，收入不平等

Consideración de las barreras estructurales e ideológicas para los programas de lucha contra la pobreza en los Estados Unidos: un análisis desinhibido y no convencional

Las circunstancias históricas y los factores ideológicos se combinan para ocultar la presencia y la gravedad de la pobreza en los Estados Unidos. Además, en los últimos años, el sistema bipartidista de los Estados Unidos se ha vuelto cada vez más no simétrico, con un segmento significativo del sistema político dedicado a la privatización, aplazando las demandas de los fundamentalistas religiosos y agotando el poder y la autoridad del gobierno (con la notable excepción de las fuerzas policiales y militares). El resultado es una presión continua para reducir el gobierno, minimizar los impuestos, reducir o eliminar la regulación, mejorar el poder de los intereses comerciales privados y confiar en que los ciudadanos se cuiden sin asistencia. Esto ha llevado a una demonización del "estado de bienestar", a un enorme aumento de la desigualdad en el ingreso, a una concentración de la riqueza al alza, a un esfuerzo significativo destinado a retirar en gran medida al gobierno de la prestación de atención médica, y al retiro de un partido político importante de Aceptación de cualquier obligación de promover el bienestar general.

PALABRAS CLAVES: sistema bipartidista, privatización, salud, desigualdad de ingresos

Introduction

It is almost a truism that the United States across the board came late to programs of social welfare. Despite former President Theodore Roosevelt's rousing call for a broad range of programs—first with his famous speech in Osawatomie, Kansas, in 1910, and then in 1912 during his third-party "Bull Moose Progressive" effort to regain the presidency—America has yet to achieve the levels of income and health maintenance achieved in the rest of the developed world. What Americans call Social Security emerged in Germany in the 1880s, and it was not enacted into law in the United States until 1935. The United States had no legislation providing for disability benefits until 1956, when President Eisenhower signed an amendment adding them to the Social Security Act.

Universal health care still is not fully implemented, despite President Lyndon Johnson's addition of Medicare, health care for the aged, to the Social Security Act in 1965; and despite President Barack Obama's legislation in 2010, the Affordable Care Act (or, under Republican terminology, calculated to demonize it, the infamous "Obamacare"). That act—created to expand coverage under private health insurance and under Medicaid, the program designed for those in poverty—moved the United States in the direction of universal health coverage, but it admittedly left much yet to be done to achieve full coverage.

To be sure, impediments have existed and continue to exist. It is important to recognize that, but also to keep things in perspective. The situation is more nuanced than the conventional wisdom has it. Theda Skocpol demonstrated in her landmark *Protecting Soldiers and Mothers* (Skocpol, 1995) that by the end of the nineteenth century, the United States had extensive programs benefiting many of its elderly, disabled, and poverty-stricken citizens. The explanation for the apparent contradiction is that the benefits were related to the ravages of the Civil War, and that war, directly and indirectly, affected an enormous number of Americans of both sexes.

The military connection reflected one of the persistent realities of American politics: much that otherwise had been virtually impossible could be achieved when justified by military considerations. In the beginning early twentieth century, there were some programs of federal assistance to the building of highways. These, generally, were supported by considerations of national defense, but discussions in the 1930s buttressed later by what became the dynamics of the Cold War brought about what was perhaps the greatest public works program of all time, the Interstate Highway System. President Eisenhower signed into law the Federal Aid Highway Act on June 29, 1956; this law is more widely known as the Interstate and Defense Highways Act of 1956.

That is not hyperbole. In designing and constructing the interstate highways, not only were they to facilitate ground transport for the military and its equipment, but also, as one scholar remarked, "superhighways can accommodate emergency landings and takeoffs of airplanes" (McNichol, 2003, p. 12; Skidmore, 2016, p. 326).

Similarly, until the 1950s, there had been no widespread support for broad federal assistance to education. To be sure, there had previously been some programs that did provide education with some support from the federal government. Most notable, perhaps, was the Morrill Act that President Lincoln signed into law in 1862, which increased the accessibility of higher education by encouraging the creation of what became America's great land-grant colleges and universities—many of them now world-class research institutions. Fears of "federal control," however, as well as resistance to taxation, had always overwhelmed any support for broader assistance. The dynamics of the Cold War, especially the launch of history's first successful space satellite, *Sputnik*, by the USSR on October 4, 1957, made possible the National Defense Education Act that President Eisenhower signed into law on September 2, 1958. The act provided support for education at all levels, and emphasized science, mathematics, and foreign languages.

The factor that enabled the acceptance of these new programs was not transportation for its own sake; possibly even less was it a concern for education. It was fear of foreign military power. Regarding anti-poverty legislation, one might conclude, perhaps with cynicism, that it is unlikely to succeed in any major way unless it can be rationalized as needed for national defense.

Even that, though—if viewed cynically—may recently have become obsolete as a consideration. One might be justified in suspecting, from the vantage point of 2018, that even the intense concern for national defense has been superseded by tribal political considerations as American "conservatives" rally around their leader who during his campaign issued a clear call for foreign interference; they disregard evidence of foreign corrupting of American elections, and dismiss any threat whatever from the alien source that had long been their strongest fear: Russia.

This article examines the difficulties in securing anti-poverty legislation in the United States. Securing such programs requires maneuvering around both structural and ideological barriers, and overcoming cultural proclivities.

Structural Barriers

Recognizing structural barriers to anti-poverty programs is simple and straightforward. Any thoughtful person familiar with the structure and function of American government should require little reflection to recognize them. The Constitution establishes a government that incorporates caution, and thus, especially where broad programs are involved, that government is not designed to encourage easy action. In this respect, anti-poverty programs are not unique. Under normal circumstances, passage of any legislation—anti-poverty measures included—tends to be a difficult process.

Bills may be introduced into either house of Congress (except that the Constitution requires revenue bills to originate in the House of Representatives, and custom requires that appropriation measures originate there also). In the originating house, they must make their way through an elaborate committee structure, be approved by a vote of the whole house, and proceed to the other chamber. There, they must embark upon a similarly difficult journey, ultimately obtaining approval from that full house as well.

After achieving approval in each house, in nearly all instances any complex program will have some variations between the versions that each house has approved. A conference committee consisting of members from each chamber then must be appointed and must approve a new version of the bill for it to become law. This must reflect a majority of the senators on the committee, and a majority also of the representatives on the committee; a committee majority, alone, is insufficient. When approved, the conference committee report goes back to each house, and both houses must approve it before it can proceed to the president.

The president then must decide whether to veto the proposed legislation or to sign it into law before 10 days have passed. If the president vetoes it, the bill is returned, with presidential objections, to the house where it originated. The measure dies unless both houses vote, each by a two-thirds majority, to override the veto. If the president takes no action, the bill becomes law with no presidential signature after 10 days have passed—providing that Congress is still in session. If Congress has adjourned during the 10-day period, though, the bill dies. That is the so-called "pocket veto," and such a veto cannot be overridden.

Assuming that the bill makes it through the process, despite the hurdles, and becomes law, the program—complicated though the course it has followed has been—it still is only halfway to success. To be sure, there is a law, but despite passage of that law, there is no funding for whatever program the new law authorizes. To obtain funding, an appropriations bill is required. Thus, a completely separate bill must be enacted to support the original bill. Such a bill must go through the same procedures as the original bill, except that it must begin in the House, not the Senate, and must go through different committees in each house.

This extraordinarily complex process is not unique to anti-poverty measures, but applies to all national legislation. To be sure, emergency legislation can be enacted quickly. FDR's New Deal began with a most impressive First 100 Days in which some 15 or so enormous programs emerged from Congress with astonishing speed, but quick action is not customary from Congress, nor can it be expected. The process is designed to discourage it. Legislation is very hard to achieve.

Anti-poverty legislation faces the same procedural difficulties as other measures, but it also encounters other challenges of its own. These are cultural and ideological.

Ideological and Cultural Barriers

Misconceptions Regarding the Extent of Poverty and Its Effects

For a number of reasons, those Americans who are not themselves afflicted with poverty often are uninformed about the extent to which it exists in the United States, and are equally ignorant of its dire effects. This first became apparent to well-read Americans in the middle of the last century, when Michael Harrington published his scathing exposé, *The Other America* (Harrington, 1962). In early 1963, Harrington's book became the subject of a quite lengthy review by Dwight MacDonald, in *The New Yorker*. MacDonald's review was itself an impressive work, and indirectly brought Harrington's powerful condemnation to President John Kennedy's attention (MacDonald, 1963).

As I said in a retrospective review of Harrington's book roughly a half century after it was published (Skidmore, 2009), Harrington "took direct issue with the 'conventional wisdom,' a term that itself was new. The great economist (and noted iconoclast) John Kenneth Galbraith had coined it only a short time before, in *The Affluent Society*, his own classic work of 1958. Appropriately, Galbraith was one of Harrington's major sources, despite Harrington's rejection of Galbraith's conclusion that America's poverty had dwindled as its affluence progressed." Thus, even Galbraith, who possessed one of the most penetrating intellects of modern times, had misjudged the extent of poverty in America—at least as Harrington read him.

The enormous effect of Harrington's work and MacDonald's vast distribution of his highly positive, and extensive, review became the subject of a fine analytical article by Linda Keefe, "Dwight MacDonald and Poverty Discourse, 1960–1965: The Art and Power of a Seminal Book Review," first published in *Poverty and Public Policy* in 2010 (Keefe, 2010). It also was reprinted, five years later, in *Poverty in America* (Skidmore, 2015). Keefe deftly traces the effect of Harrington's work as MacDonald carefully presented and interpreted it. She also goes into great depth regarding the effect on MacDonald's own career, especially as the public responded so overwhelmingly to his perceptive work.

Sadly, the attention toward poverty that began under Kennedy and escalated greatly under Lyndon Johnson, with his War on Poverty, quickly dwindled as Nixon and subsequently Reagan implemented their Southern Strategy. It dwindled even more rapidly as their Republican successors vied to go to even greater extremes than their predecessors in their pursuits of political power. From the vantage point of the twenty-first century, Keefe (2010) makes plain what has been lost. My own review, predating Keefe, ended thusly:

> It may seem that *The Other America* was premature, but perhaps it was essential that it appear when it did. Its ideas later were shoved aside, but not destroyed. Society awaits a new call, but such a call is unlikely to come from turning again to Harrington.
>
> Instead, a new voice should raise again the issues that he raised, tailoring the new appeal to the nation as it has become, and introducing new issues beyond what Harrington or other thinkers a half-century ago recognized. America seems now to have come again to the notion that "you're on your own" cannot be the foundation of a desirable society. The time seems appropriate for another voice that will encourage the placement of poverty among the few items at the top of society's political agenda. (Skidmore, 2009)

Those words came before the emergence nationally of such figures as Bernie Sanders, and certainly before anyone of substance thought of taking seriously one such as Donald Trump. Nevertheless, their relevance (if not their prescience) seems if anything to have increased. Poverty continues to demand attention even as the political system turns its back, and ignores it, even denying its importance. As a recent UN report, and the almost hysterical reaction to it, made clear, poverty remains an American phenomenon. However apparent American poverty may be outside the United States, though, it again has retreated to near invisibility within the country itself.

The *Washington Post* reported in late June of 2018 that "the U.N. says 18.5 million Americans are in 'extreme poverty.' Trump's team says just 250,000 are." To be sure, the issue is complex. Conservatives argue that the higher figures ignore programs of assistance to the poor. Whatever the accuracy of the two extremes, though, it is clear to those actually in the field (the *Post* cites a number of scholars) that the figure of one quarter million is absurdly low (Washington Post Wonkblog, 2018).

Nikki Haley, Trump's ambassador to the UN, said the report was "misleading and politically motivated." The *Los Angeles Times* quoted the report's author, Philip Alston, "the U.N.'s special rapporteur on extreme poverty and human rights," as condemning the Trump administration for "pursuing high tax breaks for the rich and removing basic protections for the poor" (Jarvie, 2018). *The Guardian* and other publications quoted Haley as saying that it is "patently ridiculous for the United Nations to examine poverty in America." *The Guardian* also noted that this furor came a mere matter of days after the United States announced, through Haley, that it would withdraw from the UN's human rights council, the first country ever to do so (Pilkington, 2018).

Whatever the merits of the controversy regarding the UN report—and however much another phenomenon, the increasingly obvious fragility of this country's most fundamental political institutions, is coming to overshadow all other considerations—it appears clear that poverty does, indeed, remain ever-present in the United States. It seems equally clear that the tendency, at least within the United States, is to overlook its presence, if not, in fact, to ignore it deliberately.

Jeffersonian Heritage

Regardless of the actual practices of the American political system, there can be little doubt that the heritage of Jeffersonianism, at least with regard to political rhetoric, reflects a widespread romantic attachment to what much of the public (even of those who believe they are reasonably informed on the subject) would consider to be the ideas of Thomas Jefferson. This attachment may either be recognized—that is, those who hold them do so knowingly—or others may have absorbed them without recognizing, or caring about, their origin. In both instances, the acceptance of popular views of Jeffersonian ideas is unlikely to encourage nuance, or to permit understanding the complexities of his thought.

Most prominently, Jefferson advocated localism, strictly limited government (especially at the national level), agrarianism, and a maximum of individual autonomy. At one level, the effect of such ideas can lead to a laudable effort to be as self-sufficient as possible, and to support individual freedom for others as well as for oneself. At another, it can lead to such antipathy toward government that it brings opposition to any collective effort to assist those in need, or to restrict the ability of private power holders to impose their will upon others. Review any of the numerous statements by the Koch brothers for examples. This means that it certainly is possible to use Jeffersonian rhetoric to oppose action calculated to alleviate poverty, and to support policies that lead to income inequality, thus leading to preferential treatment of the most powerful. That clearly is apparent in contemporary America. As I described the situation in a recent book: "The principles accepted by modern American 'conservatives' and libertarians emerged in the eighteenth century, crafted carefully to protect the people from the powerful. As they have evolved, or devolved, over the last half century or so, they now are carefully crafted to protect the powerful from the people" (Skidmore, 2017, p. 1).

In any case, they are most unlikely to be based upon a clear understanding of the nuances of Jefferson's thought, such as his preference for "ward republics" intended to enhance the ability of individuals actually to become governors, and to influence the forces that affect them directly.

However much the practice of slavery especially, and racism in general, sullied his record and rendered him justly vulnerable to the charge of hypocrisy, Jefferson's intellectual approach to authority and political equality did condemn the "peculiar institution." Regarding the evolution of anti-poverty legislation, however, Jefferson's legacy was pernicious. The habit of speaking in terms of a preference for the local, as opposed to the national (or even the state), as well as an assumption that the national government should limit itself to minimal action in the social realm, has always tended to put proposals for anti-poverty legislation at a disadvantage before they even were considered seriously. With the ascendency of southern strategies, tender treatment of wealth, and pandering toward right-wing fundamentalist populists, the obstacles facing anti-poverty measures have become almost insurmountable.

Confusion Regarding Thought of "The Founders"

Although one often hears that the United States has departed from the ideas of "The Founders" and should return to their principles, those who are so adamant on the issue tend to extol ideas that were common among those who opposed the Constitution, rather than those who supported it. Using the Founders as a guide would in any case appear to present difficulties, when one considers that the Founders as a group certainly had their differences. Jefferson and Hamilton were certainly "Founders," and more often than not, they entertained opinions that differed sharply.

Certainly, Americans throughout their history have honored Jeffersonian rhetoric: small government, strict construction of the Constitution, decentralization of power, limited taxation, and the like. Just as certainly, though, the country all the while speaking in Jeffersonian terms erected a foundation built on the principles of Jefferson's antagonists, the Federalists.

To be sure, the Federalists as a party vanished within a few decades of the Republic's creation. Nevertheless, Federalist principles, ensconced in the judiciary, built the new Republic as it evolved. The great Chief Justice John Marshall, certainly "a Founder," speaking for the Court set forth judicial review, central power, and other Federalist ideas.

Outside the judiciary, even those in the Jeffersonian tradition often asserted or acted to enhance presidential authority. President Thomas Jefferson himself, regardless of his constitutional views, did what he thought was best for the country and negotiated the enormous Louisiana Purchase. President James Madison signed into law legislation creating a national bank. Andrew Jackson, the "Old Hero," who considered himself to be an old Jeffersonian, pioneered the use of the veto as a policy measure.

Regardless of what might be thought of as Hamiltonian practices, the use of Jeffersonian rhetoric and presuppositions through the years has been troublesome for advocates of legislation designed specifically to combat poverty. As noted above, any legislation aiming at the implementation of strong national domestic policy is handicapped to begin with. Its chances for success are best if put forward with justifications relating it to national defense. The need to provide such justification creates special hurdles for measures designed primarily to reduce poverty. President Franklin D. Roosevelt was extraordinarily perceptive when he proposed "An Economic Bill of Rights" in his State of the Union addresses in 1944 and 1945. He argued that economic security was part of national security. Unfortunately, reasonable though the case certainly is, it has not been made sufficiently since then to be as effective as it needs to be to bring anti-poverty programs in the United States to levels that prevail elsewhere in industrialized countries.

Fundamentalist Misrepresentations of America's Political Heritage

"Fundamentalism," as discussed here, refers to ideological rigidity, and textual literalism. The argument is that it leads to rejection of logic, and even of fact. It is a mind-set, and it is to be found not only in religion, but in other forms of thought as well.

Although the assertion here covers many subjects, and thus is considerably broader than one normally encounters, the assertion of similarities between religious and constitutional fundamentalism is not unique to this article. Smith and Tuttle have produced a deeply thoughtful examination that deals with such similarities (note that they consider dissimilarities as well). As they remark, "given the obvious similarities between these two interpretive approaches, it is perhaps not surprising that Cass Sunstein, Morton Horwitz, and others have pejoratively used the label 'fundamentalists' to describe originalists." Moreover, they note, it therefore "is not surprising that prominent conservative Protestant fundamentalists have praised originalism as the proper approach to constitutional interpretation in the course of criticizing the Supreme Court's nonoriginalist decisionmaking" (Smith & Tuttle, 2013, pp. 694–695).

Going much further than they and most others do, the current essay takes the position that wherever it is encountered, fundamentalism instills dogma. Its tendency is toward repression. It accommodates racism, opposes measures to enhance human freedom, and almost always leads to the subjugation of women (which itself is arguably the greatest single cause of poverty throughout the world).

Constitutional Fundamentalism

As of autumn, 2018, there is and has been considerable discussion regarding Mr. Trump's selection of Brett Kavanaugh as his new nominee to the Supreme Court to replace Justice Kennedy, who retired the preceding summer. Many of the Republican commentators had stressed that the Trump appointee would, and had to, be an "originalist" and would, and had to, interpret the Constitution as authorizing only that which it asserts specifically.

Most who commented were less sophisticated than the late Justice Scalia, in that they asserted that his originalism meant "original intent" of the Founders. Justice Scalia was not so simpleminded as to believe that it is possible to discern original intent. What he meant by originalism was the somewhat more practical—but still more superficial than truly analytical—notion of "original understanding." That is, the Constitution should be interpreted in the same way as those who originally interpreted it. The difficulty, even with this definition of originalism, is that with regard to the Constitution—just as with any other fairly complex writing (scripture, of course, is a case in point)—there are always, and always have been, differing interpretations, and differing interpretations among people who are reasonable, well-intentioned, and well-informed. One may pick and choose among the Founders to support a wide variety of interpretations.

Moreover, the assertion that something must be specifically spelled out in the Constitution to be valid has itself been a source of debate throughout American political history. Witness the "Stewardship Theory," of Theodore Roosevelt, who argued that the president has the authority, even the duty, to take any action the public good requires, unless that action is forbidden by the Constitution or by the law. His successor, President Taft, who subsequently became chief justice of the Supreme Court, believed that such an approach was far too activist and that the president is bound by what the Constitution and the laws specifically authorize. This argument was centered on presidential power, but similar discussions have dealt with the power of the national government in general.

The absolutist argument, in any case, is almost assuredly unworkable. Perhaps it is illustrative to cite an example that seems ridiculous. That is this: to one who fully accepts absolutism, it should have been unconstitutional to create a U.S. Air Force without actually proposing and ratifying a constitutional amendment. The Constitution, as it stands, gives Congress the power only to raise and maintain an army and a navy.

The reason the example seems ridiculous is that the notion that a constitution can spell out specifically every detail of governing a nation-state is itself ridiculous. It was ridiculous even in 1789. In fact, the entire absolutist argument is itself nonconstitutional, in that the actual Constitution explicitly asserts that it does not include every detail. Those who assert constitutional fundamentalism themselves ignore the Ninth Amendment: "The enumeration in the Constitution, of certain rights, shall not be construed to deny or disparage others retained by the people." In other words, the Constitution clearly contains principles that it does not explicitly spell out, and says so directly.

Yet how often has one heard such arguments as, for example, "show me where in the Constitution it authorizes a system of social security" or "where in the Constitution does it authorize welfare?" Of course, such questions ignore the Preamble's assertion that a purpose of the Constitution is to "promote the general welfare." People have even been known to dismiss the importance of this phrase, because they argue that the Preamble is not "really" a part of the Constitution; it is mere window dressing. Ignoring that such a statement itself is hardly a literal reading of the Constitution, one can refer them to Article I, Section 8, where the Constitution again uses the phrase. In the very first sentence, it grants Congress the "Power To lay and collect Taxes, Duties, Imposts and Excises, to pay the Debts and provide for the common Defence and general Welfare of the United States. ..." In the last paragraph of Article I, Section 8, the Constitution further grants Congress the power "To make all Laws which shall be necessary and proper for carrying into Execution the foregoing Powers, and all other Powers vested by this Constitution in the Government of the United States. ..."

Regardless of whether it is appropriate, many Americans tend to assume that Jeffersonian rhetoric (or rhetoric that sounds Jeffersonian) is the rhetoric of the Founders. Similarly, it bears repeating that many conservatives attribute to "the Founders" not the arguments of the actual founding, but rather the arguments of those who opposed the Constitution. They argue, for example, that the purpose of the Constitution was to create a weak national government, when in reality the intention was to create a strong government at the center to replace one that had, in the minds of the Founders, too little power. That, along with a fairly common tendency to respond favorably to arguments based on constitutional fundamentalism, presents an obstacle to the passage and implementation of anti-poverty measures.

Economic Fundamentalism

Opponents of anti-poverty measures number among their prime concerns a preoccupation with cost. When cost is the prime criterion, any resulting program is likely to be entirely inadequate. As counterintuitive as it sounds, the way to achieve good programs is to plan the program that best meets the needs, and only then plan for cost; cost is a secondary consideration.

This will be resisted strongly. Every dollar the government spends, say the economic fundamentalists (and, one must concede, most others as well), must come from taxing the people, or else from borrowing, thus running at a deficit. Not putting costs first, they argue, is irresponsible, and would create a situation that is unsustainable.

The answer to this is simple, and should be obvious: concentrate on outcomes, *all things considered*. First, examine Medicare, Part D, the prescription drug benefit. Part D has its problems, but has turned out to work quite well. Violating all the strictures of economic fundamentalism, the administration of President George W. Bush shoved the program through Congress over the objections of Democrats, who argued that the program provided no financing mechanism. One should note that the program's major supporters were "conservatives"; Republicans who presumably were devoted to economic fundamentalism, but who sacrificed such principles in order to gain political advantage. The Bush administration created a program without considerations of cost—and that program works.

True, Part D prohibits Medicare officials from negotiating drug prices with manufacturers, and thus adds to the absurdly high costs of American medicine. It also is true that this results in an enormous subsidy to Big Pharma. These are flaws. They could be remedied easily—and certainly should be.

The key point is the good that Part D does. It provides a huge new benefit to the American people, an important benefit that helps them survive the unspeakably high costs of American medicine. It also, to repeat, was created with no thought of, or attention to, the expense.

Second, consider military expenditures. The very people who would argue that costs must be demonstrated to be "sustainable" when planning for social legislation never think to provide a set sum to the Department of Defense, and then say "work within those limits." Rather, the practice always has been—at least since it began during the Second World War—to provide the military with that which military officials say they need, and worry about paying for it later, if at all.

The security of the American people, in other words, is deemed important enough to violate the principles of economic fundamentalism. Certainly, one should think, the health security and economic security of the people are equally important, and thus should be considered accordingly.

Economic fundamentalists can never accept a key principle of American national government. At the state and local level this is not the case, but at the national level, the government of the United States controls its own currency. It pays its debts in dollars, borrows in dollars, and creates dollars as needed. It simply is not true that "every dollar has to come from taxation or borrowing." The U.S. government creates dollars all the time. Moreover, as a result, there is no direct relationship at the national level between government expenditures and government income.

Nevertheless, this is difficult to grasp, and somehow seems intuitively that it cannot be true. Dollars have to come from somewhere, is the sentiment. A family cannot create an IOU to pay its bills. When times are tight, families must tighten their belts. When times are tight, government must tighten its belt too, goes the conventional wisdom (President Obama himself once made a similar comment). Anything else is counterintuitive. Perhaps it is counterintuitive, but the conventional wisdom is what is wrong. "You cannot spend your way to prosperity," we hear. A national government with a strong economy, however, can—and does.

Still, the conventional wisdom creates another hurdle for anti-poverty measures. People detest having "their hard-earned money" going to others: often others who they believe are not worthy; others who don't want to work, who are of a different race or religion, who are outsiders. Until people recognize that government could halt all welfare payments and it would not reduce their taxes, or that they could triple or quadruple all such payments and that would not directly increase their taxes, they will continue to believe that they are financing others of whom they disapprove. Of course, it adds to the misconception every time politicians speak of "the taxpayer's money."

Also adding to misconceptions are assertions that come from economic "pundits," as well as politicians, that are simply contrary to observed fact. Hardly any competent economist believes that reducing taxes increases government revenue, and experience from Reagan onward demonstrates that it does not— witness the increase in revenues following tax increases under Bush I and Clinton, the enormous deficits following Reagan's tax reductions, the huge tax cuts under Bush II that were followed quickly by replacement of the budget surplus with great deficits. Witness, also, the financial disasters that resulted from slashing taxes in Louisiana and Kansas. Nevertheless, such was the propaganda that the "supply siders" spread after Reagan's tax cuts: that there still is a widespread opinion that there is a free lunch, and that a way to increase government revenues is to reduce taxes.

Similarly, pundits and conservative politicians offer austerity as the solution to economic downturns. All experience demonstrates that this is counterproductive, and destructive.

We are told that raising the minimum wage creates unemployment, yet from the famous Card and Krueger study onward, the bulk of research indicates little or no such effect (Card & Krueger, 1994). Card and Krueger had studied fast-food jobs in the Philadelphia area, part of which was in Pennsylvania, part in New Jersey. One state raised the minimum wage, and the other did not. The increase did not decrease the number of jobs. Conservatives, of course, have attacked these findings. Also, keep in mind that the economics profession as a whole is biased toward assuming such an effect, which may influence the studies its journals accept for publication. As the prominent liberal, and Nobel Laureate in Economics, Paul Krugman put it in the *New York Times* (Krugman, 2015):

> Until the Card-Krueger study, most economists, myself included, assumed that raising the minimum wage would have a clear negative effect on employment. But they found, if anything, a positive effect. Their result has since been confirmed using data from many episodes. There's just no evidence that raising the minimum wage costs jobs, at least when the starting point is as low as it is in modern America.

Krugman, too, as knowledgeable people would anticipate, has been the target of attacks from the usual suspects.

The *American Economic Review* supplies another striking example, equally revealing, possibly even more so. An enormously influential article appeared in 2010, "Growth in a Time of Debt," by two prominent economists, Carmen Reinhart and Kenneth Rogoff (2010). Their examinations of the economies of numerous countries, they asserted, demonstrated that when debt levels reach a certain point, 90 percent of GDP, they generate a severely adverse effect on economic growth, reducing it, in fact, to negative rates.

Representative Paul Ryan, then chair of the House Budget Committee, subsequently to be designated Speaker of the House—a noted austerian ideologue —used the article's conclusions as a foundation for his budget recommendations. Liberal economist Dean Baker pointed to the Reinhart and Rogoff effect as having caused enormous harm in Europe, where the austerian policies they encouraged pushed the unemployment rate "over 10 percent for the euro zone as a whole and above 20 percent in Greece and Spain." Their ideas had "certainly taken the world by storm" (see Skidmore, 2017, p. 89). Then, some two years later, the newly minted "law of finance," as some commentators and policymakers had gone so far as to label it, suddenly not only was called into question, but in the eyes of reasonable observers had crumbled into nothing but dogma.

To be sure, Reinhart and Rogoff (2010) had not gone so far as had many of those who advocated austerity did in citing their study, nor would it be wrong to recognize that there is some correlation, though not necessarily causation, between debt and growth. Discovering a "new law of finance," however, is another matter entirely.

Thomas Herndon, a doctoral student in economics at the University of Massachusetts—a mere student at an institution far down the totem pole from Harvard, the lofty and comfortable location from which Reinhart and Rogoff confidently reported their findings—had received an assignment to select an influential economics article and provide a critique. Happily for the knowledge base, if not so for Reinhart and Rogoff, Herndon chose their study.

The result, Herndon discovered, was immediate frustration. He could not make the figures work. Therefore, he went directly to Reinhart and Rogoff and sought their help. They kindly provided him with their own data. Unfortunately, those data quickly revealed significant errors in their study: exclusion of important data, coding errors, and questionable weighting. Herndon and his professors, Michael Ash and Robert Pollin, published a critical article in the *Cambridge Journal of Economics* and concluded that corrections demonstrated that the dreaded 90 percent figure had no special significance at all.

Reinhart and Rogoff conceded the errors, but continued to maintain that their conclusions were nevertheless accurate. Paul Krugman examined the controversy and concluded that the important factor seemed to be whether countries "had their own currencies, and borrowed in those currencies." Such countries cannot run out of money because they can create it as needed. Advanced economies can therefore carry large debt levels without generating crises.

The key question here, Krugman asked perceptively, is how an academic study can become so widely accepted without anyone looking at it closely enough to see obvious errors. The answer certainly is that it was such a convenient fit, and was so congenial to the conservative conventional wisdom, that no one thought to examine it—or wanted to. Erskine Bowles, for example, revealingly, said that the errors did not change his views because of his own "common sense," and his experience that debt is always an "enormous risk factor" (see Rabin-Havt & Matters, 2016; see also Skidmore, 2017, p. 90).

Some time later, John Cassidy, a thoughtful and perceptive staff writer who deals with politics and economics for *The New Yorker*, wrote "The Reinhart and Rogoff Controversy: A Summing Up." Pointing out what should have been obvious, Cassidy noted the "enormous damage to Reinhart and Rogoff's credibility, and to the intellectual underpinnings of the austerity policies with which they are associated" (Cassidy, 2013).

Cassidy noted further that the fiasco "has created another huge embarrassment for an economics profession that was still suffering from the fallout of the financial crisis and the laissez-faire policies that preceded it." As a journalist, Cassidy is less bound by disciplinary fastidiousness than are academic social scientists, and was free to ask the embarrassing—and again, the obvious—question: "After this new fiasco, how seriously should we take any economist's policy prescriptions, especially ones that are seized upon by politicians with agendas of their own?"

The question is apt. For our purposes, it is important to point out that it verifies just how irrational it is to be preoccupied with expenditures alone. More important is the overall *effect of those expenditures*—that is, the extent to which they meet the people's needs. Thus, the obsession that is so harmful to all social and anti-poverty considerations rests not firmly on fact, but actually on the unstable foundation of ideology.

Religious Fundamentalism

Religious fundamentalism might seem to be an unlikely topic to include in an article on barriers to anti-poverty legislation. Religion and poverty, as themes, have had a complex relationship far earlier than Max Weber, and even far earlier than the emergence of Protestantism. The emphasis here is not on Calvinism, on "The Protestant Ethic" that encouraged hard work as evidence that one was among "the Elect." Such doctrine may have led to an assumption that the poor did not work hard, and were therefore "undeserving." That, however, is not the major concern here.

Admittedly, in the American setting as well as in the traditions inherited from England, the notion of the "deserving" and the "undeserving" poor has had considerable force. Such emphasis can be seen in contemporary politics with regard to the "Dreamers," those noncitizens who are in this country because their parents brought them as infants or children. On the one hand, there are those who argue that they should in some manner be accommodated, because they are here without "permission" through no fault of their own. Others charge that anyone here without documentation is a "criminal," and should be deported immediately. The law becomes sacred when considering immigrants, yet not when a president pardons those who engage law enforcement officials in armed standoffs. Nor is a law "sacred" when a political party goes to great lengths—as Republicans have done with the Affordable Care Act—not only to repeal it (which is within normal political practice), but to sabotage it, and attempt to ensure its failure (which is not).

Nevertheless, as indicated, these issues are not the foremost concern of this article. Regardless of the relevance of such issues, the concern with religion here relates to something different: that is, the practice often taught in Bible colleges and fundamentalist-evangelical groups of "harmonization," along with excessive literalism. Vincent Crapanzano, an anthropologist, is one of the foremost scholars examining the effects of such literalism throughout American culture. His vital study is *Serving the Word*, but it is his subtitle that is especially appropriate: *Literalism in America from the Pulpit to the Bench* (Crapanzano, 2001).

Another anthropological scholar, Susan Friend Harding, a cultural anthropologist, similarly has studied "fundamentalist language and politics," which is the subtitle of her serious study, *The Book of Jerry Falwell* (Harding, 2000). Her work should be required reading for anyone seeking to understand the Trump phenomenon, and how it is that Trump seems to be virtually immune to the effects of his own conduct. He noted this himself during the campaign, when he remarked that he could shoot someone on 5th Avenue and not lose a vote. That seemed at the time to be humorous exaggeration; now, if studies of his supporters are valid, it appears perhaps to be literally correct. What follows is an explanation of how this can be.

Harding identifies the practice of "harmonization," the practice of adhering to biblical literalism, despite the many contradictions within scripture. Believers are taught to develop the ability to consider contradictions, rationalizing them, until they are able to "harmonize" away the conflicts. At that point, they have come to accept the whole as literally true, however logically inconsistent and impossible it is for two completely opposite notions each to be true (see Skidmore, 2002).

One fundamentalist Baptist minister some time ago, for example, responded to a question about the two versions of creation early in Genesis. In one version, God created Adam, subsequently created other animals, and ultimately created Eve, for Adam's companionship. In the other, God created whales and other animals, after which, for creation to be complete, he created Adam. The question was, which version is correct? The answer was, both. The follow-up question was, which then came first, Adam, or other animals? The answer was that they both came first. That was God's word; it therefore had to be correct. The apparent contradiction was simply the inability of the human mind to comprehend God's truth.

Whether or not literalism and harmonization are appropriate for religion is irrelevant. What is relevant is that people adhering to fundamentalist-evangelical traditions and modes of thought have become enormously influential in American society, and it seems not to be overreaching if one suspects that bringing their habits of thought—learned from their religion—into political, economic, and social matters arms them against rational argument and logic. This, if so, presents an obvious danger. It clearly is detrimental not only to the passage of social legislation—witness, for instance, the literally irrational reaction to the science of climate change—but also to the entire political process.

Consider the thoughtful comments recently in *Religion Dispatches* by Hollis Phelps of Mercer University in Georgia. Casting tact aside, Phelps titled his essay: "Maybe It's Time to Admit That the 'Grotesque Caricature' of White Evangelicals Is the Reality" (Phelps, 2018). He was led to write because of a gathering of evangelical leaders at Wheaton College in Illinois. Participants were concerned about damage to the image of evangelicals by being considered as "agents of intolerance" (as John McCain described them as early as 2008) in "the age of Trump." Although recognizing that "evangelicalism is and will remain a complex socio-political movement propped up by a religious rhetoric that emphasizes individual piety," and pointing out that many trenchant critics of Trump come from the ranks of evangelicals, Phelps says that it should be impossible to overlook the overwhelming support that evangelicals as a group have given to Trump, to ultra-right-wing policies, and to clearly extremist candidates. Modern-day evangelicalism, he says, "does not create a new problem for evangelicals and their image; it's simply casting a very bright light on what has always been there, at least for the past forty years or so." If their support for Trump seems more calculated than sincere, he remarks, "that's because it is."

Perceptively, he noted that "the line between religion and politics is flimsy at best, if not entirely non-existent." It simply is not true that "evangelicalism, in its current manifestation," is a religion corrupted by politics. Rather, it is a "social movement that works through a specific type of politics." It was there for Trump and his allies to exacerbate, but they did not create it. "Perhaps it's time," he says, for concerned evangelical leaders to recognize that evangelicalism's public image "isn't a 'grotesque caricature,' but the thing itself."

It can be nothing other than ominous that undoubtedly large numbers of active citizens, in clear defiance of reason, find that "contradiction actually strengthens faith." Harding describes the many character flaws Falwell exhibited throughout his career. "He could humiliate, deceive, and steal," she says. Writing almost two decades before the rise of Donald Trump, she could write of Falwell in terms that are eerily prescient, and sound as though they describe the contemporary White House (to experience the full effect of her findings, read "president" for "preacher"):

> The preacher is a Godly man; evidence that he has sinned, that he is unscrupulous, that he is hypocritical merely forces believers to harmonize "contradictions and infelicities according to interpretive conventions that presume, and thus reveal, God's design. Their Bible, their preacher, is thus constantly creating new truth" (p. xi). "What makes Falwell's scandalous actions productive is that they also bound people to him" (p. 100). He engages in a "process, both languaged and enacted, in which a preacher's . . . wrongdoing is productive, not a side effect; is necessary, not incidental." (p. 103; in Skidmore, 2002)

The relevance to contemporary policy, certainly including anti-poverty policy, is painfully obvious. Personal flaws of the leader, cultish or not, strengthen that leader against criticism, and demonstrate godliness. Looking at the political implications, rather than maintaining focus on religion, demonstrates that such teachings are cleverly designed to render leaders—religious, political, cultish, or all combined—above rational analysis, providing them with powerful armor against any attack. Remember, the principles that had been crafted carefully to protect the people from the powerful have now become the foundations of protection for the powerful against the people.

In Praise of Universalism: Political Weakness of Targeted Programs

One of the foremost reasons for the popularity of Social Security and Medicare is that they are virtually universal programs. They are not targeted toward the poor, or "the other." Everyone, for all practical purposes, qualifies upon reaching the requisite age. No one is forced to demonstrate poverty to participate. There thus is no stigma attached, and such programs have huge constituencies.

Programs targeted to the poor, on the contrary, tend to suffer politically. Among other things, the poor are not organized, have little or no political power, tend not to be considered sympathetically, and when the subject of legislation directed at assisting them, by definition become "the other." Therefore, their programs are fair game for budget cutters and for those who resent assisting those whom they deem "undeserving."

Social Security was not aimed at the poor, and is not technically an anti-poverty program. Nevertheless, no program in American history has had greater success in reducing poverty. Medicare, similarly, has greatly reduced poverty among the aged, and also had the accompanying effect of being one of the greatest tools against segregation in the south, when it became a powerful funding tool for hospitals that required them to cease segregating patients and discriminating against them. There are other examples that suggest the effectiveness of universal programs, as opposed to those that specifically target the poor.

Therefore, if there is a single recommendation in this article (apart from arguing for a sound and general education for democracy), it is that there should be massive programs to eliminate poverty in the United States. Such programs should be broad, aimed at all of us as citizens of a great country, and not directed specifically toward any group, the poor, or any other. They should be open to all. Their benefits also should be understood to be part of human rights, and designed so as to avoid any stigma attached to participation. They should be designed for maximum effect, not for minimum cost. It then is up to the government, to the society, to make them work, and make them sustainable.

All poverty is damaging to human development, and, to put it emotionally, to the human spirit. Whatever excuses may be offered, it is shameful for poverty to exist in a society as affluent as that in the United States.

References

Card, D., & A. Krueger. (1994). "Minimum wages and employment: A case study of the fast-food industry in New Jersey and Pennsylvania." *American Economic Review*, 84(4), 772–793.

Cassidy, J. (2013). "The Reinhart and Rogoff controversy: A summing up." *The New Yorker*, April 26.

Crapanzano, V. (2001). *Serving the word: Literalism in America from the pulpit to the bench.* New York: The New Press.

Galbraith, J. K. (1958). *The affluent society.* Boston: Houghton-Mifflin.

Harding, S. F. (2000). *The book of Jerry Falwell: Fundamentalist language and politics.* Princeton, NJ: Princeton University Press.

Harrington, M. (1962). *The other America.* New York: Touchstone Books.

Jarvie, J. (2018). *Nikki Haley calls U.N. report on poverty in U.S. "misleading and politically motivated."* Retrieved from http://www.latimes.com/world/la-fg-un-us-poverty-20180621-story.html.

Keefe, L. (2010). "Dwight MacDonald and poverty discourse: The art and power of a seminal book review." *Poverty and Public Policy*, 2(2), 145–188; reprinted in M. J. Skidmore, ed., 2015, *Poverty in America: Urban and rural inequality in the 21st century* (pp. 2–43), Washington, DC: Westphalia Press.

Krugman, P. (2015). "Liberals and wages." *New York Times*, July 17.

MacDonald, D. (1963). "Our invisible poor." *The New Yorke*, January 16, 82–132.

McNichol, D. (2003). *The roads that built America: The incredible story of the U.S. interstate system.* New York: Barnes and Noble.

Phelps, H. (2018). "Maybe it's time to admit that the 'grotesque caricature' of white evangelicals is the reality." *Religion Dispatches*, April 19.

Pilkington, E. (2018). "Nikki Haley attacks damning UN report on US poverty under Trump." *The Guardian*. Retrieved from https://www.theguardian.com/world/2018/jun/21/nikki-haley-un-poverty-report-misleading-politically-motivated.

Rabin-Havt, A., & M. Matters. (2016). *Lies, incorporated: The world of post-truth politics.* New York: Anchor Books.

Reinhart, C., & K. Rogoff. (2010). "Growth in a time of debt." *American Economic Review*, 100(2), 573–578.

Skidmore, M. J. (2002). "Review of: The Book of Jerry Falwell," in *The European Legacy*, 7(3), 415–416; reprinted in J. Skidmore, 2013, *The review as art and communication* (pp. 87–89), Cambridge: Cambridge Scholars Press.

Skidmore, M. J. (2009). "Revisiting a classic after nearly a half century." *Poverty and Public Policy*, 1(2), Article 8.

Skidmore, M. J. (2015). *Poverty in America: Urban and rural inequality and deprivation in the 21st century.* Washington, DC: Westphalia Press.

Skidmore, M. J. (2016). "Tourism, travel, and transportation." In G. Burns (Ed.), *A companion to popular culture* (pp. 322–340). Malden, MA: Wiley-Blackwell.

Skidmore, M. J. (2017). *Unworkable conservatism: Small government, freemarkets, and impracticality.* Washington, DC: Westphalia Press.

Skocpol, T. (1995). *Protecting soldiers and mothers: The political origins of social policy in the United States.* Cambridge, MA: Harvard University Press.

Smith, P. J., & R. W. Tuttle. (2013). "Biblical literalism and constitutional originalism." *Notre Dame Law Review*, 86(2), 693–764.

Washington Post Wonkblog. (2018). *The U.N. says 18.5 million Americans are in "extreme poverty." Trump's team says just 250,000 are.* Retrieved from https://www.washingtonpost.com/news/wonk/wp/2018/06/25trump_.

www.ingramcontent.com/pod-product-compliance
Lightning Source LLC
Chambersburg PA
CBHW021618270326
41931CB00008B/753